RUBRICS AND CHECKLISTS 4-8

TABLE OF CONTENTS

RUBRICS

A rubric's purpose is twofold. First, a rubric is a tool used to assess a piece of work which a student has produced. Second, a rubric is a method of expressing the distinctions between the qualities of work.

Usually criteria are recorded in the left hand column and varying degrees of the quality of work is described in the columns to the right. A rubric clarifies what makes a good piece of work excellent and provides reference for next steps to improve work.

A successful rubric:

* helps teachers describe excellence.
* helps teachers plan how to guide students to achieve this excellence.
* conveys to students what comprises excellence.
* shows students how to evaluate their own work.
* shares goals and results.
* encourages accurate, unbiased and consistent scoring.

The primary goal of using a rubric for assessment is to improve student learning. When demonstrating rubrics to the class, it is a good idea for teachers to provide examples of each standard. Students and teachers can look at the examples together and use them to guide the student's work.

Evaluating a performance assessment task involves making subjective decisions about the quality of a student's work. A set of scoring guidelines or rubric is a way to make those judgments fairly. A uniform set of defined criteria used to judge student work ensures sound measurement.

GENERAL READING: CLASS LIST

Term _____

Student Name	Independent Book Choice	Story Elements	Character Development	Specific Examples	Reading Task Focus

READING FICTION RUBRIC

LEVEL 4
When reading fiction, the student:

- ❑ Demonstrates a comprehensive recall of the text.
- ❑ Makes clear connections between their ideas and the text.
- ❑ Supports their opinions with relevant text-based information.
- ❑ Demonstrates a thorough understanding of literary basics.

LEVEL 3
When reading fiction, the student:

- ❑ Demonstrates a general recall of the text.
- ❑ Makes clear connections between their ideas and the text.
- ❑ Supports their answers with relevant text-based information.
- ❑ Demonstrates a complete understanding of literary basics.

LEVEL 2
When reading fiction, the student:

- ❑ Demonstrates an adequate recall of the text.
- ❑ Makes some connections between their ideas and the text.
- ❑ Supports their answers with some text-based information.
- ❑ Demonstrated a passable understanding of literary basics.

LEVEL 1
When reading fiction, the student:

- ❑ Demonstrates little recall of the text.
- ❑ Makes incomplete connections between their ideas and the text.
- ❑ Attempts to support their responses with negligible text-based information.
- ❑ Demonstrates slightest understanding of literary basics.

READING CONFERENCE FORM

Date _____   Student's Name _____

What is the title of the book? _____

Who is the author? _____

Have you read other books by this author? _____

_____

Why did you choose this book? _____

_____

DISCUSSION POINTS BASED ON THE STORY READ	TEACHER NOTES/COMMENTS
Does the student comprehend the text? For example: ❖ What was the story about? ❖ Who was the main character(s)? ❖ What was the plot/conflict? ❖ How was the plot/conflict resolved?	
Does the student make connections between their ideas and the text? For example: ❖ Explain your thinking about…. ❖ What does …. remind you of?	
Does the student support their opinions with relevant text-based information? ❖ What is evidence in the story to support your opinion?	
Does the student demonstrate a complete understanding of literary basics?	

READING NON-FICTION RUBRIC

LEVEL4

When reading non-fiction the student:

- ☐ Demonstrates a thorough understanding of the text.
- ☐ Makes clear associations between the text and his/her ideas.
- ☐ States relevant opinions or interpretations and supported them with extensive, explicit references to the text.

LEVEL3

When reading non-fiction the student:

- ☐ Demonstrates a developed understanding of the text.
- ☐ Makes clear connections between the text and his/her ideas.
- ☐ States relevant opinions or interpretations and supported them with references from the text.

LEVEL2

When reading non-fiction the student:

- ☐ Demonstrates an adequate understanding of the text.
- ☐ Suggests connections between the text and his/her ideas.
- ☐ States opinions or interpretations and provided some support with some references to the text.

LEVEL1

When reading non-fiction the student:

- ☐ Demonstrates a superficial understanding of text.
- ☐ Provides limited connections between the text and his/her ideas.
- ☐ States unsupported conclusions in connecting his/her ideas to the text.

CHECKLIST: READING NON-FICTION

Title _____

Author _____

I am reading to learn about _____

_____

JOT NOTES:

_____

_____

_____

_____

_____

_____

_____

_____

_____

_____

_____

_____

TIPS:

☐ Take time during your reading to sort out new information and link it to what you already know.

☐ Reread the parts you may not have understood, to try and make sense of it.

☐ Use resources such as a dictionary when you are not sure of a word or the text doesn't make sense.

☐ Decide what you still want to learn about the subject.

ORAL READING RUBRIC

	Level 1	Level 2	Level 3	Level 4
Enjoyment	Student requires prompting and encouragement to read out loud.	Student sometimes requires prompting and encouragement to read out loud.	Student enjoys reading out loud with little prompting to do so.	Student enjoys reading out loud without prompting.
Punctuation	Student struggles to read according to punctuation.	Student sometimes can read according to punctuation.	Student usually reads according to punctuation.	Student consistently reads accurately and according to punctuation.
Expression & Flow	Student rarely reads with expression or flow.	Student sometimes reads with expression and flow.	Student usually reads with expression. Flow is smooth and a good pace.	Student consistently reads with expression. Flow and pace are good.
Strategies	Student rarely uses strategies to decode text. Teacher prompts required.	Student uses some strategies to decode text. Some teacher prompts required.	Student uses various strategies to decode text. Few teacher prompts required.	Student uses various strategies to decode text, and can explain their use.
Sight vocabulary	Student has limited sight vocabulary.	Student has basic sight vocabulary.	Student has suitable sight vocabulary.	Student has well developed sight vocabulary.

TEACHER COMMENTS:

_____
_____
_____
_____
_____
_____
_____

SELF-ASSESSMENT READING RUBRIC

Think about how you are doing in reading. With a light coloured pencil or marker, highlight where you rate yourself for each category.

	Level 1	Level 2	Level 3	Level 4
Attitude	I complain about reading and I often have a negative attitude about reading activities.	Sometimes I complain about reading and I sometimes have a negative attitude about reading activities.	I usually enjoy reading. I often have a positive attitude about reading activities.	I consistently enjoy reading. I always have a positive attitude about reading activities.
Time Management	I have trouble getting my work done in the time allotted.	I sometimes have trouble getting my work, done in the time allotted.	I usually get my work done in the time allotted.	I almost always get my work done in the time allotted.
Productivity	I need teacher reminders to stay on the task.	I sometimes need teacher reminders to stay on the task.	I usually stay on task without teacher reminders.	I almost always stay on task without teacher reminders.
Ready To Work	I need teacher reminders to bring materials.	I sometimes need teacher reminders to bring materials.	I usually bring materials.	I almost always bring materials.
Pride	My work shows very little effort from me.	My work shows some effort from me.	My work shows a strong effort from me.	My work shows my best efforts.
Quality Of Work	My work usually needs to be checked or redone.	My work occasionally needs to be checked or redone.	I do high quality work.	I always do high quality work.

What I am good at: _____

What I need to work on: _____

READING RESPONSE PROMPTS

THINKING ABOUT CHARACTER:

☐ Are the characters in the story believable? Why or why not?

☐ Do you think the main character made good decisions? Why or why not?

☐ Who is the teller in the story? How would the story be different if told by another character?

☐ What character in the book do you think you are the most alike? Explain your thinking.

☐ What character in the book do you think you are the most different? Explain your thinking.

☐ Some characters have a small part in a story, but are still important. Pick one these types of characters from your story and explain their importance.

☐ If I were _____ in the story I would have / not have done the same thing because…………

☐ What do you think happened to the main character after the story was finished?

THINKING ABOUT SETTING:

☐ Where does the story take place?

☐ How would the story change if the setting was in a different place or different time?

☐ Is there a setting in the story that is familiar to you? Explain.

READING RESPONSE PROMPTS

THINKING ABOUT THE PLOT:

☐ What incident, situation or problem occurred at the beginning of the book to get the story started?

☐ Did the author give clues in the book as to the outcome of the story? Explain your thinking and give examples.

☐ What is the main idea or lesson in this story?

☐ What is the mood or feeling in the story? Give examples from the story of how the author created this mood or feeling.

☐ How does the author create suspense so that the reader wants to continue reading the story? Explain your thinking with examples.

☐ Is this story similar to any other you have read? Explain your thinking.

☐ Would you like to read another book by this author? Why or why not?

OPEN RESPONSE QUESTIONS:

☐ My favourite part of the story was when…………

☐ I was surprised when………

☐ The situation in the book reminded me of ……….

☐ I wonder why………

☐ This story was very realistic/ unrealistic because……

READING RESPONSE RUBRIC

Level 1

❖ Reading response is incomplete with only a few key concepts and ideas identified, defined and described with several errors or omissions.

❖ Few or no noteworthy facts, supporting details or quotes are included from the text to support ideas and opinion.

Level 2

❖ Reading response is more than half complete with key concepts and ideas identified, defined and described with some errors or omissions.

❖ Some noteworthy facts, supporting details or quotes are included from the text to support ideas and opinion.

Level 3

❖ Reading response is complete with key concepts and ideas identified, defined and described with few errors or omissions.

❖ Most of the noteworthy facts, supporting details or quotes are included from the text to support ideas and opinion.

Level 4

❖ Reading response is complete with key concepts and ideas fully identified, defined and described with almost no errors or omissions.

❖ Almost all noteworthy facts, supporting details or quotes are included from the text to support ideas and opinion.

READING RESPONSE CHECKLIST

I checked that:

☐   I rewrote the reading response question into a topic sentence.

☐   I answered all parts of the question.

☐   I used specific details from the reading to explain my thinking and to support my answer.

☐   I related my answer to my own experiences.

☐   I used correct spelling and grammar.

Name_____

READING RESPONSE CHECKLIST

I checked that:

☐   I rewrote the reading response question into a topic sentence.

☐   I answered all parts of the question.

☐   I used specific details from the reading to explain my thinking and to support my answer.

☐   I related my answer to my own experiences.

☐   I used correct spelling and grammar.

PERSUASIVE OPINION RUBRIC

	Level 1	Level 2	Level 3	Level 4
Opening Statement	Student does not state their opinion.	Student partially states their opinion.	Student adequately states their opinion.	Student clearly states their opinion.
Idea Development	Student presents and supports their opinion in limited ways.	Student partially presents and supports their opinion using few examples and details.	Student capably presents and supports their opinion using some examples and details.	Student thoroughly presents and supports their opinion using examples and details.
Concluding Statement	Student does not restate their opinion.	Student partially restates their opinion.	Student adequately restates their opinion.	Student clearly restates their opinion.
Organization	Student displays little organization in ordering ideas.	Student displays satisfactory organization in ordering ideas.	Student displays developed organization in ordering ideas.	Student displays complete organization in ordering ideas.
Language Conventions	Several spelling and grammar mistakes. Limited use of sentence types.	Some spelling and grammar mistakes. Few sentence types are used.	Few spelling and grammar mistakes. Some variety of sentence types are used.	Spelling and grammar is correct. A variety of sentence types are used.

_____

_____

_____

_____

_____

_____

_____

_____

CLASS LIST: PERSUASIVE OPINION

Assignment Details _____

_____

Student Name	Opening Statement	Idea Development	Closing Statement	Language Conventions	Organization	Overall Mark

WRITING: STUDENT CHECKLIST

	What to look for:
Idea development	☐ the topic has relevant information ☐ there are details, examples or descriptions ☐ ideas are clear
Arrangement	☐ ideas are organized in a logical and sequential order ☐ the introduction is engaging and captures the reader's interest ☐ the ending is conclusive and pleasing
Language	☐ descriptive details are evident ☐ verbs are the correct tense. ☐ there are a variety of sentences
Punctuation	☐ capitals ☐ periods ☐ exclamation marks ☐ question marks ☐ quotation marks
Conventions	☐ paragraphs. ☐ titles. ☐ no run-on sentences or fragments. ☐ sentences are complete and make sense.

BUSINESS LETTER

A business letter can be divided into five parts:

Company or Business Address	This tells where the letter is going. ❖ It has the address, the city, the province and the postal code.
Return Address	This tells from whom the letter is written. ❖ It has the address, the city, the province and the postal code.
Date	This tells the reader when the letter was written. ❖ It states the day and year.
Greeting	This tells to whom the letter is written. ❖ It begins with a salutation. ❖ It begins with a capital. ❖ It ends with a colon.
Body	This is the part that tells what the letter is about. ❖ It is written in paragraphs.
Closing	This is the part that ends the letter. ❖ It has a closing that begins with a capital. ❖ It ends with a comma.
Signature	This is where you sign the letter. ❖ It has a first and last name. ❖ It has signature.

BUSINESS LETTER CHECKLIST

My business letter is about _____

_____

The first heading has:

☐   my address

☐   my city

☐   my province

☐   my postal code

The second heading has:

☐   the address of the company or business

☐   the city

☐   the province

☐   the postal code

The salutation says:

☐   Dear _____;

                (Name of person or Sir/Madam)

The body has:

☐   an introduction that explains the purpose

☐   a main section that gives details

☐   an ending

☐   a closing

☐   my first and last name

NARRATIVE RUBRIC

	Level 1	Level 2	Level 3	Level 4
Introduction	The characters and setting are confusing/or incomplete.	The characters and setting are introduced. No attempt to capture the attention of the reader.	The characters and setting are introduced and some attempt to capture the attention of the reader.	The characters and setting are introduced and captures the attention of the reader.
Problem	The problem the character(s) face is unclear.	The problem the character(s) face is clear, but it is not clear why it is a problem.	The problem the character(s) face and why, is straightforward to understand.	The problem the character(s) face and why, is very clear and straightforward to understand.
Story Events	The story contains little evidence of creative events details, and descriptions that add to the reader's enjoyment.	The story contains few creative events details, and descriptions that add to the reader's enjoyment.	The story contains some creative events details, and descriptions that add to the reader's enjoyment.	The story contains many creative events details, and descriptions that add to the reader's enjoyment.
Resolution	The resolution to the story is unclear.	The resolution to the story is difficult to follow, but complete.	The resolution to the story is fairly logical and simple to understand.	The resolution to the story is logical and simple to understand.
Vocabulary & Sentence Use	Student uses limited vocabulary and limited sentence types.	Student uses basic vocabulary and few sentence types.	Student uses suitable vocabulary and some sentence types.	Student uses extended vocabulary and a variety of sentence types.

TEACHER COMMENTS:

_____

_____

_____

_____

_____

_____

NARRATIVE: REVISING MY WORK

Title _____

Introduction	☐ I introduced the main characters. ☐ I described the setting. ☐ My introduction grabs the reader's attention.
Story Events	☐ I planned and wrote the events in logical order. ☐ The events are easy to follow and to understand. ☐ The events are creative and have descriptions or details that add to the reader's enjoyment.
Resolution	☐ The problem/ adventure are resolved. ☐ The resolution is easy to follow and makes sense.
Vocabulary	☐ I used a thesaurus. (e.g. "hollered" for "said") ☐ I did not use any extra "and" or "then". ☐ I added similes.

PROOFREADING MY WORK

I checked for:

Capitals:
- ☐ at the beginning of each sentence
- ☐ in names
- ☐ in dates
- ☐ for the word "i"

Punctuation:
- ☐ . periods at the end of sentences.
- ☐ ? question marks at the end of questions.
- ☐ ! exclamation marks to show expression.
- ☐ " " quotation marks around speaking parts.
- ☐ , commas are used correctly.
- ☐ ' apostrophes are used in contractions and possessives.

**Spelling
I checked in:**
- ☐ my personal word book
- ☐ dictionaries
- ☐ other ways (spellchecker)

**Sentences
that have:**
- ☐ interesting words
- ☐ I used a thesaurus
- ☐ missing words
- ☐ extra words
- ☐ details
- ☐ no fragments or run-ons

CLASS LIST: WRITING PROCESS

Use this class list keep track of what students are working on during each writing class. At the beginning of each writing class, spend a couple of minutes to go down the class list and ask students to state where they are in the writing process. Display a class chart of the writing process for students' easy reference.

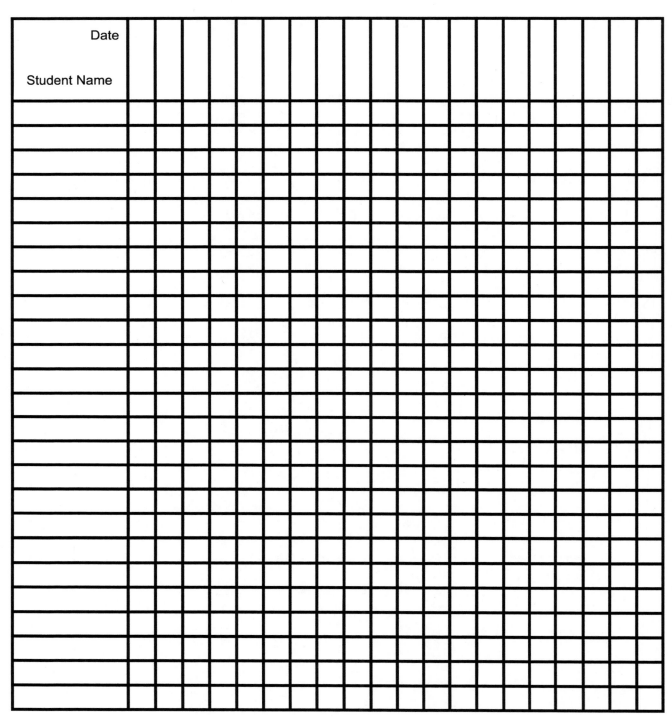

Date Student Name																						

Writing Process Stages

S- Story Plan

D- Draft

R- Revision

E- Editing

P- Peer Editing

T- Teacher Conference

G- Good Copy

AC- Ready for the Author Chair

WRITTEN RETELL RUBRIC

	Level 1	Level 2	Level 3	Level 4
Story Recall	Student's written retell reveals a partial recall of the story with few events from the story mentioned.	Student's written retell reveals a satisfactory recall of the story sequence with some events from the story mentioned.	Student's written retell reveals a capable recall of the story with most major events from the story mentioned.	Student's written retell reveals an excellent recall of the story with all important events from the story mentioned.
Story Sequence	Student displays little organization in ordering ideas into the proper story sequence.	Student displays satisfactory organization in ordering ideas into the proper story sequence.	Student displays capable organization in ordering ideas into the proper story sequence.	Student displays complete organization in ordering ideas into the proper story sequence.
Vocabulary Choice	Student includes few story details or descriptions and limited book language from the story in written retell.	Student includes some details or descriptions and some book language from the story in written retell.	Student includes many details or descriptions and book language from the story in written retell.	Student consistently includes details or descriptions and book language from the story in written retell.
Language Conventions	Student has several spelling and grammar mistakes. Student displays a limited use of sentence types.	Student has some spelling and grammar mistakes. Student uses a few sentence types.	Student has few spelling and grammar mistakes. Student uses a variety of sentence types.	Student has correct spelling and grammar. Student uses a variety of sentence types.

TEACHER COMMENTS:

_____

_____

_____

_____

_____

_____

_____

CLASS LIST: WRITTEN RETELL

Assignment Details _____

_____

Student Name	Story Recall	Story Sequence	Vocabulary Choice	Language Conventions	Overall Mark

RESEARCH REPORT RUBRIC

	Level 1	Level 2	Level 3	Level 4
Organization of Research	Student displays little organization in ordering ideas.	Student displays satisfactory organization in ordering ideas.	Student displays capable organization in ordering ideas.	Student displays complete organization in ordering ideas.
Background Research	Student includes few facts, details or descriptions.	Student includes some facts, details or descriptions.	Student includes many facts, details or descriptions.	Student includes facts, details or descriptions beyond expectations.
Language Conventions	Student has several spelling and grammar mistakes. Student displays a limited use of sentence types.	Student has some spelling and grammar mistakes. Student uses a few sentence types.	Student has few spelling and grammar mistakes. Student uses a variety of sentence types.	Student has correct spelling and grammar. Student uses a variety of sentence types.
Citation of Sources	Student cites sources in an incomplete or limited way.	Student cites sources in an adequate way.	Student cites sources in a complete way.	Student cites sources in a thorough way.

TEACHER COMMENTS:

_____
_____
_____
_____
_____
_____
_____

RESEARCH REPORT CHECKLIST

Research Report Title _____

_____

Introduction Paragraph	☐ I introduced the topic in an interesting way.
Body Paragraphs	☐ I have a topic sentence for each paragraph. ☐ Each paragraph has facts, supporting details, examples or descriptions.
Closing Paragraph	☐ I closed the research report stating the main idea in an interesting way.
Research Information	☐ The facts are written in my own words. ☐ I checked my facts to make sure they are accurate. ☐ I used a variety of sources and kept a complete accurate list.
Proofreading	☐ I checked for spelling. ☐ I checked for punctuation. ☐ I used different sentence types.
Overall Final Copy	☐ I have a title, my name and date. ☐ My report is well organized and presented clearly. ☐ My printing/writing is neat and easy to understand.

CLASS LIST: RESEARCH REPORT

Assignment Details _____

_____

Student Name	Organization of Research	Research Information	Language Conventions	Citation of Sources	Overall Mark

ORAL
COMMUNICATION

&

VISUAL
COMMUNICATION

ORAL PRESENTATION RUBRIC

	Level 1	Level 2	Level 3	Level 4
Preparation	Student is not prepared.	Student is somewhat prepared, but needs more practice.	Student is prepared and has noticeably practiced the presentation.	Student is completely prepared and has noticeably practiced the presentation.
Content Knowledge	Student shows little understanding of the topic.	Student shows a satisfactory understanding of the topic.	Student shows a good understanding of the topic.	Student shows an excellent understanding of the topic.
Assignment Requirements	Assignment requirements are incomplete.	More than half of the assignment requirements are complete.	Assignment requirements are complete.	Assignment requirements are complete and go beyond assignment expectations.
Voice	Student speaks unclearly and uses little voice expression.	Student speaks clearly for some of the time and uses satisfactory voice expression.	Student speaks clearly for most of the time and uses good voice expression.	Student speaks clearly all of the time and uses excellent voice expression.
Eye Contact	Student establishes little or no eye contact with the audience.	Student establishes some eye contact with the audience.	Student establishes good eye contact with the audience.	Student establishes consistent eye contact with the audience.

TEACHER COMMENTS:

_____

_____

_____

_____

_____

CLASS LIST: ORAL PRESENTATION

Assignment Details _____

_____

Student Name	Preparation	Content Knowledge	Assignment Requirements	Voice	Eye Contact	Overall Mark

POSTER RUBRIC

	Level 1	Level 2	Level 3	Level 4
Poster Appeal	Poor design. Layout is unattractive and messy.	Basic design. Layout and neatness are acceptable.	Interesting design. Layout and neatness are good.	Very well thought out design. Excellent layout and neatness.
Content	Few facts are accurately displayed on the poster.	Some facts are accurately displayed on the poster.	Facts are mostly accurately displayed on the poster.	Facts are accurately displayed on the poster.
Graphic Support	No graphics are related to the topic and no support of the information.	Few graphics are related to the topic and little support of the information.	Most graphics are related to the topic and support the information.	Graphics are related to the topic and support the information.
Assigned Poster Requirements	Several elements were missing. No additional information was added.	Student includes some of the necessary elements but no additional information.	Student includes most of the necessary elements as well as some additional information.	Student includes all necessary elements as well as additional information.
Time Management	Student did not use time effectively to focus on the project. Student was easily distracted.	Student used time somewhat effectively to focus on the project. Student was sometimes distracted.	Student usually used time effectively to focus on the project. Student was not easily distracted.	Student used time effectively to focus on the project. Student stayed on task.

TEACHER COMMENTS:

_____

_____

_____

_____

_____

_____

POSTER CHECKLIST

Topic: _____

Purpose of Poster: _____

Poster Appeal	☐	My layout design is attractive.
	☐	The heading grabs the reader's attention.
Content	☐	It is clear what the poster is about.
	☐	There are supporting facts, details and or descriptions.
Graphics	☐	The graphics relate to the topic.
	☐	The graphics are neat and have details.
Assigned Poster Requirements	☐	I completed all parts of the assignment.
Proofreading	☐	I checked for spelling.
	☐	I checked for punctuation.
	☐	My writing/printing is neat and easy to read.

ADDED NOTES:

_____

_____

_____

_____

CLASS LIST: POSTER

Assignment Details _____

_____

Student Name	Poster Appeal	Content	Graphics	Poster Requirements	Time Management	Overall Mark

MULTI MEDIA RUBRIC

	Level 1	Level 2	Level 3	Level 4
Project Appeal	Poor use of font, colour, graphics, effects, etc. to enrich presentation.	Some use of font, colour, graphics, effects, etc. to enrich presentation.	Good use of font, colour, graphics, effects, etc. to enrich presentation.	Excellent use of font, colour, graphics, effects, etc. to enrich presentation.
Content	Student covers topic with few or no details and examples. Student is not familiar with subject.	Student covers topic with some details and examples. Student has some subject knowledge.	Student covers topic with many details and examples. Student has good subject knowledge.	Covers topic thoroughly with details and examples. Student has thorough subject knowledge.
Creativity and Organization	Content is not organized. Creative ideas not apparent.	Content is partially organized and shows some creative and inventive ideas.	Content is organized and shows some creative and inventive ideas.	Content is well organized and shows many creative and inventive ideas.
Oral Presentation	Student delivery is awkward. Audience interest was often lost.	Student delivery is somewhat smooth. Some audience interest was maintained.	Student delivery is smooth. Audience interest was maintained most of the time.	Student is well-rehearsed with smooth delivery that consistently holds audience interest.
Technical Knowledge	Student has little knowledge about the facts or processes used in multi-media presentation.	Student has some knowledge about the facts or processes used multi-media presentation.	Student has good knowledge about the facts or processes used in multi-media presentation.	Student has accurate and well developed knowledge about the facts or processes used in multi-media presentation.

TEACHER COMMENTS:

_____

_____

_____

_____

_____

_____

CLASS LIST: MULTI MEDIA PROJECT

Assignment Details _____

_____

Student Name	Project Appeal	Content	Creativity and Organization	Oral Presentation	Technical Knowledge	Overall Mark

BROCHURE RUBRIC

	Level 1	Level 2	Level 3	Level 4
Brochure Organization	Less than half of the sections are complete and defined.	More than half of the sections are complete and defined.	Almost all of the sections in the brochure are complete and defined.	Each section of the brochure is complete and defined.
Brochure Appeal	Brochure layout is not organized and confusing for the reader.	Brochure layout is some what organized.	Brochure layout is organized and eye-catching.	Brochure layout is very organized and very eye-catching.
Content	Little content is accurate.	Some of the content is accurate.	All of the content is accurate.	All of the content is accurate with added detail.
Graphics	Little or no graphics to go with text.	Satisfactory graphics to go with text.	Good graphics to go with text.	Excellent graphics to go with text.
Proofreading	There are several spelling or grammar mistakes.	There are some spelling or grammar mistakes.	There are few spelling or grammar mistakes.	There are no spelling or grammar mistakes.

TEACHER COMMENTS:

_____

_____

_____

_____

_____

_____

_____

BROCHURE CHECKLIST

BROCHURE PLAN

☐ I folded a paper the same way the brochure will be folded and presented.

☐ I planned the brochure layout in pencil. For example, I wrote the heading on the top of the front of the brochure. Underneath the heading, I wrote the information that will follow.

☐ I planned and sketched where graphics could support the information.

ROUGH COPY

☐ I wrote a rough copy for each section of the brochure.

☐ I reread my rough copy for meaning and then added, deleted, or changed words to make my writing more interesting and clear.

EDITING

I checked for:

☐ capitals at the beginning of sentences or for names and for your headings and subheadings.

☐ periods, question marks, or exclamation marks.

☐ commas used correctly.

☐ correct spelling.

☐ complete sentences.

GOOD COPY

☐ I discussed with my teacher final changes that need to be made.

☐ I organized my information on the brochure paper.

☐ I made my brochure visually appealing by using interesting fonts, colours, and adding pictures.

☐ I made sure I wrote or typed clearly so the brochure is easy to read.

CLASS LIST: BROCHURE

Assignment Details _____

_____

Student Name	Brochure Organization	Brochure Appeal	Content	Graphics	Proofreading	Overall Mark

MATHEMATICS

DAILY MATH WORK RUBRIC

	Level 1	Level 2	Level 3	Level 4
Understanding of Math Concepts	Student demonstrates a limited understanding of math concepts in daily work.	Student demonstrates a satisfactory understanding of taught in daily work.	Student demonstrates a complete understanding of math concepts in daily work.	Student demonstrates a thorough understanding of math concepts in daily work.
Application of Skills Taught	Student rarely applies skills taught in daily work without teacher assistance.	Student applies skills taught in daily work with several errors and omissions.	Student applies skills taught in daily work with few errors and omissions.	Student consistently applies skills taught in daily work with almost no errors and omissions.
Math Terminology	Student rarely uses appropriate math terms during math discussions and activities.	Student sometimes uses appropriate math terms during math discussions and activities.	Student usually uses appropriate math terms during math discussions and activities.	Student consistently uses appropriate math terms during math discussions and activities.
Class Preparation	Student rarely comes prepared with materials and assignments done.	Student sometimes comes prepared with materials and assignments done.	Student usually comes prepared with materials and assignments done.	Student consistently comes prepared with materials and assignments done.

TEACHER COMMENTS:

_____
_____
_____
_____
_____
_____
_____

CLASS LIST: DAILY MATH WORK

Math Focus: _____

Student Name	Understanding of Concepts	Application of Skills Taught	Math Terminology	Class Preparation

MATH WORK CHECKLIST

I did the following: Name: _____

- ☐ I drew pictures or diagrams to help me solve the problem.
- ☐ I showed all the steps in solving the problem.
- ☐ I named the operations I used to solve the problem.
- ☐ I used math language to explain my thinking.

···

MATH WORK CHECKLIST

I did the following: Name: _____

- ☐ I drew pictures or diagrams to help me solve the problem.
- ☐ I showed all the steps in solving the problem.
- ☐ I named the operations I used to solve the problem.
- ☐ I used math language to explain my thinking.

···

MATH WORK CHECKLIST

I did the following: Name: _____

- ☐ I drew pictures or diagrams to help me solve the problem.
- ☐ I showed all the steps in solving the problem.
- ☐ I named the operations I used to solve the problem.
- ☐ I used math language to explain my thinking.

PROBLEM SOLVING CHECKLIST

Name _____

☐ I carefully read the problem.

☐ I listed known numbers, and important information.

☐ I drew a labeled diagram to help solve the problem.

☐ I showed my work for every step in solving the problem.

☐ I stated the solution, and showed the units.

☐ I used math language to explain my thinking.

☐ I printed neatly, and spaced out my work.

☐ I checked my calculations over.

....

PROBLEM SOLVING CHECKLIST

Name _____

☐ I carefully read the problem.

☐ I listed known numbers, and important information.

☐ I drew a labeled diagram to help solve the problem.

☐ I showed my work for every step in solving the problem.

☐ I stated the solution, and showed the units.

☐ I used math language to explain my thinking.

☐ I printed neatly, and spaced out my work.

☐ I checked my calculations over.

QUALITY MATH NOTE BOOK CHECKLIST

Name _____

- ☐ There is a title and date on each page.
- ☐ Work is complete and neatly organized.
- ☐ Calculations are labeled and done in pencil.
- ☐ Questions are copied and the solutions are underneath.

....

QUALITY MATH NOTE BOOK CHECKLIST

Name _____

- ☐ There is a title and date on each page.
- ☐ Work is complete and neatly organized.
- ☐ Calculations are labeled and done in pencil.
- ☐ Questions are copied and the solutions are underneath.

....

QUALITY MATH NOTE BOOK CHECKLIST

Name _____

- ☐ There is a title and date on each page.
- ☐ Work is complete and neatly organized.
- ☐ Calculations are labeled and done in pencil.
- ☐ Questions are copied and the solutions are underneath.

MATH PROBLEM SOLVING RUBRIC

	Level 1	Level 2	Level 3	Level 4
Application of Problem Solving Strategies	Student shows little or no attempt to solve the problem.	Student uses partially appropriate strategies and math procedures to solve the problem with several errors or omissions.	Student appropriate strategies and math procedures to solve the problem with few errors or omissions.	Student appropriate strategies and math procedures to solve the problem accurately.
Communication of Mathematical Thinking	Little or no attempt to solve the problem	Stated some steps in solving the problem using math terms and diagrams in a limited way.	States steps in solving the problem using some math terms and diagrams	Clearly stated steps in solving the problem using math terms and diagrams.
Organization	Work is not and organized with few or no labeled calculations.	Work is somewhat organized with some labeled calculations.	Work is neat and organized with labeled calculations with a few omissions.	Work is neat and organized with labeled calculations.
Time Management	Student did not use time effectively to focus on the problem. Student was easily distracted.	Student used time somewhat effectively to focus on the problem. Student was sometimes distracted.	Student usually used time effectively to focus on the problem. Student was not easily distracted.	Student used time effectively to focus on the problem. Student stayed on task.

TEACHER COMMENTS:

_____
_____
_____
_____
_____
_____
_____

CLASS LIST: PROBLEM SOLVING

Math Focus: _____

Student Name	Application of Strategies	Communication of Thinking	Organization	Overall Mark

MATH JOURNAL RUBRIC

Level 1

- ❖ Math journal response is incomplete with only a few key concepts and ideas identified, defined and described with several errors or omissions.

Level 2

- ❖ Math journal response is more than half complete with key concepts and ideas identified, defined and described with some errors or omissions.

Level 3

- ❖ Math journal response is complete with key concepts and ideas identified, defined and described with few errors or omissions.

- ❖ Most of the noteworthy facts, supporting details or quotes are included from the text to support ideas and opinion.

Level 4

- ❖ Math journal response is complete with key concepts and ideas fully identified, defined and described.

- ❖ Almost all noteworthy facts, supporting details or quotes are included from the text to support ideas and opinion.

CLASS LIST: MATH DAILY WORK

Math Focus: _____

Student Name	Math Journal	Math Notebook	Homework Completion	Overall Mark

VISUAL ARTS

DANCE/ MOVEMENT

DRAMA

GENERAL VISUAL ARTS RUBRIC

	Level 1	Level 2	Level 3	Level 4
Art Appreciation	Student expresses opinions about art in limited ways. Teacher prompts are needed.	Student sometimes expresses opinions about art with some teacher prompts.	Student usually expresses opinions about art with few teacher prompts.	Student consistently expresses opinions about art.
Critical Analysis	Student does not use evidence from artwork to support their interpretation.	Student supports their interpretation using little evidence from the art work.	Student supports their interpretation using satisfactory evidence from the art work.	Student supports their interpretation using extensive evidence from the art work.
Creative Work	Student applies less than half of the skills, techniques and concepts taught.	Student applies over half of the skills techniques and concepts taught.	Student applies most of the skills techniques and concepts taught.	Student applies almost all of the skills techniques and concepts taught.
Use of Tools and Materials	Student needs constant reminders to use tools and materials appropriately.	Student needs some reminders to use tools and materials appropriately.	Student needs little reminders to use tools and materials appropriately.	Student rarely needs reminders to use tools and materials appropriately.
Communication	Student rarely uses correct terminology.	Student sometimes uses correct terminology.	Student usually uses correct terminology.	Student consistently uses correct terminology.

TEACHER COMMENTS:

_____

_____

_____

_____

_____

_____

_____

CLASS LIST: GENERAL VISUAL ARTS

Student Name	Art Appreciation	Critical Analysis	Creative Work	Use of Tools	Communication

DANCE/MOVEMENT RUBRIC

	Level 1	Level 2	Level 3	Level 4
Understanding of Concepts	Student rarely performs all steps correctly.	Student sometimes performs all steps correctly.	Student usually performs all steps correctly.	Student consistently performs all steps correctly.
Application of Skills	Student applies skills learned in limited ways to own creative works.	Student applies skills learned in some ways to own creative works.	Student applies skills learned in complete ways to own creative works.	Student applies skills learned in extended ways to own creative works.
Rhythm	Student rarely stays in rhythm and holds head up and faces forward.	Student sometimes stays in rhythm and holds head up and faces forward.	Student usually stays in rhythm and holds head up and faces forward.	Student consistently stays in rhythm and holds head up and faces forward.
Participation	Student rarely shows enthusiasm and energy during activities.	Student sometimes shows enthusiasm and energy during activities.	Student usually shows enthusiasm and energy during activities.	Student consistently shows enthusiasm and energy during activities.
Communication of Concepts	Student rarely uses correct terminology when describing or interpreting their own and others' work.	Student sometimes uses correct terminology when describing or interpreting their own and others' work.	Student usually uses correct terminology when describing or interpreting their own and others' work.	Student consistently uses correct terminology when describing or interpreting their own and others' work.

TEACHER COMMENTS:

_____
_____
_____
_____
_____
_____
_____

CLASS LIST: DANCE/MOVEMENT

Student Name	Understanding of Concepts	Application of Skills	Rhythm	Participation	Communication of Concepts

DRAMA RUBRIC

	Level 1	Level 2	Level 3	Level 4
Understanding of Concepts	Student demonstrates a limited understanding of voice and audience by speaking and writing in role as characters in a story.	Student demonstrates a satisfactory understanding of voice and audience by speaking and writing in role as characters in a story.	Student demonstrates a good understanding of voice and audience by speaking and writing in role as characters in a story.	Student demonstrates a thorough understanding of voice and audience by speaking and writing in role as characters in a story.
Application of Skills	Student applies skills learned in limited ways to own creative works.	Student applies skills learned in some ways to own creative works.	Student applies skills learned in complete ways to own creative works.	Student applies skills learned in extended ways to own creative works.
Voice	Student rarely varies intonation or expression.	Student sometimes intonation or	Student usually intonation or holds head up and faces forward.	Student consistently intonation or holds head up and faces forward.
Performance	Student performs with limited feeling and expression and fails to engage the audience.	Student performs with some feeling and expression and has a limited engagement of the audience.	Student performs with feeling and expression and engages the audience.	Student performs with impressive feeling and expression and has completely engages the audience.
Participation	Student rarely shows enthusiasm and energy during activities.	Student sometimes shows enthusiasm and energy during activities.	Student usually shows enthusiasm and energy during activities.	Student consistently shows enthusiasm and energy during activities.
Communication of Concepts	Student rarely uses correct terminology when describing or interpreting their own and others' work.	Student sometimes uses correct terminology when describing or interpreting their own and others' work.	Student usually uses correct terminology when describing or interpreting their own and others' work.	Student consistently uses correct terminology when describing or interpreting their own and others' work.

CLASS LIST: DRAMA

Student Name	Understanding of Concepts	Application of Skills	Voice	Participation	Communication of Concepts

SCIENCE
&
SOCIAL
STUDIES

GENERAL SCIENCE RUBRIC

	Level 1	Level 2	Level 3	Level 4
Comprehension of Science Concepts	Student displays a limited understanding of concepts and how they relate to daily life.	Student displays a satisfactory understanding of concepts and how they relate to daily life.	Student displays a good understanding of concepts and how they relate to daily life.	Student displays a thorough understanding of concepts and how they relate to daily life.
Procedure Skills	Student applies few of the required skills and needs teacher support.	Student applies some of the required skills and needs some teacher support.	Student applies most of the required skills and needs infrequent teacher support.	Student applies almost all of the required skills and needs no teacher support.
Safety	Student uses tools, equipment, and materials correctly only with teacher supervision.	Student uses tools, equipment, and materials correctly with some teacher supervision.	Student uses tools, equipment, and materials correctly with little teacher supervision.	Student uses tools, equipment, and materials correctly without teacher supervision.
Communication Skills	Student rarely uses correct science terminology when discussing science concepts.	Student sometimes uses correct science terminology when discussing science concepts.	Student usually uses correct science terminology when discussing science concepts.	Student consistently uses correct science terminology when discussing science concepts.

TEACHER COMMENTS:

_____

_____

_____

_____

_____

_____

_____

CLASS LIST: GENERAL SCIENCE

SCIENCE FOCUS: _____

Student Name	Comprehension of Science Concepts	Procedure Skills	Safety	Communication	Overall Mark

SCIENCE EXPERIMENT RUBRIC

	Level 1	Level 2	Level 3	Level 4
Understanding of Concept	Student displays a limited understanding of the experiment concept and how it works.	Student displays a satisfactory understanding of the experiment concept and how it works.	Student displays a good understanding of the experiment concept and how it works.	Student displays a thorough understanding of the experiment concept and how it works.
Experiment Design	Student applies few of the required skills and strategies to carry out the experiment successfully. The experiment is incomplete.	Student applies some of the required skills and strategies to carry out the experiment successfully. The experiment is complete.	Student applies most of the required skills and strategies to carry out the experiment successfully. The experiment is complete.	Student applies almost all of required skills and strategies to carry out the experiment successfully. The experiment is complete.
Concepts and Skills Connections	Student shows little understanding of how the experiment connects to a real world application within a familiar context.	Student shows some understanding of how the experiment connects to a real world application within a familiar context.	Student shows good understanding of how the experiment connects to a real world application within a familiar context.	Student shows complete understanding of how the experiment connects to a real world application within a familiar context.
Safety	Student uses tools, equipment, and materials correctly only with teacher supervision.	Student uses tools, equipment, and materials correctly with some teacher supervision.	Student uses tools, equipment, and materials correctly with little teacher supervision.	Student uses tools, equipment, and materials correctly without teacher supervision.
Communication Skills	Student rarely uses correct science terminology introduced in the experiment.	Student sometimes uses correct science terminology introduced in the experiment.	Student usually uses correct uses correct science terminology introduced in the experiment.	Student consistently uses correct science terminology introduced in the experiment.

TEACHER COMMENTS:

_____

_____

_____

_____

CLASS LIST: SCIENCE EXPERIMENT

Experiment: _____

Student Name	Understanding of Concept	Experiment Design	Concept and Skills Connections	Safety	Communication	Overall Mark

GENERAL SOCIAL STUDIES RUBRIC

	Level 1	Level 2	Level 3	Level 4
Comprehension of Social Studies Concepts	Student displays a limited understanding of concepts.	Student displays a satisfactory understanding of concepts.	Student displays a good understanding of concepts.	Student displays a thorough understanding of concepts.
Mapping Skills	Student applies few of the required mapping skills and needs teacher support.	Student applies some of the mapping required skills and needs some teacher support.	Student applies most of the mapping required skills and needs infrequent teacher support.	Student applies almost all of the required mapping skills and needs no teacher support.
Social Studies Concepts and Skills Connections	Student relates concepts to personal experience or prior knowledge or the outside world in limited ways.	Student relates some concepts to personal experience or prior knowledge or the outside world.	Student relates most concepts to personal experience or prior knowledge or the outside world.	Student relates almost all concepts to personal experience or prior knowledge or the outside world.
Communication Skills	Student rarely uses correct social studies terminology and symbols.	Student sometimes uses correct social studies terminology and symbols	Student usually uses correct social studies terminology and symbols	Student consistently uses correct social studies terminology and symbols

TEACHER COMMENTS:

_____

_____

_____

_____

_____

_____

_____

CLASS LIST: GENERAL SOCIAL STUDIES

Social Studies Focus _____

Student Name	Comprehension of Concepts	Mapping Skills	Social Studies Connections	Communication Skills	Overall Mark

MAP MAKING RUBRIC

	Level 1	Level 2	Level 3	Level 4
Neatness	Few of the labels or features can be read easily.	Some of the labels or features can be read easily.	Most of the labels or features can be read easily.	Almost all of the labels or features can be read easily.
Spelling	Almost all of the words on the map are spelled incorrectly.	Few of the words on the map are spelled correctly.	Many of the words on the map are spelled correctly.	Almost all of the words on the map are spelled correctly.
Mapping Skills	When shown a map, the student can identify few features or places.	When shown a map, the student can identify some features or places.	When shown a map, the student can identify most features or places.	When shown a map, the student can accurately identify features or places.
Scale	Features on the map are not drawn to scale and there are no indications on the map.	Features on the map are not drawn to scale but scale is indicated on the map.	Features on the map are drawn close to scale and this is indicated on the map.	Features on the map are drawn to scale and this is clearly indicated on the map.
Map Legend	The legend is not evident or difficult to read.	The legend contains a set of symbols, but is confusing to understand.	The legend contains a set of symbols, including a compass rose and is complete.	The legend contains a complete set of symbols, including a compass rose and is easy to read.
Colour & Shading	Student does not use shading to show differences in information. Few features are coloured.	Student uses shading to show some differences in information. Some features are coloured.	Student uses shading to show most of the differences in information. Most features are coloured completely.	Student uses consistent shading to show almost all of the differences in information. All features are coloured completely.

CLASS LIST: MAP MAKING

Assignment Details _____

_____

Student Name	Neatness	Spelling	Mapping Skills	Scale	Map Legend	Overall Mark

PHYSICAL EDUCATION

PHYSICAL EDUCATION RUBRIC

	Level 1	Level 2	Level 3	Level 4
Understanding of Physical Education Concepts	Student demonstrates a limited understanding of concepts.	Student demonstrates a satisfactory understanding of concepts.	Student demonstrates a complete understanding of concepts.	Student demonstrates a thorough understanding of concepts.
Application of Skills Taught	Student applies few of the required skills.	Student applies some of the required skills.	Student applies most of the required skills.	Student applies almost all of the required skills.
Participation	Student rarely participates actively. Constant teacher encouragement is needed.	Student sometimes participates actively. Some teacher encouragement is needed.	Student usually participates actively. Little teacher encouragement is needed.	Student almost always participates actively without teacher encouragement
Sportsmanship	Student behavior interferes with own learning. Student needs encouragement to be a team player.	Student behavior occasionally interferes with own learning. Student will sometimes share, help and encourage others.	Student behavior rarely interferes with own learning. Student will usually share, help and encourage others.	Student acts as a team leader. Student will consistently share, help, and encourage others.
Safety	Student requires constant reminders regarding safety or the safe use of equipment and facilities.	Student requires some reminders regarding safety or the safe use of equipment and facilities.	Student requires few reminders regarding safety or the safe use of equipment and facilities.	Student requires almost no reminders regarding safety or the safe use of equipment and facilities.

TEACHER COMMENTS:

_____

_____

_____

CLASS LIST: PHYSICAL EDUCATION

Physical Education Focus: _____

Student Name	Understanding Concepts	Application of Skills	Participation	Sportsmanship	Safety	Overall Mark

STUDENT FITNESS SURVEY

Complete this survey to learn more about your fitness habits.

	Rarely	Sometimes	Often
Do you spend time outside after school playing, riding your bike, or doing some active activity before or after supper?			
Do you participate in an organized sport at least once a week?			
Are you involved in at least one extra-curricular sport in school?			
Do you participate in active activities (like baseball, skipping, tag, etc.) during recess?			
Do you participate in sports with your family?			
Do you walk or ride your bike to and from school?			
Do you have fun when you are participating in sports?			
Do you participate in team sports?			
Do you participate in individual sports?			
Do you give 100% when you play sports?			

What does this fitness survey reveal about your fitness level? Explain.

_____

_____

_____

_____

_____

LEARNING SKILLS

LEARNING SKILLS RUBRIC

	Level 1	Level 2	Level 3	Level 4
Attendance	Student is late more than twice a week and/or attends class infrequently.	Student is occasionally late and/or attends class most of the time.	Student is rarely late and/or attends class regularly.	Student is always prompt and/or attends class regularly.
Behavior	Student needs constant teacher reminders about appropriate behavior.	Student sometimes needs teacher reminders about appropriate behavior.	Student rarely needs teacher reminders about appropriate behavior.	Student almost never needs teacher reminders about appropriate behavior.
Class Preparation	Student is rarely prepared and organized for class.	Student is sometimes prepared and organized for class.	Student is usually prepared and organized for class.	Student is almost always prepared and organized for class.
Listening Skills	Student rarely listens to others and speaks out of turn. Constant teacher reminders are needed.	Student sometimes listens to others and sometimes speaks out of turn. Some teacher reminders are needed.	Student usually listens to others and rarely speaks out of turn. Few teacher reminders are needed.	Student almost always listens to others and almost never speaks out of turn.
Time Management	Student rarely finishes work in the allotted time.	Student sometimes finishes work in the allotted time.	Student usually finishes work in the allotted time.	Student almost always finishes work in the allotted time.
Learning Attitude	Student rarely displays a positive attitude towards learning.	Student sometimes displays a positive attitude towards learning.	Student usually displays a positive attitude towards learning.	Student consistently displays a positive attitude towards learning.

CLASS LIST: LEARNING SKILLS

Time Period_____

Student Name	Attendance	Behaviour	Class Preparation	Listening Skills	Time Management	Learning Attitude

CLASS LIST: STUDENT PARTICIPATION

Subject _____

Date Student Name																			

Level 1 Student rarely contributes to class discussions and activities by offering ideas and asking questions.

Level 2 Student sometimes contributes to class discussions and activities by offering ideas and asking questions.

Level 3 Student usually contributes to class discussions and activities by offering ideas and asking questions.

Level 4 Student consistently contributes to class discussions and activities by offering ideas and asking questions.

CLASS LIST: HOMEWORK COMPLETION

Subject _____

	Date																						
Student Name																							

Level 1 Less than the half of the required homework is complete.
Level 2 More than half of the required homework is complete.
Level 3 Homework is complete.
Level 4 Homework is complete and has added detail.

GeoWat Innovative Publishing ©2005

HOMEWORK CHECKLIST
FOR FAMILIES

Dear Parents and Guardians,

Support your child's learning at home by incorporating the following homework checklist.

- ❖ Establish a regular time for homework each day.

- ❖ Do not allow TV or video games during homework time.

- ❖ Follow a daily routine, to help your child learn time management.

- ❖ Expect your child to take responsibility for their learning.

- ❖ Encourage your child to keep an agenda to track of homework, tests and special events.

- ❖ Be positive about homework, projects or tests. A positive attitude will create less anxiety for your child.

- ❖ Practice with your child reading directions independently.

- ❖ Take time with your child to review completed and graded assignments. Give positive and constructive feedback.

Your cooperation is greatly appreciated!

Kind regards,

_____

WEB PLANNER FOR_____

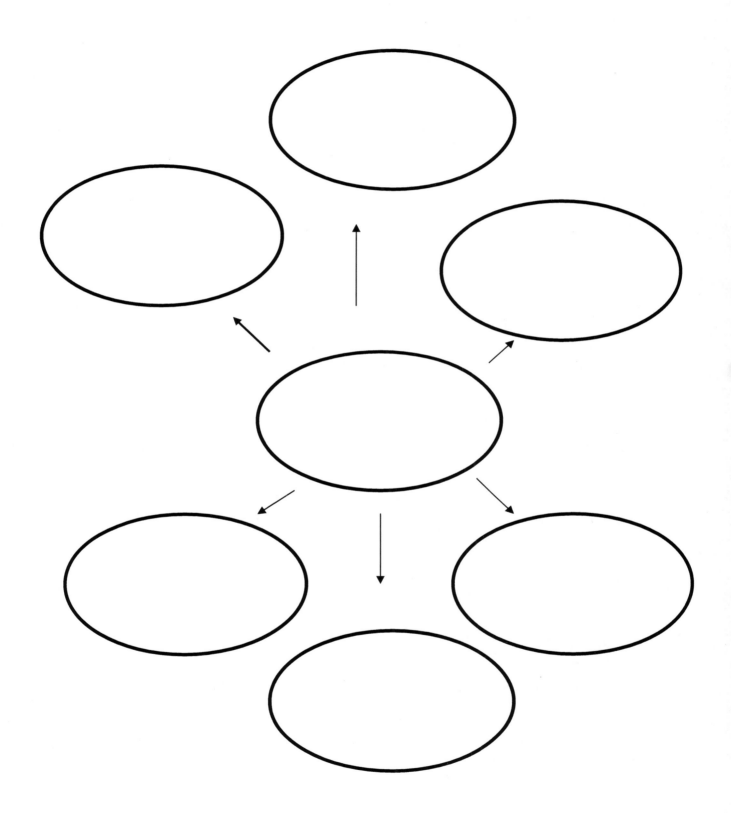

WONDERFUL JOB!

Congratulations to

_____

GREAT EFFORT!

Keep up the effort!

_____

Quality Worker

★ ★ ★ ★ ★ ★

NOTE TO TEACHERS: HOW TO USE THIS BOOK

JUMP was founded in the belief that all children, even those who have traditionally struggled at school, can learn mathematics. If you don't share this belief, you will probably leave some of your students behind, even if you are using these materials with the help of a team of tutors.

If you believe that some of the students in your class are not capable of learning math, we recommend that you read *The Myth of Ability: Nurturing Mathematical Talent in Every Child,* or consult the JUMP website (at www.jumpmath.org) for testimonials from teachers who have tried the program, and for a report on current research on the program. Please also read the Introduction to the Teacher's Manual which explains in detail how to implement the program. As well, please check our website periodically for information on newly-developed JUMP materials. (NOTE: We are presently developing enriched units and units on problem solving.)

To prepare your students to use this book, you should set aside 40 to 50 minutes a day for 3 weeks to teach them the material in the JUMP Fractions Unit. You may print individual copies of the unit from the JUMP website at no charge and you can order classroom sets (at cost) from the University of Toronto Press. NOTE: For large numbers, this option is cheaper than photocopying. The Fractions Unit has proven to be a remarkably effective tool for instilling a sense of confidence and enthusiasm about mathematics in students. The unit has helped many teachers discover a potential in their students that they might not otherwise have seen. In a recent survey, all of the teachers who used the Fractions Unit for the first time acknowledged afterwards that they had underestimated the abilities of some of their students. (For details of this study, see the JUMP website at www.jumpmath.org.)

Organization of the Workbooks

In some sections of these books (particularly in Part 1), you will find material that goes back a year or two before grade level. This is intentional: learning mathematics can take a great deal of practice (even for mathematicians!) but, in traditional math programs, students are often expected to recall material instantly even when they haven't seen it for a year. If you feel your students already know the material on a particular worksheet, you can skip the worksheet, or assign it to students who need review while other students work on something else. NOTE: See our website for a guide that tells you which curriculum requirements (for Eastern Canada, Ontario and Western Canada) are covered by each worksheet.

Do not assume that JUMP is merely a remedial program or does not teach math conceptually simply because it provides students with adequate practice and review. If you read both parts of the workbook from cover to cover (along with the accompanying activities and extensions in the Teacher's Manual) you will see that students are expected to advance to a very high conceptual level, in some areas beyond grade level. We would recommend that you complete Part 1 as soon as possible, so that you have time to cover all the material in Part 2.

In this new edition of the workbooks, we have attempted to provide an effective balance of concrete and symbolic work, and guided and independent work. If a worksheet is marked with an...

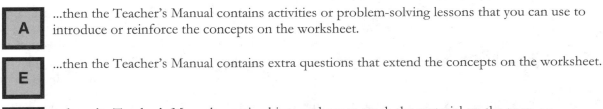

A ...then the Teacher's Manual contains activities or problem-solving lessons that you can use to introduce or reinforce the concepts on the worksheet.

E ...then the Teacher's Manual contains extra questions that extend the concepts on the worksheet.

M ...then the Teacher's Manual contains hints on how to teach the material on the page.

N ...then students will need a notebook to answer some of the questions on the page. (We would recommend that students always have a grid paper notebook on hand, for answering extra questions and questions that require additional room.)

Purpose of the Workbooks

Guided discovery is a fundamental approach in the JUMP program. Allow students to discover the concepts by themselves as much as possible. Bear in mind that in mathematics, more than in any other subject, discoveries can be made in steps. Even when you are guiding students in small steps, you can encourage them to discover the next step themselves. When you ask the class a question, allow students time to think about the answer: don't automatically pick the first person who raises their hand. Give hints and encouragement until every hand is up.

The workbooks were developed primarily as an assessment tool for teachers. On many of the worksheets, concepts and skills have been broken down into the most basic elements of understanding or perception, so you can see where students have missed steps in their understanding and can provide effective help.

We would encourage you not to simply assign questions from the workbooks.

Here are some suggestions:

- Before you assign a question from the workbook, you should verify that your students are prepared to answer the question without your help (or with minimal help). Give a short diagnostic quiz of four or five questions similar to the ones on the worksheet. Quizzes needn't count for marks but students should complete quizzes by themselves, without talking to their neighbours (otherwise you won't be able to verify if they know how to do the work independently). The quizzes will help you identify which students need an extra review before you move on. If any of your students finish a quiz early, assign extra questions similar to the ones on the quiz. On most worksheets, only one or two new concepts or skills are introduced, so that you should find it easy to verify that all of your students can answer the questions. Use the worksheet to assess comprehension and application of concepts and skills.

- If you have assistance in your classroom, try to have quizzes marked immediately. On days when you don't have assistance, check the work of students who might need extra help first, then take up the answers to the quiz at the board with the entire class (or use peer tutors to help with the marking).

- Students who finish a worksheet early should be assigned bonus questions similar to the questions on the worksheet, or extension questions from the manual. Write the bonus questions on the board (or have extra worksheets prepared) and ask students to answer the questions in their notebooks. While students are working independently on the bonus questions, you can spend extra time with anyone who needs help.

- Use the activities and games in the manual to extend ideas. If your students are confident and motivated, let them work independently to discover the ideas. Some worksheets can be used as a tool to verify that all students have the skills required to try an activity, others as an assessment tool to verify that all students have understood the concepts introduced by the activity.

In designing these books we have made an effort to address only one or two skills per page, so you should find it easy to create extra questions when necessary: just change the numbers in an existing question or add an extra element to a problem on the worksheet. For instance, if you have just taught students how to add a pair of three digit numbers, you might ask students who finish early to add a pair of four- or five-digit numbers. This extra work is the key to the JUMP program. Let students know how impressed you are with their abilities when you assign more challenging questions, and you will find that even students who previously had trouble focusing will race to finish their work so they can answer a bonus question too.

The bonus questions you create should generally be simple extensions of the material on the worksheet: if you create questions that are too hard or require too much background, you may have to help students who should be working independently. At times, though, you will want to assign more challenging questions: that is why we have provided extension questions in this edition. Four years of in-class implementations of JUMP have shown that a teacher can always keep faster students engaged with extra work. But if, instead of assigning bonus and extension questions, you allow some students to work ahead of others in the workbooks, you will never be able to build the momentum and excitement that comes when an entire class experiences success together.

On worksheets where several new concepts are introduced, a stop sign indicates a place where students should stop working until you have taught the material that comes after the stop sign. The pages entitled "Problems and Puzzles" or "Explorations in..." or "Concepts in..." contain more challenging word problems and activities for class or independent work. (Read the problems aloud to your students if they have trouble with the language.) You needn't assign all the questions on the page at once.

During the first few months of the program, set aside five to ten minutes every few days to work with students who need extra help. As students catch up and become more confident about their abilities, they will need less help. We would encourage you not to look on extra time you spend teaching math as time taken away from other subjects. A number of JUMP pilots have shown that the confidence and sense of focus students gain from succeeding at math will quickly spill over into other subjects.

We've found that the JUMP program works best when teachers give their students a great deal of praise and encouragement. If you teach in steps and allow enough practice and repetition, you'll find you won't be giving false encouragement.

If a student doesn't understand your explanation, assume that there is something lacking in your explanation, not in your student.

The worksheets are intended as models for teachers to improve upon: we hope you will take responsibility for providing students with warm-up questions and bonus questions, and for filling in the gaps in our materials wherever you find them. We have made a serious effort to introduce skills and concepts in small steps and in a coherent order, so a committed teacher should have no trouble seeing where they need to create extra questions for practice or where they need to fill in a missing step in the development of the ideas. This book is a work in progress: each year we are taught how to improve our materials by the hundreds of students and teachers who participate in the JUMP program. We would welcome any suggestions you have for improving the worksheets. All proceeds from the sale of these books have been donated to JUMP by the authors, so that the program can be made available to more children.

TABLE OF CONTENTS

NOTE: All acknowledgements are listed in Part 2.

Copyright © 2006, JUMP Math
JUMP Math: Workbook 8, Part 1 – ISBN 1-897120-32-X

PA8-1: Increasing Sequences

In an **increasing sequence**, each number is greater than the one before it.

Deborah wants to continue the number pattern: 6 , 8 , 10 , 12 , _?_

She finds the **difference** between the first two numbers: 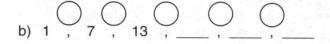   6 , 8 , 10 , 12 , _?_

6   7   8

She finds that the difference between the other numbers in the pattern is also 2. So the pattern was made by adding 2:   6 , 8 , 10 , 12 , ?

To continue the pattern, Deborah adds 2 to the last number in the sequence.

So the final number in the pattern is 14:   6 , 8 , 10 , 12 , 14

- -

1.   Extend the following patterns:

   NOTE: It is important to start by finding the gap between the numbers.

a) 4 , 7 , 10 , ___ , ___ , ___   b) 1 , 7 , 13 , ___ , ___ , ___

c) 1 , 6 , 11 , ___ , ___ , ___   d) 3 , 7 , 11 , ___ , ___ , ___

e) 4 , 9 , 14 , ___ , ___ , ___   f) 7 , 12 , 17 , ___ , ___ , ___

g) 1 , 11 , 21 , ___ , ___ , ___   h) 6 , 14 , 22 , ___ , ___ , ___

i) 41 , 44 , 47 , ___ , ___ , ___   j) 89 , 97 , 105 , ___ , ___ , ___

k) 13 , 20 , 27 , ___ , ___ , ___   l) 8 , 20 , 32 , ___ , ___ , ___

2.   Use an increasing sequence to solve this problem:

   A plant is 9 cm high. It grows 6 cm each week.

   a)   How high will it be after 4 weeks? _____

   b)   After how many weeks will the plant be 45 cm high? _____

In a **decreasing sequence**, each number is less than the one before it.

Inder wants to continue the number pattern:

25 , 23 , 21 , _?_

She finds the **difference** between the first two numbers:

25   24   23

25 ②23 , 21 , _?_

She finds that the difference between the other numbers in the pattern is also 2. So the pattern was made by subtracting 2.

The final number in the pattern is 19:

25 ②23 , 21 , _19_

---

1.   Extend the following patterns:
     NOTE: It is important to start by finding the gap between the numbers.

a) 19 , 16 , 13 , ____ , ____ , ____   b) 21 , 15 , 9 , ____ , ____ , ____

c) 51 , 46 , 41 , ____ , ____ , ____   d) 33 , 29 , 25 , ____ , ____ , ____

e) 53 , 48 , 43 , ____ , ____ , ____   f) 85 , 81 , 77 , ____ , ____ , ____

g) 61 , 50 , 39 , ____ , ____ , ____   h) 99 , 91 , 83 , ____ , ____ , ____

i) 72 , 65 , 58 , ____ , ____ , ____   j) 61 , 57 , 53 , ____ , ____ , ____

k) 91 , 82 , 73 , ____ , ____ , ____   l) 108 , 99 , 90 , ____ , ____ , ____

Use decreasing sequences to solve these problems:

2.   Paula has a roll of 87 stamps. She uses 8 each day for 7 days.
     How many are left?

3.   Sarah has saved $48. She spends $9 each day.
     How much money does she have left after 5 days?

PA8-3: Extending Patterns and Identifying Rules

1. Continue the following sequences by <u>adding</u> or <u>subtracting</u> the number given:

   a) (add 4)   48, 52, _____, _____, _____   b) (add 8)   26, 34, _____, _____, _____

   c) (subtract 3)   25, 22, _____, _____, _____   d) (subtract 5)   43, 38, _____, _____, _____

   e) (subtract 6)   85, 79, _____, _____, _____   f) (add 5)   89, 94, _____, _____, _____

   g) (subtract 9)   78, 69, _____, _____, _____   h) (add 13)   50, 63, _____, _____, _____

   i) (add 9)   74, 83, _____, _____, _____   j) (subtract 11) 115, 104, _____, _____, _____

2. What amount was added or subtracted to create the sequence?

   a) 71, 69, 67, 65   subtract _____   b) 55, 63, 71, 79   add _____

   c) 496, 492, 488, 484   _____   d) 167, 158, 149, 140,   _____

   e) 512, 505, 498, 491, 484 _____   f) 681, 668, 655, 642, 629   _____

3. Use the first three numbers in the pattern to find the rule. Then fill in the blanks:

   a) 52, 57, 62, _____, _____, _____   The rule is: <u>Start at 52 and add 5.</u>

   b) 82, 79, 76, _____, _____, _____   The rule is: _____

   c) 824, 836, 848, _____, _____, _____   The rule is: _____

   d) 1 011, 1 003, 995, _____, _____, _____   The rule is: _____

4. Create a pattern of your own. Give the rule you used:

   _____ , _____ , _____ , _____ , _____   My rule is: _____

5.   **7, 13, 19, 25, 31...**

   Tim says the pattern rule is: "Start at 7 and subtract 6 each time."
   Jack says the rule is: "Add 7 each time."
   Hannah says the rule is: "Start at 7 and add 6 each time."

   a) Whose rule is correct? _____

   b) What mistakes did the others make? _____

   _____

   _____

Claude makes an **increasing pattern** with squares. He records the number of squares in each figure in a chart or T-table. He also records the number of squares he adds each time he makes a new figure:

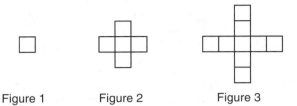

Figure 1   Figure 2   Figure 3

Figure	# of Squares
1	1
2	5
3	9

4 ← Number of squares added each time
4 ←

The number of squares in the figures are 1, 5, 9, …

Claude writes a rule for this number pattern:

RULE: Start at 1 and add 4 each time.

---

1. Claude makes other growing patterns with squares.
    How many squares does he add to make each new figure?
    Write your answer in the circles provided. Then write a rule for the pattern:

a)

Figure	Number of Blocks
1	2
2	7
3	12

Rule:
Start at _____
and add _____.

b)

Figure	Number of Blocks
1	2
2	9
3	16

Rule:

c)

Figure	Number of Blocks
1	1
2	4
3	7

Rule:

2. Extend the number pattern. How many blocks would be used in Figure 6?

a)

Figure	Number of Blocks
1	6
2	11
3	16

b)

Figure	Number of Blocks
1	2
2	6
3	10

c)

Figure	Number of Blocks
1	3
2	9
3	15

1. At the end of Week 1, Ryan has $150 in his savings account. He spends $15 each week.

   a) How much money will he have left at the end of Week 5?

   _____

   b) At the end of which week will he have no money left?

   _____

Week	Savings
1	$150
2	
3	
4	
5	

Make charts in your notebook to solve the following questions.

2. The water in a rain barrel is 18 cm deep at 5 pm. 3 cm of rain falls each hour. How deep is the water at 9 p.m.?

3. A marina rents kayaks for $8 for the first hour and $6 for every hour after that. How much would it cost to rent a kayak for 6 hours?

4.

   a) Make a chart as shown;

   b) How many shaded squares will be needed for a figure with 7 unshaded squares?

   c) How many squares will be need for a figure with 15 shaded squares?

Number of Unshaded Squares	Number of Shaded squares	Number of Squares
1	5	6

5. a) How much fuel will be left in the airplane after 25 minutes?

   b) How far from the airport will the plane be after 30 minutes?

   c) How much fuel will be left in the airplane when it reaches the airport?

Minutes	Litres of Fuel	Distance from Airport (km)
0	1200	525
5	1150	450
10	1100	375

6. Halley's Comet returns to Earth every 76 years. It was last seen in 1986.

   a) List the next three dates it will return to Earth.

   b) When was the first time Halley's comet was seen in the 1900's?

1. Find the <u>amount</u> by which the sequence <u>increases</u> or <u>decreases</u>. Write a number in the circle, with a '+' sign if the sequence increases and a '−' sign if it decreases. The first one has been done for you:

a) 3 , 7 , 5 , 12 , 8
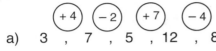
    (+4) (−2) (+7) (−4)

b) 4 , 9 , 5 , 14 , 19

c) 2 , 9 , 10 , 20 , 29

d) 9 , 2 , 7 , 0 , 10

e) 4 , 6 , 8 , 7 , 12

f) 17 , 16 , 19 , 10 , 11

g) 56 , 47 , 45 , 39 , 31

h) 45 , 54 , 59 , 63 , 55

2. Match each sequence with the sentence that describes it. This sequence....

a) **A** ... increases by 5 each time.
   B ... increases by different amounts.

   _____ 11 , 16 , 21 , 26 , 31

   _____ 9 , 15 , 17 , 34 , 37

b) **A** ... increases by 7 each time.
   B ... increases by different amounts.

   _____ 12 , 19 , 26 , 33 , 40

   _____ 6 , 13 , 18 , 26 , 33

c) **A** ... decreases by different amounts.
   B ... decreases by the same amount.

   _____ 21 , 20 , 18 , 15 , 11

   _____ 13 , 10 , 7 , 4 , 1

d) **A** ... decreases by 13 each time.
   B ... decreases by different amounts.

   _____ 72 , 59 , 46 , 33 , 20

   _____ 48 , 35 , 22 , 15 , 3

BONUS:

e) **A** ... increases by 5 each time.
   B ... decreases by different amounts.
   C ... increases by different amounts.

   _____ 23 , 28 , 29 , 35 , 43

   _____ 27 , 24 , 20 , 19 , 16

   _____ 34 , 39 , 44 , 49 , 54

f) **A** ... increases and decreases.
   B ... increases by the same amount.
   C ... decreases by different amounts.
   D ... decreases by the same amount.

   _____ 41 , 39 , 35 , 23 , 7

   _____ 10 , 14 , 9 , 6 , 5

   _____ 38 , 36 , 34 , 32 , 30

   _____ 28 , 31 , 34 , 37 , 40

3. Write a rule for each pattern. Use the words <u>add</u> or <u>subtract</u>, and say what number the pattern starts with:

a)   4 , 7 , 10 , 13   _Start at 4 and add 3._ _____

b)   13 , 19 , 25 , 31   _____

c)   48 , 45 , 42 , 39   _____

d)   54 , 49 , 44 , 39   _____

4. Write a rule for each pattern:
    NOTE: One sequence doesn't have a rule – see if you can find it.

a) 31 , 36 , 41 , 46   _____

b) 27 , 19 , 11 , 3   _____

c) 59 , 51 , 47 , 34 , 19   _____

d) 97 , 104 , 111 , 118   _____

5. Describe each pattern as <u>increasing</u>, <u>decreasing</u> or <u>repeating</u>:

a) 2 , 4 , 8 , 16 , 32 , 64   _____   b) 12 , 7 , 3 , 12 , 7 , 3   _____

c) 25 , 9 , 1 , 25 , 9 , 1   _____   d) 2 , 6 , 10 , 14 , 17   _____

e) 19 , 17 , 15 , 13 , 12   _____   f) 63 , 58 , 53 , 44 , 43   _____

Answer the following questions in your notebook.

6. Write the first five numbers in the pattern:

a) Start at 51 and add 6.   b) Start at 89 and subtract 7.   c) Start at 31 and add 8.

7. Create an increasing number pattern. Give the rule for your pattern.
    Do the same for a decreasing number pattern.

8. Create a repeating pattern using: a) letters   b) shapes   c) numbers

9. Create a pattern and ask a friend to find the rule for your pattern.

jump math
MULTIPLYING POTENTIAL

Patterns & Algebra 1

TEACHER: Review ordinal numbers before beginning this page.

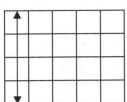

Columns run up and down.

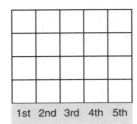

1st 2nd 3rd 4th 5th

Columns are numbered left to right (in this exercise).

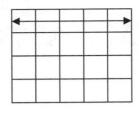

Rows run sideways.

1st
2nd
3rd
4th

Rows are numbered from top to bottom (in this exercise).

- -

1. Shade...

a)

1	5	9
9	13	17
17	21	25

the 2nd row

b)

1	5	9
9	13	17
17	21	25

the 1st column

c)

1	5	9
9	13	17
17	21	25

the 3rd column

d)

1	5	9
9	13	17
17	21	25

the diagonals
(one is shaded here)

Answer the questions below in your notebook.

2. For each chart below, describe any patterns you see in the numbers:
    NOTE: You should use the words "rows", "columns", and "diagonals" in your answer.

a)

3	5	7
7	9	11
11	13	15

b)

5	11	17	23
11	17	23	29
17	23	29	35
23	29	35	41

c)

13	16	19	22
10	13	16	19
7	10	13	16
4	7	10	13

3. Make up your own pattern and describe it:

4. Place the letters X and Y so that each row and each column has two Xs and two Ys in it:

5. a) Which row of the chart has a decreasing pattern (looking left to right)?

    b) Which column has a repeating pattern?

    c) Write pattern rules for the first and second column.

    d) Describe the relationship between the numbers in the third and fourth columns.

    e) Describe one other pattern in the chart.

    f) Name a row or column that does not appear to have any pattern.

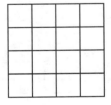

27	19	11	9	9
22	17	12	10	16
17	15	13	11	9
12	13	14	12	16
7	11	15	13	9

Patterns & Algebra 1

PA8-8: Extensions

1. In a magic square, the numbers in each row, column, and diagonal all add up to the same number (the "magic number" for the square):

   What is the magic number for this square? _____

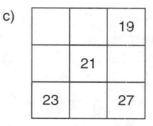

2. Complete the magic squares:

   a)   b)   c)

3. Here are some number pyramids:

   Can you find the rule by which the patterns in the pyramids were made? Describe it here:

4. Using the rule you described in Question 3, find the missing numbers:

   a) 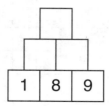   b) 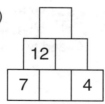   c) 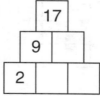   d) 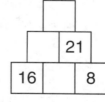   e)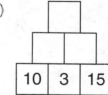

   f)   g)   h)   i)   j)

   k)   l)   m)

jump math
MULTIPLYING POTENTIAL.

E   Patterns & Algebra 1

PA8-9: 2-Dimensional Patterns (Advanced)

TEACHER:

For this worksheet, each student will need two copies of the hundreds charts from the Teacher's Guide.

1. Shade the numbers along any column of a hundreds chart.

   Write a rule for the pattern you see.

   Look at any other column. How do you explain what you see?

2. This picture shows part of a hundreds chart:

   Fill in the missing numbers using the pattern you found in Question 1.

	56	

3. Shade a 2 × 2 square as shown.

   Then add the pair of numbers on the "left to right" diagonal:

   Then add the pair on the "right to left" diagonal.

   "left to right" diagonal

   Try this again with different 2 × 2 squares. What do you observe?

4. Shade a 4-point square around any number on the chart (as shown).

   Add the pair of shaded numbers above and below the middle number.

   Add the pair of shaded numbers to the right and left of the middle number.

   Try this with several different 4 point squares.

   Can you explain what you notice?

5. Shade a 3 × 3 square as shown at left.

   a) Take the average of the two numbers above and below the centre square.

   What do you notice?

   b) Add the six numbers that lie in the columns shown:

   Repeat this with several 3 × 3 squares.

   What relation does the sum have to the number in the centre box?

BONUS:

6. a) Using a calculator, find the sums of the first 3 columns:

   b) Why are the sums equal?

   c) Describe any patterns you see in the hundreds chart.

1	2	3	4	5	6	7	8	9	10
20	19	18	17	16	15	14	13	12	11
21	22	23	24	25	26	27	28	29	30
40	39	38	37	36	35	34	33	32	31
41	42	43	44	45	46	47	48	49	50
60	59	58	57	56	55	54	53	52	51
61	62	63	64	65	66	67	68	69	70
80	79	78	77	76	75	74	73	72	71
81	82	83	84	85	86	87	88	89	90
100	99	98	97	96	95	94	93	92	91

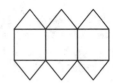

Brandon makes a garden path using square and triangular stones. He uses 2 triangular stones for every 1 square stone:

He writes an equation that shows how to calculate the number of triangles from the number of squares:

squares × 2 = triangles

or (for short): **2 × s = t**

Squares (s)	2 × s = t	Triangles (t)
1	2 × $\boxed{1}$ = 2	2
2	2 × $\boxed{2}$ = 4	4
3	2 × $\boxed{3}$ = 6	6

----

1. Each chart represents a different design for a path. Complete the charts:

a)

Squares (s)	3 × s = t	Triangles (t)
1	3 × $\boxed{1}$ = 3	4
2	3 × $\boxed{}$ = 6	
3	3 × $\boxed{}$ = 9	

b)

Squares (s)	4 × s = t	Triangles (t)
1	4 × $\boxed{}$ =	
2	4 × $\boxed{}$ =	
3	4 × $\boxed{}$ =	

2. Write a rule (or formula) to show how to calculate the number of triangles from the number of squares:

a)

Squares	Triangles
1	4
2	8
3	12

Multiply by 4

4 × s = t

b)

Squares	Triangles
1	5
2	10
3	15

c)

Squares	Triangles
1	7
2	14
3	21

d)

Squares	Triangles
1	6
2	12
3	18

3. Wendy makes broaches using squares (s) and triangles (t). Complete the chart and then write a formula (such as 4 × s = t) for each design:

a)

Squares (s)	Triangles (t)
1	
2	
3	

b)

Squares (s)	Triangles (t)
1	
2	
3	

Patterns & Algebra 1

In the auditorium of her school, Sandra notices that the number of chairs in each row is always four greater than the number of the row.

She writes an equation that shows how to calculate the number of chairs from the row number:

row number + 4 = number of chairs (or **r + 4 = c** for short)

Row	r + 4 = c	Chairs
1	☐1 + 4 = 5	5
2	☐2 + 4 = 6	6
3	☐3 + 4 = 7	7

Row 1
Row 2
Row 3

- -

4. Each chart represents a different arrangement of chairs. Complete the charts:

a)

Row	r + 5 = c	Chairs
1	☐1 + 5 = 6	6
2	☐ + 5 =	
3	☐ + 5 =	

b)

Row	r + 9 = c	Chairs
1	☐ + 9 =	
2	☐ + 9 =	
3	☐ + 9 =	

5. Find the number you must add to the row number to get the number of chairs. Write a formula using **r** for the row number and **c** for the number of chairs:

a)

Row	Chairs
1	5
2	6
3	7

Add 4

r + 4 = c

b)

Row	Chairs
1	8
2	9
3	10

c)

Row	Chairs
1	9
2	10
3	11

d)

Row	Chairs
7	11
8	12
9	13

6. Complete the charts. Then, in the box provided, write a formula for each arrangement of chairs:

a)

Row	Chairs

b)

Row	Chairs

TEACHER:
In T-tables, it is common to use the titles "input" and "output," or "term number" and "term." We will use both forms.

10. Apply the given rule to the numbers in the input column. Write your answer in the output column:

a)

INPUT	OUTPUT
2	
3	
4	

Rule: Add 5 to each input number.

b)

INPUT	OUTPUT
7	
8	
9	

Rule: Subtract 4 from each input number.

c)

INPUT	OUTPUT
3	
6	
9	

Rule: Multiply the input number by 7.

d)

TERM NUMBER	TERM
36	
24	
44	

Rule: Divide each term number by 4.

e)

TERM NUMBER	TERM
18	
19	
20	

Rule: Add 11 to each term number.

f)

TERM NUMBER	TERM
6	
7	
8	

Rule: Multiply each term number by 6.

11. For each chart, give a rule that tells you how to make the output numbers from the input numbers. See Question 10, above, for sample rules:

a)

INPUT	OUTPUT
3	10
4	11
5	12

Rule:

b)

INPUT	OUTPUT
5	8
7	10
9	12

Rule:

c)

INPUT	OUTPUT
1	9
2	18
3	27

Rule:

d)

TERM NUMBER	TERM
3	12
2	8
1	4

Rule:

e)

TERM NUMBER	TERM
2	16
4	32
6	48

Rule:

f)

TERM NUMBER	TERM
18	15
14	11
20	17

Rule:

Complete the T-table for each pattern.

Then write a rule that tells you how to calculate the output numbers from the input number. For instance, a rule could be: "Multiply the input by 3" or " Add 1 to the input".

1.

Number of Vertical Lines	Number of Horizontal Lines

2.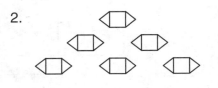

Number of Squares	Number of Triangles

3.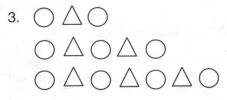

Number of Triangles	Number of Circles

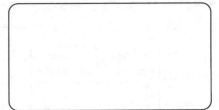

4.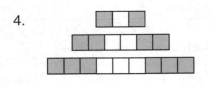

Number of White squares	Number of Grey squares

5.

Number of Diamonds	Number of Grey Squares

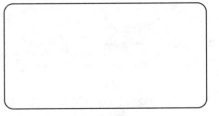

6. In your notebook, make a T-table and write a rule for the number of rectangles and triangles:

Figure 1   Figure 2   Figure 3

7. How many triangles are needed for 9 rectangles in the pattern in Question 6? How do you know?

PA8-12: Finding Rules for Patterns

1. Write a rule for the number of blocks in each figure, as shown in part a):

a)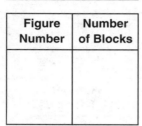

Figure 1   Figure 2   Figure 3

Figure Number	Number of Blocks
1	2
2	4
3	6

RULE: 2 × Figure Number

b)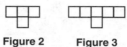

Figure 1   Figure 2   Figure 3

Figure Number	Number of Blocks

c)

Figure 1   Figure 2   Figure 3

Figure Number	Number of Blocks

d)

Figure 1   Figure 2   Figure 3

Figure Number	Number of Blocks

In each example above, you can find the **total number of blocks** by *multiplying* the **Figure Number** by the **number of blocks in the first figure**.

In such cases, the number of blocks is said to increase **directly** with the Figure Number.

2. Circle the sequences where the number of blocks varies directly with the Figure Number:

a)
Figure Number	Number of Blocks
1	4
2	8
3	12

b)
Figure Number	Number of Blocks
1	5
2	11
3	17

c)
Figure Number	Number of Blocks
1	6
2	12
3	18

d)
Figure Number	Number of Blocks
1	7
2	14
3	23

3. In each pattern below, the number of *shaded* blocks increases directly with the Figure Number. The *total* number of blocks however does not increase directly.

    i)   Write a rule for the number of *shaded* blocks in each sequence.

    ii)   Write a rule for the *total number* of blocks in each sequence.

a)

Figure 1   Figure 2   Figure 3

Rule for the number of shaded blocks:

    2 × Figure Number

Rule for the total number of blocks:

    2 × Figure Number + 1

b)

Figure 1   Figure 2   Figure 3

Rule for the number of shaded blocks:

Rule for the total number of blocks:

Answer the remaining question in your notebook.

c)

  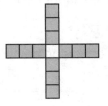

Figure 1   Figure 2   Figure 3

d)

Figure 1   Figure 2   Figure 3

e)

  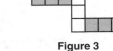

Figure 1   Figure 2   Figure 3

f)

Figure 1   Figure 2   Figure 3

4. Shade the part of the figure that varies <u>directly</u> with the Figure Number. (For practice seeing the part that varies <u>directly</u>, see Questions 2 and 3). Then write:

    i) a rule for the number of shaded blocks;

    ii) and a rule for the total number of blocks.

a)

Figure 1   Figure 2   Figure 3

b)

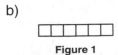

Figure 1   Figure 2   Figure 3

5. Draw a sequence of figures that might go with the following tables. Shade the part that varies directly with the Figure Number:

a)

Figure Number	Number of Blocks
1	3
2	5
3	7

b)

Figure Number	Number of Blocks
1	5
2	8
3	11

c)

Figure Number	Number of Blocks
1	6
2	10
3	14

Sudha counts the number of blocks in a sequence as follows:

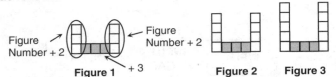

Figure 1   Figure 2   Figure 3

<u>Expression:</u>
Figure Number + 2 + Figure Number + 2 + 3

Nan counts the number of blocks as follows:

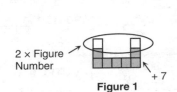

Figure 1   Figure 2   Figure 3

<u>Expression:</u>
2 × Figure Number + 7

6. a) Do Suhda's and Nan's expressions give the same number of blocks for each figure? Explain.

    b)

 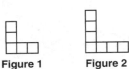

Figure 1   Figure 2   Figure 3

Show <u>two different ways</u> of calculating the number of blocks in this sequence (using the Figure Number).

INPUT	OUTPUT
1	5
2	8
3	11

In the T-table shown, the output is calculated from the input by <u>two</u> operations.

To find the rule, follow the steps below:

Step 1
Find the step (or gap) between the numbers in the OUTPUT column.

INPUT	INPUT × GAP	OUTPUT	
1		5	
2		8	⟩3
3		11	⟩3

Step 2
Multiply the INPUT numbers by the gap.

INPUT	INPUT × GAP	OUTPUT	
1	3	5	
2	6	8	⟩3
3	9	11	⟩3

Step 3
What must you add to each number in the second column?

INPUT	INPUT × GAP	OUTPUT	
1	3	5	
2	6	8	⟩3
3	9	11	⟩3

Add 2

Step 4
Write a rule for the T-table – **Rule:** Multiply by ___3___ and add ___2___.

TEACHER:
In T-tables, it is common to use the titles "input" and "output," or "term number" and "term." We will use both forms.

- -

1. Use the steps above to find the rule that tells you how to calculate the OUTPUT from the INPUT:

a)

INPUT	INPUT × GAP	OUTPUT	
1		3	○
2		5	
3		7	○

Add ____

Rule: Multiply by _____ and add _____.

b)

INPUT	INPUT × GAP	OUTPUT	
1		8	○
2		12	
3		16	○

Add ____

Rule: Multiply by _____ and add _____.

c)

INPUT	INPUT × GAP	OUTPUT	
1		7	○
2		10	
3		13	○

Add ____

Rule: Multiply by _____ and add _____.

d)

INPUT	INPUT × GAP	OUTPUT	
1		12	○
2		19	
3		26	○

Add ____

Rule: Multiply by _____ and add _____.

2. Write a rule that tells you how to calculate the OUTPUT (or Term) from the INPUT (or Term Number):

a)

INPUT	INPUT × GAP	OUTPUT
1		9
2		14
3		19

Multiply by _____ and add _____ .

b)

INPUT	INPUT × GAP	OUTPUT
1		12
2		18
3		24

Multiply by _____ and add _____ .

c)

TERM NUMBER	TERM NUMBER × GAP	TERM
1		7
2		11
3		15

Multiply by _____ and add _____ .

d)

TERM NUMBER	TERM NUMBER × GAP	TERM
1		7
2		12
3		17

Multiply by _____ and add _____ .

3. Write a rule that tells you how to calculate the OUTPUT (or Term) from the INPUT (or Term Number):
NOTE: In this case, you will have to subtract rather than add.

a)

INPUT	INPUT × GAP	OUTPUT
1		4
2		9
3		14

Multiply by _____ and subtract _____ .

b)

INPUT	INPUT × GAP	OUTPUT
1		2
2		5
3		8

Multiply by _____ and subtract _____ .

c)

TERM NUMBER	TERM NUMBER × GAP	TERM
1		0
2		4
3		8

Multiply by _____ and subtract _____ .

d)

TERM NUMBER	TERM NUMBER × GAP	TERM
1		5
2		11
3		17

Multiply by _____ and subtract _____ .

4. Complete the tables using the rules given. The first entry in part a) has been done for you:

a)
Input	Output
1	4
2	
3	
4	

Rule: Multiply by 3 and
add 1.

b)
Input	Output
1	
2	
3	
4	

Rule: Multiply by 5 and
subtract 4.

c)
Input	Output
2	
3	
4	
5	

Rule: Multiply by 7 and
add 5.

d)
Input	Output
2	
4	
6	
8	

Rule: Multiply by 4 and
subtract 2.

e)
Input	Output
15	
12	
10	
21	

Rule: Multiply by 2 and
add 3.

f)
Input	Output
48	
36	
116	
72	

Rule: Divide by 4 and
add 3.

5. Write the rule that tells you how to make the Output from the Input. Each rule involves <u>two</u> operations:
multiplication and addition, or multiplication and subtraction.
**HINT: Start by finding the <u>gap</u>. Multiply the gap by the Input. Then find what number you must add to (or subtract
from) the result to get the Output.**

a)
Input	Output
1	6
2	9
3	12

Rule:

b)
Input	Output
1	6
2	11
3	16

Rule:

c)
Input	Output
1	6
2	10
3	14

Rule:

d)
Input	Output
1	9
2	13
3	17

Rule:

e)
Input	Output
1	1
2	4
3	7

Rule:

f)
Input	Output
1	32
2	42
3	52

Rule:

6. Write a rule that tells you how to make the Output from the Input:
   NOTE: Each rule may involve either one or two operations.

a)

Input	Output
1	2
2	7
3	12
4	17

Rule:

b)

Input	Output
1	4
2	10
3	16
4	22

Rule:

c)

Input	Output
1	5
2	6
3	7
4	8

Rule:

d)

Input	Output
1	11
2	13
3	15
4	17

Rule:

e)

Input	Output
0	4
1	8
2	12
3	16

Rule:

f)

Input	Output
1	7
2	14
3	21
4	28

Rule:

BONUS:

7. Find the rule by guessing and checking:
   HINT: If you subtract the Input from the Output and you always get the same number, you know the rule only involves addition or subtraction. Otherwise the rule will involve multiplication and possibly addition or subtraction.

a)

Input	Output
5	28
6	33
7	38
8	43

Rule:

b)

Input	Output
8	13
4	5
3	3
7	11

Rule:

c)

Input	Output
10	21
9	19
3	7
1	3

Rule:

d)

Input	Output
4	7
5	9
6	11
7	13

Rule:

e)

Input	Output
77	63
78	64
79	65
80	66

Rule:

f)

Input	Output
2	7
4	13
6	19
8	25

Rule:

1. For each pattern, draw Figure 4 and fill in the T-table.

    Then write a rule that tells you how to calculate the output from the input:

a)   1   2   3   4

Figure	Number of Triangles
1	
2	
3	
4	

Rule for T-table: _____

Use your rule to predict how many triangles will be needed for Figure 9: _____

b)   1   2   3   4

Figure	Perimeter
1	
2	
3	
4	

Rule for T-table: _____

Use your rule to predict the perimeter of Figure 11: _____

c)   1   2   3   4

  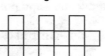

Figure	Number of Squares
1	
2	
3	
4	

Rule for T-table: _____

Use your rule to predict the number of squares needed for Figure 10: _____

d)   1   2   3   4

Figure	Perimeter
1	
2	
3	
4	

Rule for T-table: _____

Use your rule to predict the perimeter of Figure 23: _____

1. A **term number** gives the position of a term in a pattern. For instance, in part a), the term circled is <u>term number</u> 5 since it is the fifth term in the sequence.

   State the term number of each number circled below:

   a) 8, 11, 14, 17, (20) 23   b) 4, 6, 8, (10) 12, 14, 16   c) 58, 54, 50, 46, 42, (38)

   <u>   term number 5   </u>   _____   _____

   > The sequences above (and in the previous five sections) are called **linear patterns**.
   >
   > A pattern is linear if you can find the value of the term by multiplying (or dividing) the term number by a fixed amount and then by adding or subtracting by a fixed amount.

2. Describe each linear pattern below in <u>two</u> ways:

   i) Give a **stepwise rule** that tells you the first term of the sequence and what you need to add or subtract to each term to get the next term.

   ii) Give a **general rule** that tells you how to calculate any term from the term number.

   a) 1, 3, 5, 7

   Stepwise rule: <u> Start at 1 and add 2. </u>

   _____

   General rule: <u> Multiply the term number </u>
   <u> by 2 and subtract 1. </u>

   b) 3, 7, 11, 15, 19

   Stepwise rule: _____

   _____

   General rule: _____

   _____

   c) 12, 17, 22, 27, 32

   Stepwise rule: _____

   _____

   General rule: _____

   _____

   d) 12, 10, 8, 6, 4

   Stepwise rule: _____

   _____

   General rule: _____

   _____

Answer the remaining questions in your notebook.

   e) 7, 12, 17, 22, 27   f) 18, 15, 12, 9, 6   g) 10, 15, 20, 25, 30   h) 5, 11, 17, 23, 29

3. Make a table of values for the number of blocks or toothpicks in each pattern. Then write a <u>stepwise rule</u> and a <u>general rule</u> for the pattern:

   a)

   b)

BONUS:

4. For each sequence below…

   i) Find the gap between successive terms.   ii) Describe how the gap changes.

   iii) Write a stepwise rule: identify the first term and then describe how to create successive terms.

   iv) Can you write a <u>general rule</u> for each pattern (i.e. a rule that tells you how to calculate the term from the term number)? Why or why not?

   a) 3, 4, 6, 9, 13   b) 6, 7, 9, 13, 21, 37

1. Write the correct symbol (+ or ×) in the circle to make the equation true:

   a) 5 (+) 2 = 7   b) 4 ( ) 15 = 19   c) 5 ( ) 3 = 8   d) 3 ( ) 5 = 15

   e) 9 ( ) 1 = 10   f) 8 ( ) 5 = 13   g) 2 ( ) 4 = 8   h) 8 ( ) 6 = 14

   i) 5 ( ) 4 = 9   j) 8 ( ) 5 = 40   k) 7 ( ) 3 = 21   l) 7 ( ) 1 = 7

2. Write the correct symbol (+, –, or ×) in the circle to make the equation true:

   a) 8 ( ) 3 = 24   b) 7 ( ) 3 = 4   c) 3 ( ) 3 = 9   d) 7 ( ) 1 = 6

   e) 4 ( ) 7 = 11   f) 4 ( ) 4 = 16   g) 9 ( ) 3 = 6   h) 9 ( ) 3 = 12

   i) 9 ( ) 5 = 14   j) 8 ( ) 1 = 9   k) 4 ( ) 7 = 28   l) 5 ( ) 14 = 19

NOTE: For some questions below, you will need to do long division or multiply large numbers. Do any rough work in your notebook.

3. Continue the following sequences by <u>multiplying</u> each term by the given number:

   a) 3 (×3) , 9 , ____ , ____ , ____   b) 1 (×4) , 4 , ____ , ____ , ____

   c) 4 (×2) , 8 , ____ , ____ , ____   d) 1 (×8) , 8 , ____ , ____ , ____

4. Each term in the sequence below was made by <u>multiplying</u> the previous term by a fixed number. Find the number and continue the sequence:

   a) 2 (×) , 8 , 32 , ____ , ____   b) 3 (×) , 6 , 12 , ____ , ____

   c) 1 (×) , 5 , 25 , ____ , ____   d) 2 (×) , 6 , 18 , ____ , ____

5. Each of the sequences below was made by <u>multiplication</u>, <u>addition</u>, or <u>subtraction</u>. Continue the sequence:

   a) 3 , 7 , 11 , ____ , ____   b) 5 , 8 , 11 , ____ , ____   c) 18 , 14 , 10 , ____ , ____

   d) 3 , 6 , 12 , ____ , ____   e) 16 , 20 , 24 , ____ , ____   f) 1 , 3 , 9 , ____ , ____

6. In your notebook, write a rule for each sequence in Question 5.
   HINT: The rule for the first sequence is: "Start at 3 and add by 4."

PA8-17: Patterns with Increasing & Decreasing Steps
      – Part II
      page 24

1. In the sequences below, the step or gap between the numbers increases. Can you see a pattern in the way the gap increases? Use the pattern to extend the sequence:

a) 3 , 5 , 8 , 12 , ____ , ____

b) 4 , 5 , 7 , 10 , 14 , ____ , ____

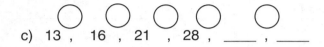

c) 13 , 16 , 21 , 28 , ____ , ____

d) 7 , 9 , 13 , 19 , 27 , ____ , ____

2. In the sequences below, the gap between the numbers decreases. Can you see a pattern in the way the gap decreases? Use the pattern to extend the sequence:

a) 28 , 22 , 17 , 13 , ____ , ____

b) 52 , 42 , 34 , 28 , ____ , ____

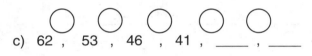

c) 62 , 53 , 46 , 41 , ____ , ____

d) 310 , 280 , 255 , 235 , 220 , ____ , ____

3. Complete the T-table for Figure 3 and Figure 4. Then use the pattern in the gap to predict the number of triangles needed for Figures 5 and 6:

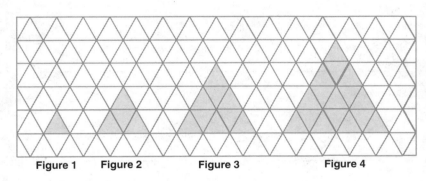

Figure 1   Figure 2   Figure 3   Figure 4

Figure	Number of Triangles
1	1
2	4
3	
4	
5	
6	

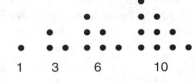

Write the number of triangles added each time here.

4. a) The Ancient Greeks investigated numbers that could be arranged in geometric shapes. The first four **triangular** numbers are shown in the figures below:

      i) Find the 5th and 6th triangular numbers by drawing a picture:

      ii) Describe the pattern in the triangular numbers. How does the step change?

          1   3   6   10

      iii) Find the 8th triangular number by extending the pattern you found in part ii).

      iv) Add any two consecutive triangular numbers. What kind of number do you get?

5. In each sequence below, the step changes in a regular way (it increases, decreases, or increases and decreases). Write a rule for each pattern:

a) 2 $\overset{+3}{}$, 5 $\overset{+5}{}$, 10 $\overset{+7}{}$, 17 $\overset{+9}{}$, 26

Rule: Start at 2. Add 3, 5, 7 … (the step increases by 2)

b) 7 $\overset{+4}{}$, 11 $\overset{-2}{}$, 9 $\overset{+4}{}$, 13 $\overset{-2}{}$, 11

Rule : Start at 7. Add 4, then subtract 2. Repeat.

c) 1 , 2 , 4 , 7 , 11

Rule: _____

d) 6 , 8 , 5 , 7 , 4

Rule: _____

e) 24 , 23 , 20 , 15 , 8

Rule: _____

f) 17 , 20 , 25 , 32 , 41

Rule: _____

Answer the following questions in your notebook.

6. Write a rule for each pattern. Then give the value of the 5th term.

a) 0 , 3 , 8 , 15

b) 1 , 3 , 9 , 27

7. Write a rule for the number of shaded squares or triangles in each figure. Use your rule to predict the number of shaded parts in the 5th figure.

HINT: To count the number of triangles in the last figure in part b), try skip counting by 3s.

a)

  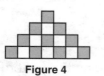

Figure 1   Figure 2   Figure 3   Figure 4

b)

Figure 1   Figure 2   Figure 3   Figure 4

8. Create a pattern with a step that increases and decreases.

Answer the following questions in your notebook.

1. a) Pick any number greater than 1 on **Pascal's Triangle**.
   Add the two numbers directly above it.
   Try this again several times.
   Do you see a pattern?

   b) Use the pattern you found in
   part a) to fill in the missing numbers
   in the triangle.

   c) What is the second number
   in the 15th row of
   Pascal's Triangle?
   **HINT: What is the pattern
   in the 2nd diagonal?**

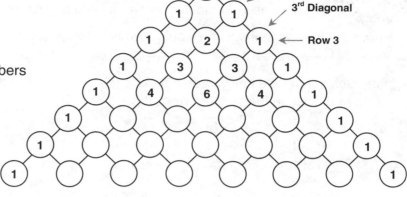

Pascal's Triangle

   d) Describe the pattern in the
   3rd diagonal of Pascal's Triangle.

   e) Add the numbers in each row of Pascal's Triangle. What pattern do you see in the sums?

   f) Using the pattern you found in part e), predict the sum of the numbers in Row 10.

   g) Describe any other patterns you see in Pascal's Triangle.

2. Every 6th person who arrives at a book sale receives a free calendar, and every 8th person receives a free book. Which of the first 50 people receive a book and a calendar?

3. a) How many shaded squares will be on the
   perimeter of the 10th figure? How do you know?

   b) How many white squares there will be in a figure that
   has a perimeter of 32 shaded squares?

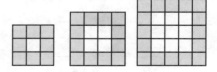

4. Describe any patterns you see in the chart:
   HINT: Look at the rows, columns and diagonals.

1	2	3	4	5	6
12	11	10	9	8	7
13	14	15	16	17	18
24	23	22	21	20	19
25	26	27	28	29	30
36	35	34	33	32	31

5.
$$2 = 1 \times 2$$
$$2 + 4 = 2 \times 3$$
$$2 + 4 + 6 = 3 \times 4$$
$$2 + 4 + 6 + 8 = 4 \times 5$$

   a) Describe any patterns you see in the
   sums shown.

   b) Using the patterns you found in
   part a), find the sum of the first
   ten even numbers.

Figure 1

There are eight dots in Figure 1.

Each pair of dots is joined by exactly 1 line segment (●——●).

How can you find out how many line segments there are without counting every line?

A mathematician would start with fewer dots and use a pattern to make a prediction.

1. For each set of dots below, use a ruler to join every pair of dots with a straight line. Write the number of lines in the space provided:

a)

1 dot

_____ lines

b)

2 dots

_____ lines

c)

3 dots

_____ lines

d)

4 dots

_____ lines

TEACHER:
Check that every student has the correct answer to Question 1 before moving on.

2. Write the numbers you found in Question 1 on the lines above their appropriate letter (a, b, c or d). Find the gaps between the numbers and write your answers in the circles provided:

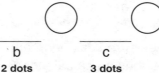

a   b   c   d
1 dot 2 dots 3 dots 4 dots

3. Predict the gaps and numbers in the sequence. Write your predictions below:

1 dot 2 dots 3 dots 4 dots 5 dots 6 dots

4. Test your predictions by joining the dots in each figure:

Were you right?

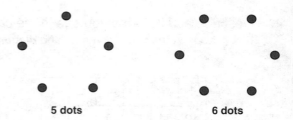

5 dots   6 dots

5. a) Use the rule you discovered to calculate the number of line segments in Figure 1:

_____

b) If you joined every pair of dots in a set of 10 dots, how many lines would you need?

_____

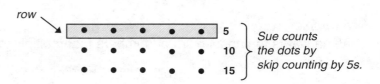

When you multiply a pair of numbers, the result is called the **product** of the numbers. You can represent a product using an **array**:

row → 5 ·· 10 ·· 15

Sue counts the dots by skip counting by 5s.

Sue writes a multiplication statement for the array: **3 × 5 = 15**   (3 and 5 are called **factors** of 15)

----

1. Write a multiplication statement for each array:

a)

b)

c)

___3___ rows

___4___ dots in each row

___3 × 4 = 12___

_____ rows

_____ dots in each row

_____

_____

_____

_____

2. Write a product for each array:

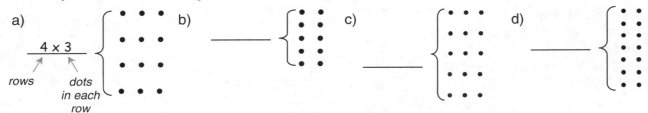

a)   4 × 3   {   b) _____ {   c) _____ {   d) _____ {

rows   dots in each row

Answer the questions below in your notebook.

3. Draw arrays for these products:

a) 2 × 5   b) 3 × 7   c) 4 × 6   d) 1 × 8   e) 4 × 2

4. There are <u>three</u> ways to arrange 4 dots in an array.

So there are only three ways to write 4 as a product of two factors:

· · · ·   1 × 4 = 4   2 × 2 = 4   4 × 1 = 4

How many ways can you write each number as a product of two factors?
HINT: Draw arrays to help.

a) 6   b) 8   c) 9   d) 10   e) 12

5. The numbers that appear beside the arrays in Question 4 are called the **factors** of 4. The factors of 4 are the numbers 1, 2, and 4.

Write a list of factors for the numbers 6, 8, 9, 10, and 12.

NS8-2: Organized Lists

Example:
Alana wants to find all pairs of numbers that multiply to give 15.

There are no numbers that will multiply by 2 or 4 to give 15,
so Alana leaves those rows in her chart blank.

The numbers in the last row of the chart are the same as those
in the 3rd row so Alana knows she has found all pairs:

$$1 \times 15 = 15 \quad \text{and} \quad 3 \times 5 = 15$$

1st Number	2nd Number
1	15
2	-
3	5
4	-
5	3

----

1. Find all pairs of numbers that multiply to give the number in bold:

a) 6

1st	2nd

b) 8

1st	2nd

c) 10

1st	2nd

2. Find all the ways to make the amounts using quarters and dimes:

   NOTE: Some entries in your chart may not work.

a) 80¢

quarters	dimes
0	
1	
2	

b) 105¢

quarters	dimes

3. Find all widths and lengths of all non-congruent rectangles with area 12 units:

Width	Length
1	

4. Complete the chart to find all rectangles whose side lengths are whole numbers and that have perimeter 12 units:

Width	Length
1	

Answer the remaining questions in your notebook.

5. Make a chart to find all the pairs of numbers that multiply to give a product of:

   a) 12   b) 14   c) 20   d) 24

6. Find all rectangles with side lengths that are whole numbers that have:

   a) perimeter 14 units.   b) area 10 square units.

   c) perimeter 12 units and area 9 square units.

NS8-3: Prime Numbers and Composite Numbers

A **prime** number has <u>two</u> distinct factors (no more, no less): itself and 1.

A **composite** number has <u>more than two</u> distinct factors: at least one number **other than** itself and 1

- -

1. a)   How many distinct factors does the number 1 have? _____   b)   Is 1 a prime number? _____

2. List all prime numbers less than 15: _____

3. List all the composite numbers between 20 and 30: _____

4. What is the greatest prime number less than 30? _____

5. Circle the prime numbers:

   a)   6   7   2   9   5   1   b)   4   3   11   12   19   14

   c)   12   24   15   13   8   20   d)   27   18   12   17   29   31

6. Eratosthenes was a Libyan scholar who lived over 2 000 years ago. He developed a method to systematically identify prime numbers.
   It is called **Eratosthenes' Sieve**.

   Follow the directions below to identify the prime numbers from 1 to 100:

   a)   Cross out the number 1 (it is not prime).

   b)   Circle 2, and cross out all the multiples of 2.

   c)   Circle 3, and cross out all the multiples of 3 (that haven't already been crossed out).

   d)   Circle 5, and cross out all the multiples of 5 (that haven't already been crossed out).

   e)   Circle 7, and cross out all the multiples of 7 (that haven't already been crossed out).

   f)   Circle all remaining numbers

   You've just used Eratosthenes' Sieve to find all the prime numbers from 1 to 100!

1	2	3	4	5	6	7	8	9	10
11	12	13	14	15	16	17	18	19	20
21	22	23	24	25	26	27	28	29	30
31	32	33	34	35	36	37	38	39	40
41	42	43	44	45	46	47	48	49	50
51	52	53	54	55	56	57	58	59	60
61	62	63	64	65	66	67	68	69	70
71	72	73	74	75	76	77	78	79	80
81	82	83	84	85	86	87	88	89	90
91	92	93	94	95	96	97	98	99	100

7. The prime numbers 3 and 5 differ by 2.
   Find 3 other pairs of prime numbers less than 20 that differ by 2:

1. List all the factors of each number. The first one is done for you.

   a) 12: _1, 2, 3, 4, 6, 12_____   b) 18: _____

   c) 14: _____   d) 25: _____

   e) 6: _____   f) 16: _____

   g) 24: _____   h) 35: _____

   i) 60: _____   j) 70: _____

2. Put a check mark in front of the numbers that are composite numbers.

   ___ 40   ___ 19   ___ 22   ___ 11   ___ 7   ___ 15   ___ 50   ___ 100

3. Write a number between 0 and 20 that has:

   a) two factors: _____   b) four factors: _____   c) five factors _____

4. Cross out any number that is not a multiple of 3: | 15   17   20   24   30   40 |

5. Write the three numbers less than 40, which have 2 and 5 as factors: _____   _____   _____

6. Write three consecutive numbers which are also all composite numbers: ⬚   ⬚   ⬚

7. Write five odd multiples of 3, between 10 and 40: _____   _____   _____   _____   _____

Show your work for the remaining questions in your notebook.

8. I am a prime number less than 10.
   If you add 10 or 20 to me, the result is a prime number.
   What number am I?

9. Find the sum of the first five composite numbers.

10. How many prime numbers are there between 30 and 50?

NS8-5: Prime Factorization

Any **composite** number can be written as a product of prime numbers. This expression is called the **prime factorization** of the original number.

10×2 is not a prime factorization of 20 (because the number 10 is composite). But $5 \times 2 \times 2$ is a prime factorization of 20.

----

1. You can find a prime factorization for a number by using a **factor tree**.

   Here is how you can make a factor tree for the number 20:

   Step 1
   Find any pair of numbers (not including one) that multiply to give 20:

   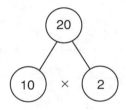

   Step 2
   Repeat Step 1 for the numbers on the "branches" of the tree:

   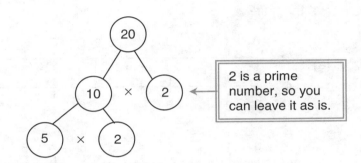

   Complete the factor tree for the numbers below:

   a) 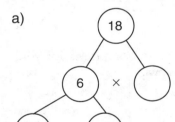   b) 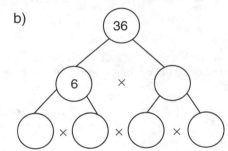   c)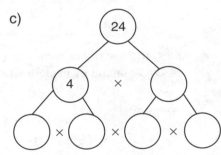

2. Write a prime factorization for each number below. The first one is started for you:

   HINT: It helps to first find any factorization and then factor any composite numbers in the factorization.

   a) $20 = 10 \times 2 =$ b) $12 =$

   c) $9 =$ d) $15 =$

Show your work for the remaining questions in your notebook.

3. Using a factor tree, find prime factorizations for:

   a) 30   b) 36   c) 27   d) 28   e) 75

4. Here are some branching patterns for factor trees:

   Can you find a factor tree for the number 24 that looks different from the tree in Question 1 c)?

   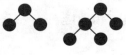 

NS8-6: Lowest Common Multiples

The multiples of 2 and 3 are marked with Xs on the number lines below:

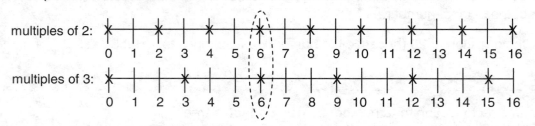

| 0 is a multiple |
| of <u>every</u> number. |

The **lowest common multiple (LCM)** of 2 and 3 is 6: 6 is the least non-zero number that 2 and 3 <u>both</u> divide into evenly.

---

1. Mark the multiples of the given numbers on the number lines. What is the lowest common multiple of the pair?

    a) 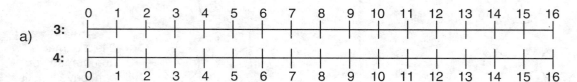   LCM = _____

    b) 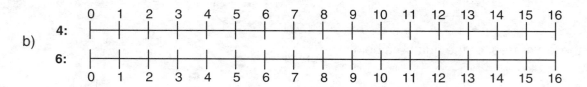   LCM = _____

2. Find the lowest common multiple of each pair of numbers. The first one has been done for you:
    HINT: Count up by the largest number until you find a number that both numbers divide into.

    a) 3 and 5

    3: 3, 6, 9, 12, **15**, 18

    5: 5, 10, **15**, 20

    LCM = _15___

    b) 4 and 10

    LCM = _____

    c) 3 and 9

    LCM = _____

    d) 2 and 6

    LCM = _____

    Find the remaining lowest common multiples in your notebook.

    e) 2 and 10   f) 3 and 6   g) 3 and 12   h) 4 and 8   i) 8 and 10

    j) 5 and 15   k) 6 and 10   l) 3 and 10   m) 6 and 8   n) 6 and 9

3. Landon cuts the lawn at 24 Maple St. every 4th day, starting on August 4.
    He cuts the lawn at 102 Deerfield Drive every 5th day, starting on August 5.

    What is the first day that Landon will cut the lawns at both places? _____

If a factor is shared by two numbers, it is called a **common factor** of the numbers. For instance, 3 is a common factor of 12 and 18.

The **greatest common factor** (GCF) of two numbers is the greatest number that is a factor of both numbers. For instance, 6 is the GCF of 12 and 18.

---

1. Find the factors of each number below by drawing all non-congruent rectangles (with whole number sides) that have an area equal to the number:

   a) 12   b) 10

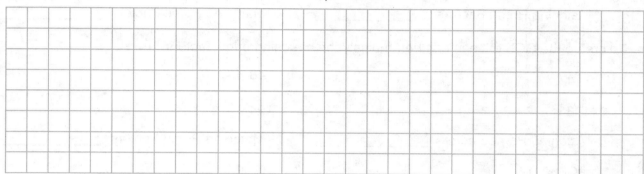

2. Find all factors of each number by dividing by the whole numbers in increasing order. When can you stop dividing? (First divide by 2, then 3, then 4, etc.) Show which whole numbers divide evenly into each number, as shown in a):

   a) 68

   $68 \div 1 = 68$
   $68 \div 2 = 34$
   $68 \div 4 = 17$

   Factors: __1, 2, 4, 17, 34, 68__

   b) 28

   Factors: _____

   c) 46

   Factors: _____

   d) 54

   Factors: _____

3. List the factors of each number in increasing order. Draw lines to match any common factors. Circle the GCF:

   a) 12: 1, 2, 3, 4, ⑥ 12
       18: 1, 3, ⑥ 9, 18

   b) 14:
       42:

   c) 24:
       36:

   d) 13:
       25:

4. The prime factorization of each number is given. Draw lines to match common prime factors:

    a) $180 = 2 \times 2 \times 3 \times 3 \times 5$
        $120 = 2 \times 2 \times 2 \times 3 \times 5$

        Matching Prime Factors: __2, 2, 3, 5__

    b) $60 = 2 \times 2 \times 3 \times 5$
        $50 = 2 \times 5 \times 5$

        Matching Prime Factors: _____

    c) $42 = 2 \times 3 \times 7$

        $72 = 2 \times 2 \times 2 \times 3 \times 3$

        Matching Prime Factors: _____

    d) $90 = 2 \times 3 \times 3 \times 5$

        $140 = 2 \times 2 \times 5 \times 7$

        Matching Prime Factors: _____

5. To create the GCF of each number, multiply the matching prime factors.

    a) $84 = 2 \times 2 \times 3 \times 7$
        $108 = 2 \times 2 \times 3 \times 3 \times 3$

        Matching Prime Factors: __2, 2, 3__

        GCF: __12__

    b) $48 =$

        $24 =$

        Matching Prime Factors: _____

        GCF: _____

6. Write a prime factorization for each number, then find the GCF of each pair.

    a) 44 and 55   b) 27 and 39   c) 82 and 94   d) 110 and 140   e) 68 and 96

7. 2 and 5 are common factors of a pair of numbers between 101 and 121. What are the numbers?

8. What is the least number that has factors 2, 3, 4, and 5? (Is it $2 \times 2 \times 3 \times 5$ or $2 \times 3 \times 4 \times 5$?)

9. The lowest common multiple of 18 and 42 is 126. What is the next greatest common multiple?

10. To find the LCM of a pair of numbers, follow the steps shown below for the numbers 84 and 120:

Step 1
Write a prime factorization for each number:

$84 = 2 \times 2 \times 3 \times 7$

$120 = 2 \times 2 \times 2 \times 3 \times 5$

Step 2
Draw lines to match common prime factors. Circle the factors that are left over:

$84 = 2 \times 2 \times 3 \times \boxed{7}$
$120 = 2 \times 2 \times \boxed{2} \times 3 \times \boxed{5}$

Step 3
Multiply the matched prime factors and the factors that are left over – the result is the LCM of 84 and 120:

$\underbrace{2 \times 2 \times 3}_{\substack{\text{matched} \\ \text{(common)} \\ \text{prime factors}}} \times \underbrace{2 \times 5 \times 7}_{\substack{\text{leftover} \\ \text{prime factors}}} = 12 \times 70 = \mathbf{840}$

Find the LCM of the following pairs of numbers:

a) 18, 20
b) 24, 36
c) 48, 56

The **power** 2^3 is a short form for repeated multiplication: $2 \times 2 \times 2$.

$$\underset{\text{base}}{\nearrow}2\overset{\nwarrow \text{exponent}}{^3}$$

The **exponent** in a power tells you how many times to write the **base** in a product.

> *Example:*
> $5^3 = \underbrace{5 \times 5 \times 5}_{\textbf{3} \text{ fives}}$ $7^2 = \underbrace{7 \times 7}_{\textbf{2} \text{ sevens}}$

- -

1. Write the exponent and base for each power:

   a) 2^3

   base: ____ exponent: ____

   b) 3^2

   base: ____ exponent: ____

   c) 7^4

   base: ____ exponent: ____

2. Write each power as a product:

   a) $9^2 =$

   b) $7^3 =$

   c) $8^4 =$

3. Write each product as a power:

   a) $3 \times 3 \times 3 =$

   b) $4 \times 4 \times 4 \times 4 =$

   c) $9 \times 9 =$

   d) $8 \times 8 \times 8 \times 8 =$

4. Evaluate:

   a) The second power of 8

   b) The third power of 3

   c) The fourth power of 2

5. The table shows the buttons you should push on a calculator to calculate a power:

		Press
2^2	2×2	2 × =
2^3	$2 \times 2 \times 2$	2 × = =
2^4	$2 \times 2 \times 2 \times 2$	2 × = = =

   a) How many times would you press the = button to calculate each power?

   i) 2^7: ____ times   ii) 5^3: ____ times   iii) 8^5: ____ times   iv) 3^{15}: ____ times

   b) Write each power as a product and then use a calculator to find the answers:

   i) $6^3 =$

   ii) $5^3 =$

   iii) $9^3 =$

6. Write each number as a power:

   a) $8 = 2^3$

   b) $27 =$

   c) $49 =$

   d) $36 =$

   e) $16 =$

   f) $32 =$

   g) $64 =$

   h) $81 =$

7. Fill in the missing number:

   a) $2^{\square} = 16$

   b) $3^{\square} = 81$

   c) $\square^4 = 81$

   d) $\square^3 = 27$

   e) $\square^5 = 32$

   f) $2^{\square} = 8$

   g) $4^{\square} = 16$

   h) $5^{\square} = 125$

   i) $\square^2 = 64$

   j) $\square^3 = 64$

   k) $\square^2 = 49$

   l) $6^{\square} = 36$

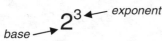

1. Evaluate. Show your work, as in part a) below:

a) 5×2^2

$= \dfrac{5 \times 4}{20}$

$= \underline{\hspace{1cm}}$

b) 3×2^3

$= \underline{\hspace{2cm}}$

$= \underline{\hspace{1cm}}$

c) 2×4^2

$= \underline{\hspace{2cm}}$

$= \underline{\hspace{1cm}}$

d) 2×5^2

$= \underline{\hspace{2cm}}$

$= \underline{\hspace{1cm}}$

e) $2^2 \times 3^2$

$= \underline{\hspace{2cm}}$

$= \underline{\hspace{1cm}}$

f) $3^2 \times 2^3$

$= \underline{\hspace{2cm}}$

$= \underline{\hspace{1cm}}$

g) $10^2 \times 5^2$

$= \underline{\hspace{2cm}}$

$= \underline{\hspace{1cm}}$

h) $2^2 + 3^2$

$= \underline{\hspace{2cm}}$

$= \underline{\hspace{1cm}}$

i) $7^2 + 6^2$

$= \underline{\hspace{2cm}}$

$= \underline{\hspace{1cm}}$

j) $8^2 - 2^2$

$= \underline{\hspace{2cm}}$

$= \underline{\hspace{1cm}}$

2. Answer the following questions by regrouping and using the fact that:

25 × 4 = 100   **5 × 2 = 10**   **50 × 2 = 100**

a) $5 \times 5 \times 3 \times 2$

b) $25 \times 3 \times 7 \times 4$

c) $5 \times 3 \times 2 \times 7$

d) $3 \times 25 \times 11 \times 4$

e) 75×8

f) 45×14

g) 5×22

h) 35×18

i) $2 \times 2 \times 5$

j) $2 \times 2 \times 2 \times 5 \times 5$

k) $2 \times 2 \times 2 \times 2 \times 5 \times 5 \times 5$

l) $2^5 \times 5^4$

Answer the remaining questions in your notebook.

3. Write each number in exponential form:
   HINT: For instance, $180 = 2 \times 2 \times 3 \times 3 \times 5 = 2^2 \times 3^2 \times 5$

a) $900 = 2 \times 2 \times 3 \times 3 \times 5 \times 5$

b) $294 = 2 \times 3 \times 7 \times 7$

c) $1800 = 2 \times 2 \times 2 \times 3 \times 3 \times 5 \times 5$

4. a) Write the first six powers of 2.
   b) What is the pattern in the ones digit of your answers?
   c) What is the ones digit of the following powers?   i) 2^{10} ii) 2^{15}

5. Write the first six powers of 5. What is the ones digit of 5^{20}? Explain.

6. Write each number in standard form. Then write the numbers in order from least to greatest.

a) $2^2 \times 3^3$

b) 4×11^2

c) $2 \times 5^2 \times 7$

d) $2^3 \times 6^2$

7. Are the prime factors of 6 and 6^2 the same or different? Explain.

8. What is the greatest common factor of 3^4 and 3^5?

9. What is the lowest common multiple of 3^4 and 3^5?

10. Calculate these differences: $1^2 - 0^2$ $2^2 - 1^2$ $3^2 - 2^2$ $4^2 - 3^2$ $5^2 - 4^2$
    a) What pattern do you see in the results?   b) Use the pattern to predict the value of $9^2 - 8^2$.

11. Use the pattern – shown in parts a) through c) – to predict the number of zeroes in each expression:

a) $10^2 = 100$

b) $10^3 = 1\,000$

c) $10^4 = 10\,000$

d) $10^5 = $ _____

e) $10^7 = $ _____

f) $10^8 = $ _____

12. Write each number as a power of 10:

a) $10\,000 = \underline{\ 10^4\ }$

b) $1\,000\,000 = $ _____

c) $10\,000\,000 = $ _____

13. Write each number as a power of 10. Show your work, as in part a) below:

a) $1\,000 \times 10\,000$

= __10 000 000__ = __10^7__

b) $10\,000 \times 1\,000\,000$

= _____ = _____

c) $10\,000\,000 \div 1\,000$

= _____ = _____

d) $10 \times 1\,000 \times 10\,000$

= _____ = _____

14. Write each number in expanded form: (i) using *multiples* of 10   (ii) using *powers* of 10

a) 78 752

= __$7 \times 10\,000 + 8 \times 1\,000 + 7 \times 100 + 5 \times 10 + 2$__

= __$7 \times 10^4 + 8 \times 10^3 + 7 \times 10^2 + 5 \times 10 + 2$__

b) 36 982

= _____

= _____

c) 4 025 901

= _____

= _____

13. Write each number in standard form:

a) $7 \times 10^4 + 3 \times 10^3 + 5 \times 10^2$

= __7 350__

b) $4 \times 10^5 + 3 \times 10^4 + 4 \times 10^3 + 5 \times 10^2 + 1 \times 10 + 9$

= _____

c) $3 \times 10^3 + 5 \times 10$

= _____

d) $9 \times 10^5 + 5 \times 10^3 + 3 \times 10 + 7$

= _____

e) $9 \times 10^5 + 3 \times 10^2 + 7$

= _____

f) $7 \times 10^8 + 9 \times 10^7$

= _____

14. Write > or < in the square to show which number is greater:

a) $5 \times 10^4 + 2 \times 10^3 + 7$ ☐ $5 \times 10^4 + 2 \times 10^2 + 7$

b) $9 \times 10^5 + 3 \times 10^3 + 2 \times 10^2$ ☐ $9 \times 10^5 + 7 \times 10^3 + 2 \times 10^2$

Fractions name equal parts of a whole.

This pie is cut into 4 equal parts; 3 parts out of 4 are shaded:

So $\frac{3}{4}$ of the pie is shaded.

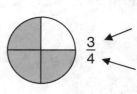

The **numerator** (3) tells you how many parts are counted.

$\frac{3}{4}$

The **denominator** (4) tells you how many equal parts are in a whole.

1. Draw lines to divide each figure into equal parts. Then say what fraction of each figure is shaded:

   a)   b)    c)   d)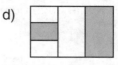

2. Divide each line into the given parts, as done in part a) below:

   a) Thirds

   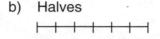

   b) Halves

   c) Thirds

   d) Quarters

   e) Fifths

Fractions can name parts of a set:

$\frac{3}{5}$ of the figures are pentagons, $\frac{1}{5}$ are squares and $\frac{1}{5}$ are circles:

1. Fill in the blanks:

   a) $\frac{4}{10}$ of the figures are _____.   b) $\frac{3}{10}$ of the figures are _____.

   c) _____of the figures are squares.   d) _____ of the figures are triangles.

   d) $\frac{8}{10}$ of the figures are _____.   f) _____ of the figures are unshaded.

2. A baseball team wins 12 games, loses 5 games, and ties 2 games. What fraction of the games did the team:

   a) win? _____   b) lose? _____   c) tie? _____

3.

	Whole Numbers from 2 to 9	Whole Numbers from 10 to 16
Prime Numbers	2, 3,	
Composite Numbers		

   a) Fill in the chart (the first part is started for you);

   b) What fraction of the whole numbers from 2 to 9 are composite?

   c) What fraction of the whole numbers from 2 to 16 are prime?

Mattias and his friends ate the amount of pie shown:

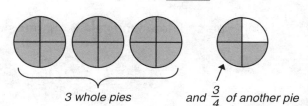

They ate three and three quarter pies altogether (or $3\frac{3}{4}$ pies).

3 whole pies   *and $\frac{3}{4}$ of another pie*

$3\frac{3}{4}$ is called a **mixed fraction** because it is a mixture of a whole number and a fraction.

----

1. Follow the example to find the <u>mixed</u> fraction for each picture:

a)

<u> 2 </u> whole pies and $\frac{1}{3}$ of

another pie = $2\frac{1}{3}$ pies

b)

___ whole pie and ___ of

another pie = _____ pies

c)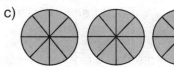

___ whole pies and ___ of

another pie = _____ pies

2. Write each fraction as a <u>mixed</u> fraction:

a)

b)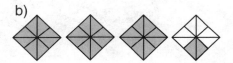

c)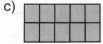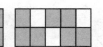

d)

3. Shade the amount of area given in bold:
   NOTE: There may be more figures than you need.

a) $2\frac{2}{3}$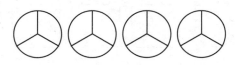

b) $3\frac{1}{4}$

c) $1\frac{5}{6}$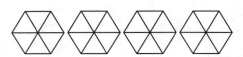

d) $2\frac{4}{5}$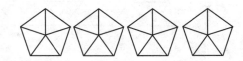

Answer the remaining questions in your notebook.

4. Sketch:

   a) $2\frac{1}{3}$ pies   b) $3\frac{3}{4}$ squares   c) $1\frac{3}{5}$ pies   d) $2\frac{5}{6}$ rectangles   e) $3\frac{7}{8}$ circles

5. Order from smallest to largest: $4\frac{2}{3}$, $4\frac{1}{4}$ and $3\frac{3}{4}$.

6. Which is closer to 5, $5\frac{3}{4}$ or $4\frac{2}{3}$? Explain.

Huan-Yue and her friends ate **9** quarter-sized pieces of pizza:

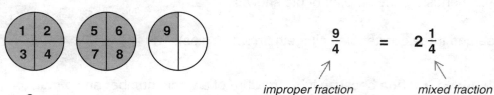

$$\frac{9}{4} = 2\frac{1}{4}$$

improper fraction *mixed fraction*

Altogether, they ate $\frac{9}{4}$ pizzas.

When the numerator of a fraction is larger than the denominator, the fraction represents *more than a whole*. Such fractions are called **improper fractions**.

- -

1. Write these fractions as <u>improper</u> fractions:

a)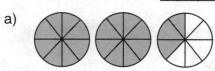

b)

c)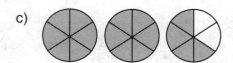

d)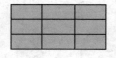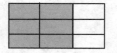

e)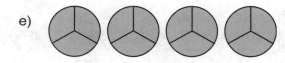

f)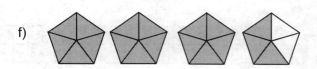

2. Shade one piece at a time until you have shaded the amount of pie given in bold:

a) $\frac{13}{4}$

b) $\frac{5}{2}$

c) $\frac{8}{3}$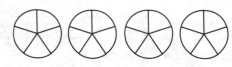

d) $\frac{15}{5}$

Answer the remaining questions in your notebook.

3. Sketch: a) $\frac{7}{3}$ pies b) $\frac{13}{4}$ squares c) $\frac{9}{2}$ parallelograms d) $\frac{11}{6}$ rectangles e) $\frac{17}{8}$ circles

4. Order from smallest to largest: $\frac{7}{4}$, $\frac{9}{4}$, $\frac{9}{3}$, $\frac{10}{3}$.

5. Which fractions are improper fractions? How do you know? a) $\frac{5}{7}$ b) $\frac{13}{11}$ c) $1\frac{9}{8}$ d) $\frac{8}{3}$

1. Write these fractions as <u>mixed</u> fractions and as <u>improper</u> fractions:

   a)
   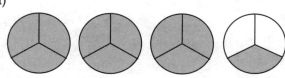

   b)
   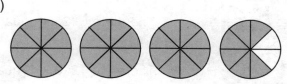

   c)
   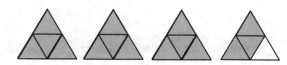

   d)
   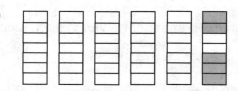

   e)
   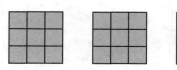

   f)
   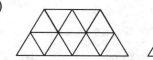
   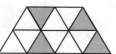

2. Shade the amount of pie given in bold. Then write an <u>improper</u> fraction for the amount of pie:

   a) $4\frac{1}{2}$

   Improper Fraction: _____

   b) $3\frac{3}{5}$
   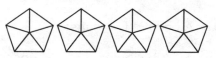

   Improper Fraction: _____

3. Shade the amount of area given in bold. Then write a <u>mixed</u> fraction for the amount of area shaded:

   a) $\frac{11}{3}$

   Mixed Fraction: _____

   b) $\frac{11}{4}$
   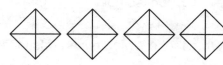

   Mixed Fraction: _____

   c) $\frac{17}{6}$
   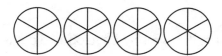

   Mixed Fraction: _____

   d) $\frac{21}{8}$
   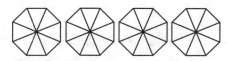

   Mixed Fraction: _____

4. In your notebook, draw a picture to find out which fraction is greater:

   a) $3\frac{1}{2}$, $2\frac{2}{3}$, $\frac{5}{3}$
   b) $1\frac{4}{5}$, $2\frac{1}{4}$, $\frac{11}{5}$
   c) $\frac{13}{4}$, $\frac{7}{2}$, $2\frac{2}{3}$
   d) $\frac{15}{8}$, $\frac{13}{5}$, $\frac{7}{3}$

5. How could you use division to find out how many <u>whole</u> pies are in $\frac{24}{7}$ of a pie? Explain.

NS8-14: More Mixed Fractions

 There are 4 quarter pieces in 1 pie.

 There are 8 (2 × 4) quarters in 2 pies.

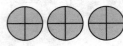 There are 12 (3 × 4) quarters in 3 pies.

How many quarter pieces are in $3\frac{3}{4}$ pies?

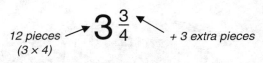

12 pieces (3 × 4) $\longrightarrow 3\frac{3}{4} \longleftarrow$ + 3 extra pieces

So there are 15 quarter pieces altogether.

---

1. Find the number of **halves** in each amount:

   a) 1 pie = _____ halves

   b) 3 pies = _____ halves

   c) 5 pies = _____ halves

   d) $2\frac{1}{2}$ pies = _____ halves

   e) $4\frac{1}{2}$ pies = _____ halves

   f) $6\frac{1}{2}$ pies = _____

2. Find the number of **thirds** in each amount:

   a) 1 pie = _____ thirds

   b) 2 pies = _____ thirds

   c) 3 pies = _____ thirds

   d) $1\frac{1}{3}$ pies = _____ thirds

   e) $3\frac{2}{3}$ pies = _____

   f) $5\frac{1}{3}$ pies = _____

3. A box holds 4 cans:

   a) 2 boxes hold _____ cans

   b) $2\frac{1}{2}$ boxes hold _____ cans

   c) $4\frac{3}{4}$ boxes hold _____ cans

4. A bag holds 16 peas:

   a) $1\frac{1}{16}$ boxes hold _____ peas

   b) $2\frac{1}{2}$ boxes hold _____ peas

   c) $3\frac{1}{4}$ boxes hold _____ peas

5. Write the following mixed fractions as improper fractions:

   a) $2\frac{2}{3} = \frac{}{3}$

   b) $3\frac{1}{2} = \frac{}{2}$

   c) $5\frac{4}{5} =$

   d) $4\frac{3}{4} =$

   e) $5\frac{2}{7} =$

BONUS:

6. Envelopes come in packs of 6. Alice used $2\frac{5}{6}$ packs. How many envelopes did she use? _____

7. How many quarters are there in $4\frac{1}{2}$ dollars? _____

8. Maia and her friends ate $2\frac{3}{4}$ pizzas. How many quarter-sized pieces did they eat? _____

9.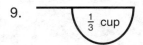

   A $\frac{1}{3}$ cup

   B $\frac{1}{6}$ cup

   Cindy needs $3\frac{2}{3}$ cups of flour.

   a) How many scoops of cup A would she need? _____

   b) How many scoops of cup B would she need? _____

Number Sense 1

NS8-15: More Mixed and Improper Fractions

How many whole pies are there in $\frac{13}{4}$ pies?

There are 13 pieces altogether, and each pie has 4 pieces.
So you can find the number of whole pies by dividing 13 by 4:   **13 ÷ 4 = 3 remainder 1**

There are 3 whole pies and 1 quarter left over: $\frac{13}{4} = 3\frac{1}{4}$

----

1. Find the number of whole pies in each amount by dividing:

    a) $\frac{4}{2}$ pies = _____ whole pies   b) $\frac{15}{3}$ pies = _____ whole pies   c) $\frac{16}{4}$ pies = _____ whole pies

    d) $\frac{21}{7}$ pies = _____ whole pies   e) $\frac{25}{5}$ pies = _____ whole pies   f) $\frac{30}{6}$ pies = _____ whole pies

2. Find the number of whole pies and the number of pieces remaining by dividing:

    a) $\frac{5}{2}$ pies = ___2___ whole pies and ___1___ half pie = ___$2\frac{1}{2}$___ pies

    b) $\frac{11}{2}$ pies = _____ whole pies and _____ half pie = _____ pies

    c) $\frac{13}{3}$ pies = _____ whole pies and _____ third = _____ pies

    d) $\frac{17}{4}$ pies = _____ whole pies and _____ fourth = _____ pies

Answer the following questions in your notebook.

3. Write the following improper fractions as mixed fractions:

    a) $\frac{5}{2}$ b) $\frac{14}{3}$ c) $\frac{17}{6}$ d) $\frac{21}{4}$ e) $\frac{29}{5}$ f) $\frac{31}{7}$ g) $\frac{70}{9}$ h) $\frac{61}{8}$

4. Write a mixed and improper fraction for the number of litres:

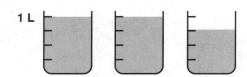

5. Write a mixed and improper fraction for the length of the rope:

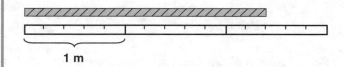

6. Order from smallest to biggest: $\frac{7}{3}$, $\frac{9}{4}$, $\frac{5}{2}$

7. Between which two whole numbers is $\frac{21}{8}$?

8. How much greater than a whole is: a) $\frac{11}{7}$ b) $\frac{8}{5}$ c) $\frac{5}{3}$ d) $\frac{19}{10}$

9. Which fractions are greater than 3 but less than 4?   a) $\frac{17}{4}$ b) $\frac{5}{3}$ c) $\frac{16}{5}$ d) $\frac{5}{2}$ e) $\frac{11}{6}$

Dan has 6 cookies. He wants to give $\frac{2}{3}$ of his cookies to his friends. To do so, he shares the cookies equally onto 3 plates:

There are 3 equal groups, so each group is $\frac{1}{3}$ of 6.

There are 2 cookies in each group, so $\frac{1}{3}$ of 6 is 2.

There are 4 cookies in two groups, so $\frac{2}{3}$ of 6 is 4.

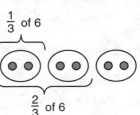

$\frac{1}{3}$ of 6

$\frac{2}{3}$ of 6

-----

1. Write a fraction for the amount of dots shown. The first one has been done for you:

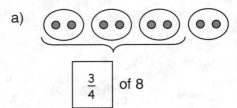

a) $\boxed{\frac{3}{4}}$ of 8

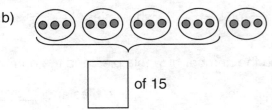

b) $\boxed{}$ of 15

2. Fill in the missing numbers:

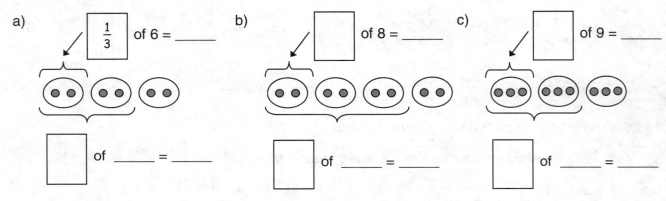

a) $\boxed{\frac{1}{3}}$ of 6 = _____

$\boxed{}$ of _____ = _____

b) $\boxed{}$ of 8 = _____

$\boxed{}$ of _____ = _____

c) $\boxed{}$ of 9 = _____

$\boxed{}$ of _____ = _____

d) $\boxed{}$ of _____ = _____

e) $\boxed{}$ of _____ = _____

3. Draw a circle to show the given amount. The first one has been done for you:

a) $\frac{2}{3}$ of 6

b) $\frac{3}{4}$ of 8

4. Fill in the correct number of dots in each circle, then draw a larger circle to show the given amount:

a) $\frac{2}{3}$ of 12

b) $\frac{1}{3}$ of 15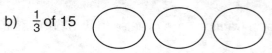

5. Find the fraction of the whole amount by sharing the cookies equally:

   HINT: Draw the correct number of plates then place the cookies one at a time. Then circle the correct amount.

   a) Find $\frac{2}{3}$ of 9 cookies.　　　　　　　b) Find $\frac{3}{5}$ of 10 cookies.

   $\frac{2}{3}$ of 9 is _____　　　　　　　$\frac{3}{5}$ of 10 is _____

6. Andy finds $\frac{2}{3}$ of 12 as follows:

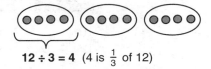 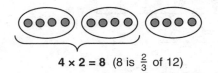

Step 1 He finds $\frac{1}{3}$ of 12 by dividing 12 by 3:

$12 \div 3 = 4$ (4 is $\frac{1}{3}$ of 12)

Step 2 Then he multiplies the result by 2:

$4 \times 2 = 8$ (8 is $\frac{2}{3}$ of 12)

Find the following amounts using Andy's method:

a) $\frac{2}{3}$ of 9 =　　b) $\frac{3}{4}$ of 8 =　　c) $\frac{2}{3}$ of 15 =　　d) $\frac{2}{5}$ of 10 =　　e) $\frac{3}{5}$ of 25 =

f) $\frac{3}{7}$ of 21 =　　g) $\frac{5}{7}$ of 28 =　　h) $\frac{3}{8}$ of 24 =　　i) $\frac{3}{4}$ of 12 =　　j) $\frac{1}{3}$ of 27 =

7. 24 students are on a soccer team. $\frac{3}{8}$ are girls. How many girls are on the team?_____

8. A bookstore with 18 copies of a book sold $\frac{5}{6}$ of the books.

   a) How many books were sold? _____　　　　b) How many books were left? _____

9. Shade $\frac{5}{8}$ of the squares. Draw stripes in $\frac{1}{4}$ of the squares.
   How many squares are blank? _____

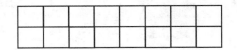

Answer the following questions in your notebook.

10. Una has a collection of 28 insects. $\frac{1}{4}$ are butterflies. $\frac{2}{7}$ are moths. The rest are beetles. How many insects are beetles?

11. Eldon started practicing piano at 7:45. He played scales for $\frac{1}{6}$ of an hour, popular songs for $\frac{2}{5}$ of an hour, and his solo for $\frac{1}{4}$ of an hour. At what time did he stop playing?

Aidan shades $\frac{2}{6}$ of the squares in an array:

He then draws heavy lines around the squares to group them into 3 equal groups:

He sees that $\frac{1}{3}$ of the squares are shaded.

The pictures show that two sixths are equal to one third: $\frac{2}{6} = \frac{1}{3}$

Two sixths and one third are **equivalent fractions**.

----

1. Group the squares to make an equivalent fraction:

   a)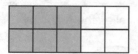
   $$\frac{6}{10} = \frac{}{5}$$

   b)
   $$\frac{4}{6} = \frac{}{3}$$

   c)
   $$\frac{10}{12} = \frac{}{6}$$

2. 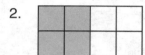   Write three equivalent fractions for the amount shaded here:

   _____ _____ _____

3. Group the buttons to make an equivalent fraction:

   a)
   $$\frac{4}{6} = \frac{}{}$$

   b)
   $$\frac{3}{6} = \frac{}{}$$

   c)
   $$\frac{2}{6} = \frac{}{}$$

   d)
   $$\frac{6}{9} = \frac{}{}$$

   e)
   $$\frac{6}{10} = \frac{}{}$$

4. Cut each pie into smaller pieces to make an equivalent fraction:

   a)
   $$\frac{2}{3} = \frac{}{6}$$

   b)
   $$\frac{2}{3} = \frac{}{9}$$

   c)
   $$\frac{3}{4} = \frac{}{12}$$

5. a) Draw lines to cut the pies into:

   b) Then fill in the numerators of the equivalent fractions:

   $$\frac{1}{2} = \frac{}{4} = \frac{}{6} = \frac{}{8}$$

   4 pieces   6 pieces   8 pieces

6. Draw shaded and un-shaded circles in your notebook (as in Question 3). Group the circles to show:

   a) six eighths is equivalent to three quarters

   b) four fifths is equivalent to eight tenths

NS8-18: Reducing Fractions

A fraction is reduced to **lowest terms** when the only whole number that will divide into its numerator and denominator is the number 1. $\frac{2}{4}$ is *not* in lowest terms (because 2 divides into 2 and 4) but $\frac{1}{2}$ is in lowest terms.

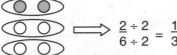 

$$\frac{2 \div 2}{6 \div 2} = \frac{1}{3} \qquad\qquad \frac{4 \div 4}{8 \div 4} = \frac{1}{2}$$

You can reduce a fraction to lowest terms by dividing a set of counters representing the fraction into equal groups.

Step 1: Count the number of counters in each group.

Step 2: Divide the numerator and denominator of the fraction by the number of counters in each group.

- -

1. Reduce these fractions by grouping:

a) $\frac{2}{4} = \frac{}{2}$ b) $\frac{3}{9} = \frac{}{3}$ c) $\frac{4}{6} = \frac{}{3}$

2. Show how you would reduce the fractions by dividing:

a) $\frac{2 \div}{4 \div} = \frac{}{}$ b) $\frac{3 \div}{9 \div} = \frac{}{}$ c) $\frac{4 \div}{6 \div} = \frac{}{}$

3. Reduce the fractions below by dividing:

a) $\frac{2}{10} = \frac{}{}$ b) $\frac{2}{6} = \frac{}{}$ c) $\frac{2}{8} = \frac{}{}$ d) $\frac{2}{12} = \frac{}{}$

e) $\frac{3}{9} = \frac{}{}$ f) $\frac{3}{15} = \frac{}{}$ g) $\frac{4}{12} = \frac{}{}$ h) $\frac{6}{9} = \frac{}{}$

i) $\frac{4}{6} = \frac{}{}$ j) $\frac{10}{15} = \frac{}{}$ k) $\frac{20}{25} = \frac{}{}$ l) $\frac{8}{12} = \frac{}{}$

4.

Hair Colour	Number of Students
Black	10
Brown	8
Blonde	4
Red	2

The chart to the left shows the hair colour of a class of students.

a) What fraction of the students have brown hair? _____

b) What colour of hair do one sixth of the students have? _____

c) What fraction of the students have black or red hair? _____

E

Number Sense 1

1. Mark the number line with Xs, as shown in a), to create an equivalent fraction for the part shaded:

a)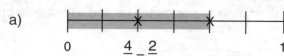

$$\frac{4}{6} = \frac{2}{3}$$

b)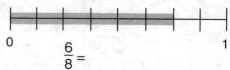

$$\frac{6}{8} =$$

c)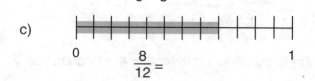

$$\frac{8}{12} =$$

d)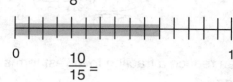

$$\frac{10}{15} =$$

2. Subdivide the line into ten equal parts using a ruler and then mark the following fractions:

A) $\frac{3}{10}$ B) $\frac{7}{10}$ C) $\frac{9}{10}$ D) $\frac{1}{2}$ E) $\frac{2}{5}$

3.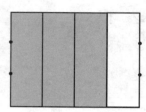

$$\frac{3}{4} =$$

Use a ruler to join the dots with horizontal lines to create an equivalent fraction.

4.

Use a ruler to divide the box into smaller boxes to show that $\frac{1}{3} = \frac{2}{6}$

5. $\frac{5}{6}$ of a pizza is covered in olives ⬤ . $\frac{1}{3}$ of the pizza is covered in mushrooms ⬆ .

Each piece has a topping. Complete the picture:

How many pieces are covered in olives **and** mushrooms? _____

6. Equivalent fractions are said to be in the same **family**.
    Write two fractions in the same family as the fraction in each triangle:

a) 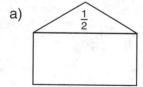   b) 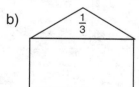   c) 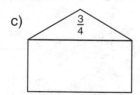   d)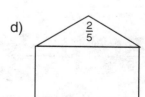

7. In each question, circle the **pair** of fractions that are in the same family: a) $\frac{1}{2}$ $\frac{4}{6}$ $\frac{5}{10}$ b) $\frac{3}{15}$ $\frac{16}{20}$ $\frac{4}{5}$ c) $\frac{2}{3}$ $\frac{4}{6}$ $\frac{1}{4}$

8. Find two fractions from the fraction family of $\frac{4}{12}$ with numerators smaller than 4: _____

9. Find five fractions from the fraction family of $\frac{12}{24}$ with numerators smaller than 12: _____

NS8-20: Adding and Subtracting Fractions (Introduction)

1. Imagine moving the shaded pieces from pies A and B into pie plate C. Show how much of pie C would be filled then write a fraction for pie C:

A 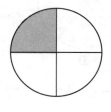   **B** 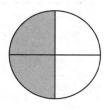   **C**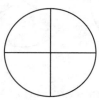

$$\frac{1}{4} \quad + \quad \frac{2}{4} \quad = \quad \underline{\quad}$$

2. Imagine pouring the liquid from cups A and B into cup C.
   Shade the amount of liquid that would be in C.
   Then complete the addition statements:

a)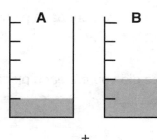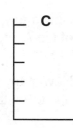

$$\frac{\underline{\quad}}{5} \quad + \quad \frac{\underline{\quad}}{5} \quad = \quad \underline{\quad}$$

b)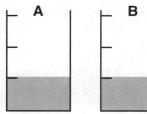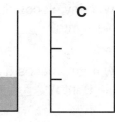

$$\frac{\underline{\quad}}{3} \quad + \quad \frac{\underline{\quad}}{3} \quad = \quad \underline{\quad}$$

3. Add:

a) $\frac{3}{5} + \frac{1}{5} =$ b) $\frac{2}{4} + \frac{1}{4} =$ c) $\frac{3}{7} + \frac{2}{7} =$ d) $\frac{5}{8} + \frac{2}{8} =$

e) $\frac{3}{11} + \frac{7}{11} =$ f) $\frac{5}{17} + \frac{9}{17} =$ g) $\frac{11}{24} + \frac{10}{24} =$ h) $\frac{18}{57} + \frac{13}{57} =$

4. Show how much pie would be left if you took away the amount shown.
   Then complete the fraction statement:

a)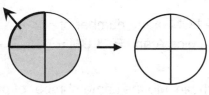

$$\frac{3}{4} \quad - \quad \frac{1}{4} \quad = \quad \underline{\quad}$$

b)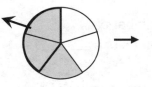

$$\frac{3}{5} \quad - \quad \frac{2}{5} \quad = \quad \underline{\quad}$$

5. Subtract:

a) $\frac{2}{3} - \frac{1}{3} =$ b) $\frac{3}{5} - \frac{2}{5} =$ c) $\frac{6}{7} - \frac{3}{7} =$ d) $\frac{5}{8} - \frac{2}{8} =$

e) $\frac{9}{12} - \frac{2}{12} =$ f) $\frac{6}{19} - \frac{4}{19} =$ g) $\frac{9}{28} - \frac{3}{28} =$ h) $\frac{17}{57} - \frac{12}{57} =$

1.

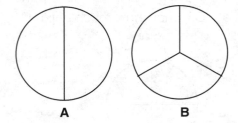

A   B

How many pieces are in pie A? _____

How many pieces are in pie B? _____

Find the LCM of the number of
pieces in pies A and B: **LCM** = _____

Cut pie A and pie B into this many pieces.

How many pieces did you cut each piece
of pie A into? _____

How many pieces did you cut each piece
of pie B into? _____

2.

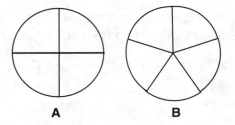

A   B

How many pieces are in pie A? _____

How many pieces are in pie B? _____

Find the LCM of the number of
pieces in pies A and B: **LCM** = _____

Cut pie A and pie B into this many pieces.

How many pieces did you cut each piece
of pie A into? _____

How many pieces did you cut each piece
of pie B into? _____

3.

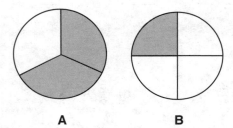

A   B

Write the name of each fraction:

A - _____   B - _____

Find the LCM of the number of
pieces in pies A and B: **LCM** = _____

Cut each pie into the same number of pieces,
given by the LCM.

Now write a new name for each fraction:

A - _____   B - _____

4.

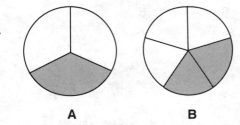

A   B

Write the name of each fraction:

A - _____   B - _____

Find the LCM of the number of
pieces in pies A and B: **LCM** = _____

Cut each pie into the same number of pieces,
given by the LCM.

Now write a new name for each fraction:

A - _____   B - _____

5.
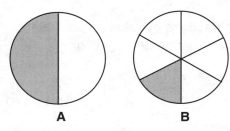

Write the name of each fraction:

A - _____   B - _____

Find the LCM of the number of pieces in pies A and B: **LCM = _____**

Cut each pie into the same number of pieces, given by the **LCM**.

Now write a new name for each fraction:

A - _____   B - _____

6.
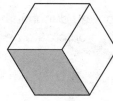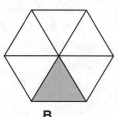

Write the name of each fraction:

A - _____   B - _____

Find the LCM of the number of pieces in pies A and B: **LCM = _____**

Cut each figure into the same number of pieces, given by the **LCM**.

Now write a name for each fraction:

A - _____   B - _____

7.
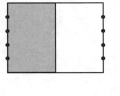

Write the name of each fraction:

A - _____   B - _____

Find the LCM of the number of pieces in figures A and B: **LCM = _____**

Draw horizontal or vertical lines to join the dots.

Now write a new name for each fraction:

A - _____   B - _____

8.
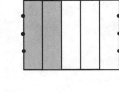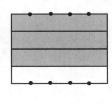

Write the name of each fraction:

A - _____   B - _____

Find the LCM of the number of pieces in figures A and B: **LCM = _____**

Draw horizontal or vertical lines to join the dots.

Now write a new name for each fraction:

A - _____   B - _____

When you multiply the numerator and denominator of a fraction by the same number, you create an equivalent fraction:

$$\frac{1}{2} = \frac{1 \times 5}{2 \times 5} = \frac{5}{10}$$

You are cutting each piece into 5 parts

You can add fractions by creating equivalent fractions with the same denominator:

$$\frac{1}{2} + \frac{2}{5} \qquad \frac{5 \times 1}{5 \times 2} + \frac{2 \times 2}{5 \times 2} = \frac{5}{10} + \frac{4}{10} = \frac{9}{10}$$

Find the LCM of the denominators or **lowest common denominator (LCD):** LCM = 10

Create equivalent fractions with denominator 10

---

1. Find the LCD of each pair of fractions. Then show what numbers you would multiply each fraction by in order to add:

   a) LCD = __6__

   $$\frac{3 \times 1}{3 \times 2} + \frac{2 \times 2}{3 \times 2}$$

   b) LCD = _____

   $$\frac{3}{4} + \frac{1}{8}$$

   c) LCD = _____

   $$\frac{1}{20} + \frac{1}{5}$$

   d) LCD = _____

   $$\frac{3}{4} + \frac{2}{3}$$

   e) LCD = _____

   $$\frac{3}{7} + \frac{1}{3}$$

   f) LCD = _____

   $$\frac{1}{4} + \frac{1}{6}$$

   g) LCD = _____

   $$\frac{2}{5} + \frac{1}{10}$$

   h) LCD = _____

   $$\frac{1}{8} + \frac{1}{7}$$

2. Add or subtract the fractions by changing them to equivalent fractions:

   a) $\frac{2}{5} + \frac{1}{4}$

   b) $\frac{4}{15} + \frac{2}{3}$

   c) $\frac{2}{3} - \frac{1}{8}$

   d) $\frac{2}{3} - \frac{1}{12}$

   =

   =

   =

   =

   =

   =

   =

   =

3. Add or subtract the fractions in your notebook by first finding the LCD:

   a) $\frac{3}{4} + \frac{1}{8}$

   b) $\frac{1}{6} + \frac{11}{24}$

   c) $\frac{5}{28} - \frac{1}{7}$

   d) $\frac{2}{7} + \frac{1}{8}$

   e) $\frac{4}{9} - \frac{1}{6}$

4. You can show addition in a number line:

   Example : $\frac{1}{2} + \frac{1}{3}$ The LCD of $\frac{1}{2}$ and $\frac{1}{3}$ is 6...

   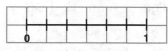

   ... so draw a number line divided into 6 parts.

   Change each fraction to an equivalent fraction:

   $$\frac{1}{2} = \frac{3}{6}, \quad \frac{1}{3} = \frac{2}{6}$$

   Draw arrows to show the addition on the number line:

   $$\frac{1}{2} + \frac{1}{3} = \frac{5}{6}$$

   In your notebook, represent the following sums on a number line (as in the example):

   a) $\frac{1}{2} + \frac{1}{5}$

   b) $\frac{2}{3} + \frac{1}{4}$

   c) $\frac{1}{10} + \frac{1}{2}$

Answer the questions below in your notebook.

5. Add or subtract:

   a) $\frac{1}{6} + \frac{5}{12}$ b) $\frac{17}{25} - \frac{3}{5}$ c) $\frac{6}{7} - \frac{1}{4}$ d) $\frac{4}{9} + \frac{2}{5}$ e) $\frac{5}{8} - \frac{7}{12}$

   f) $\frac{2}{3} + \frac{1}{4} + \frac{1}{2}$ g) $\frac{3}{15} + \frac{2}{3} + \frac{1}{5}$ h) $\frac{7}{15} + \frac{1}{3} - \frac{3}{5}$ i) $\frac{1}{4} + \frac{17}{20} - \frac{3}{5}$

6. Tabitha ate $\frac{1}{4}$ of a sub and Jordan ate $\frac{2}{3}$ of the sub.
   How much of the sub was left over?

7. Craig had $48 dollars. She spent $\frac{1}{4}$ of her money on a book and $\frac{3}{8}$ on a pair of gloves:

   a) How many dollars did Craig spend on the gloves?

   b) How much money does he have left over?

8. Trevor has $\frac{2}{3}$ of an hour to write a test. If he finishes the test in $\frac{1}{2}$ of an hour
   then how much time would remain?

9. Roberto, Kendra, and Imran painted a wall. Roberto painted $\frac{2}{5}$ of the wall and Kendra painted $\frac{2}{6}$:
   a) What fraction of the wall did Imran paint?

   b) They each painted a rectangular section, from top to bottom.
      The wall is 30 m long. How long was each person's section?

10. Olivia says the lowest common denominator for $\frac{1}{4}$ and $\frac{1}{10}$ is 40. Is this correct?

11. What mistake did Jared make when subtracting $\frac{11}{12} - \frac{2}{3} = \frac{9}{9}$? How can you tell by estimating that
    the answer is not correct?

12. The chart shows how the students in a Grade 8 class get to school:

    a) What fraction of the students walk to school?

    b) There are 30 students in the class.
       How many cycle to school?

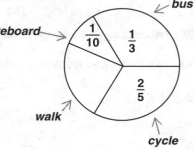

NS8-23: Adding & Subtracting Mixed Fractions

After a party, Chang's class has $2\frac{1}{2}$ pizzas left over.

Alicia's class has $3\frac{1}{3}$ pizzas left over.

To find out how much pizza is left over, Chang adds:

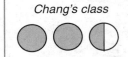

Chang's class

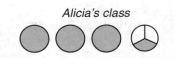

Alicia's class

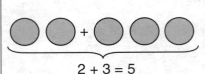

$2 + 3 = 5$

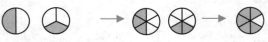

$\frac{1}{2} \times \frac{3}{3} + \frac{1}{3} \times \frac{2}{2} = \frac{3}{6} + \frac{2}{6} = \frac{5}{6}$

There are $5\frac{5}{6}$ pizzas left over.

Here is how Chang shows his calculation: $2\frac{1}{2} + 3\frac{1}{3} = 2\frac{1}{2}\times\frac{3}{3} + 3\frac{1}{3}\times\frac{2}{2} = 2\frac{3}{6} + 3\frac{2}{6} = 5\frac{5}{6}$

NOTE: Sometimes the fractional part will add to more than one whole pie. See Question 3 below for this case.

- -

1. Add or subtract:

   a) $2\frac{1}{5} + 2\frac{2}{5} =$

   b) $3\frac{3}{6} + 2\frac{1}{6} =$

   c) $5\frac{7}{8} - 3\frac{2}{8} =$

   d) $7\frac{9}{15} - 4\frac{4}{15} =$

2. Add by changing the fractions to equivalent fraction. Show your work as in a):

   a) $2\frac{1}{2}\times\frac{3}{3} + 1\frac{1}{3}\times\frac{2}{2}$

   $= 2\frac{3}{6} + 1\frac{2}{6}$

   $= 2\frac{5}{6}$

   b) $3\frac{1}{4} + 1\frac{1}{3}$

   c) $5\frac{1}{3} + 2\frac{2}{5}$

   d) $2\frac{2}{7} + 4\frac{1}{2}$

   e) $4\frac{1}{6} + 3\frac{2}{5}$

   f) $2\frac{3}{8} + 4\frac{1}{3}$

   g) $1\frac{1}{4} + 2\frac{3}{7}$

   h) $4\frac{1}{5} + 2\frac{4}{7}$

   i) $8\frac{5}{9} + 5\frac{1}{5}$

3. If you add $1\frac{1}{2} + 2\frac{2}{3}$ you will find that $1\frac{1}{2} + 2\frac{2}{3} = 3\frac{7}{6}$. How can you simplify this answer?

   CHALLENGE: Try working out a solution before you answer the questions below.

   a) Change the improper fractions to mixed fractions:

   i) $\frac{7}{6} = 1\frac{1}{6}$

   ii) $\frac{11}{5} =$

   iii) $\frac{13}{7} =$

   iv) $\frac{7}{4} =$

   v) $\frac{13}{8} =$

   vi) $\frac{13}{10} =$

   vii) $\frac{14}{9} =$

   viii) $\frac{11}{6} =$

b) Rewrite each fraction in proper form as shown in i) below. Show the steps:

i) $3\frac{7}{6} = 3 + \frac{7}{6}$ 　　　ii) $2\frac{4}{3} =$ 　　　iii) $4\frac{8}{5} =$

$= 3 + 1\frac{1}{6}$ 　　$= 4\frac{1}{6}$ 　　　$=$ 　　$=$ 　　　$=$ 　　$=$

iv) $2\frac{5}{4} =$ 　　　v) $3\frac{10}{9} =$ 　　　vi) $4\frac{12}{7} =$

$=$ 　　$=$ 　　　$=$ 　　$=$ 　　　$=$ 　　$=$

c) Add by changing the fractions to equivalent fractions. Simplify your answer as in part b) above:

i) $2\frac{2}{5} + \frac{2}{3}$ 　　　ii) $3\frac{2}{3} + \frac{5}{6}$ 　　　iii) $4\frac{3}{4} + 2\frac{3}{5}$

iv) $5\frac{1}{6} + 5\frac{7}{8}$ 　　　v) $3\frac{7}{8} + 4\frac{1}{2}$ 　　　vi) $4\frac{5}{6} + 3\frac{4}{9}$

4. Subtract. Show your work. The first one is done for you:

a) $3\frac{2}{3} - 1\frac{1}{2}$ 　　　b) $5\frac{3}{4} - 3\frac{2}{3}$ 　　　c) $4\frac{4}{5} - 2\frac{3}{4}$

$= 3\frac{4}{6} - 1\frac{3}{6}$

$= 2\frac{1}{6}$

5. $\frac{4}{5}$ is greater than $\frac{1}{3}$.

How can you subtract $4\frac{1}{3} - 2\frac{4}{5}$?

CHALLENGE: Try to work out a solution before you look below.

a) Rewrite each fraction below by regrouping as shown: $4\frac{1}{3} = 3 + \frac{3}{3} + \frac{1}{3} = 3\frac{4}{3}$

i) $5\frac{1}{4} = 4 + \frac{4}{4} + \frac{1}{4}$ 　　　　　ii) $5\frac{1}{2} = 4 +$

$= 4\frac{5}{4}$

iii) $1\frac{1}{6} =$ 　　　　　iv) $2\frac{3}{4} =$

b) For the fractions below, try to do the steps you did in part a) in your head:

i) $5\frac{2}{3} = 4\frac{5}{3}$ ii) $7\frac{3}{5} =$ iii) $4\frac{1}{6} =$ iv) $2\frac{7}{10} =$

c) Subtract by rewriting the first mixed fraction as in part b):

i) $3\frac{1}{5} - 1\frac{3}{4} = 2\frac{6}{5} - 1\frac{3}{4}$ ii) $4\frac{1}{3} - 2\frac{3}{5}$

$= 2\frac{24}{20} - 1\frac{15}{20} = 1\frac{9}{20}$

iii) $2\frac{1}{4} - 1\frac{2}{3}$ iv) $7\frac{1}{2} - 3\frac{9}{10}$

Answer the following questions in your notebook.

6. You can add or subtract mixed fractions by first changing the mixed fractions to improper fractions:

> *Example:* $3\frac{2}{3} + 1\frac{1}{2} = \frac{11}{3} + \frac{3}{2} = \frac{2 \times 11}{2 \times 3} + \frac{3 \times 3}{2 \times 3} = \frac{22}{6} + \frac{9}{6} = 5\frac{1}{6}$

Add or subtract by first changing the mixed fractions to improper fractions:

a) $3\frac{1}{3} + 5\frac{3}{4}$ b) $1\frac{1}{5} - \frac{2}{3}$ c) $3\frac{1}{4} - 2\frac{5}{6}$ d) $5\frac{1}{8} - 3\frac{1}{3}$

e) $1\frac{3}{5} + 2\frac{1}{6}$ f) $2\frac{4}{7} + 3\frac{1}{4}$ g) $4\frac{2}{3} + 2\frac{4}{5}$ h) $4\frac{1}{10} - 3\frac{4}{5}$

7. Sonjay cycled $6\frac{7}{8}$ km in the first hour, $5\frac{1}{2}$ km the second hour, and $4\frac{3}{4}$ km the third hour. How many km did he cycle in three hours?

8. A cafeteria sold $2\frac{5}{8}$ cheese pizzas, $4\frac{1}{3}$ vegetable pizzas, and $3\frac{1}{4}$ deluxe pizzas at lunchtime. How many pizzas did they sell altogether?

9. Gerome bought $5\frac{3}{4}$ metres of cloth. He used $3\frac{4}{5}$ to make a banner. How many metres of cloth were left over?

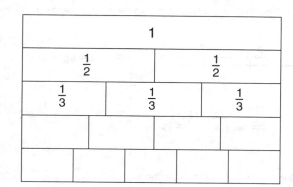

1. Fill in the missing numbers on the fraction strips.
   Then write > (greater than) or < (less than) between each pair of numbers below:

   a) $\dfrac{1}{3}$ ☐ $\dfrac{2}{5}$ b) $\dfrac{2}{3}$ ☐ $\dfrac{3}{4}$

   c) $\dfrac{1}{2}$ ☐ $\dfrac{3}{5}$ d) $\dfrac{3}{5}$ ☐ $\dfrac{2}{3}$

2. Turn the fractions into equivalent fractions with the same denominator (by finding the LCM of both denominators). Then write =, <, or > between:

   a) $\dfrac{5 \times 1}{5 \times 2}$ ☐ $\dfrac{7}{10}$ b) $\dfrac{1}{5}$ ☐ $\dfrac{3}{10}$ c) $\dfrac{3}{8}$ ☐ $\dfrac{1}{4}$ d) $\dfrac{3}{4}$ ☐ $\dfrac{11}{16}$

   $\dfrac{5}{10}$ < $\dfrac{7}{10}$ ☐

   e) $\dfrac{1}{2}$ ☐ $\dfrac{1}{3}$ f) $\dfrac{2}{3}$ ☐ $\dfrac{2}{5}$ g) $\dfrac{3}{4}$ ☐ $\dfrac{1}{3}$ h) $\dfrac{5}{6}$ ☐ $\dfrac{11}{18}$

   ☐   ☐   ☐   ☐

   i) $\dfrac{2}{5}$ ☐ $\dfrac{1}{4}$ j) $\dfrac{5}{6}$ ☐ $\dfrac{4}{5}$ k) $\dfrac{3}{8}$ ☐ $\dfrac{21}{40}$ l) $\dfrac{19}{24}$ ☐ $\dfrac{3}{4}$

   ☐   ☐   ☐   ☐

3. Write the fractions in order from least to greatest:
   HINT: First write each fraction with the same denominator.

   a) $\dfrac{1}{2}$ $\dfrac{2}{5}$ $\dfrac{3}{10}$

   $\dfrac{\ }{10}$ $\dfrac{\ }{10}$ $\dfrac{3}{10}$

   b) $\dfrac{1}{2}$ $\dfrac{5}{6}$ $\dfrac{2}{3}$

   ☐ ☐ ☐

   c) $\dfrac{3}{4}$ $\dfrac{1}{2}$ $\dfrac{7}{8}$

   ☐ ☐ ☐

4. Write these fractions in the boxes below (in order from least to greatest): $\dfrac{1}{3}, \dfrac{3}{4}, \dfrac{1}{2}, \dfrac{5}{6}, \dfrac{1}{4}, \dfrac{2}{3}, \dfrac{1}{12}, \dfrac{1}{6}, \dfrac{5}{12}$

☐ ☐ ☐ ☐ ☐ ☐ ☐ ☐ ☐ 1

5. A recipe for soup calls for $\dfrac{2}{3}$ of a can of tomatoes. A recipe for spaghetti sauce calls for $\dfrac{5}{6}$ of a can. Which recipe uses more tomatoes?

Sayaka subtracts $6 - 3\frac{2}{3}$ on a number line as follows:

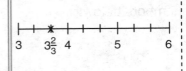

She draws an arrow which shows the difference between $3\frac{2}{3}$ and the nearest whole number (4)

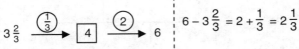

She sees that :

$$6 - 3\frac{2}{3} = 2 + \frac{1}{3} = 2\frac{1}{3}$$

She marks the number she is subtracting ($3\frac{2}{3}$) on a number line

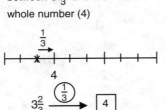

She draws an arrow to show the difference between 4 and 6 (= 2)

1. Follow Sayaka's steps to find the difference. The first question is started for you:

a)
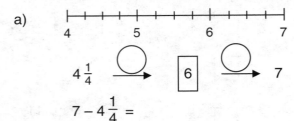

$4\frac{1}{4}$ → ◯ → $\boxed{6}$ → ◯ → 7

$$7 - 4\frac{1}{4} =$$

b)
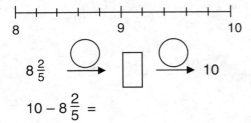

$8\frac{2}{5}$ → ◯ → ☐ → ◯ → 10

$$10 - 8\frac{2}{5} =$$

2. Find the differences:

a) $6\frac{3}{5}$ → ◯ → ☐ → ◯ → 8

$$8 - 6\frac{3}{5} =$$

b) $5\frac{5}{6}$ → ◯ → ☐ → ◯ → 9

$$9 - 5\frac{5}{6} =$$

c) $6\frac{5}{8}$ → ◯ → ☐ → ◯ → 11

$$11 - 6\frac{5}{8} =$$

3. Find the differences mentally:

a) $4 - 1\frac{1}{7} =$

b) $9 - 6\frac{7}{9} =$

c) $12 - 7\frac{3}{10} =$

d) $23 - 20\frac{5}{8} =$

4. Find the difference by following the steps shown:

a)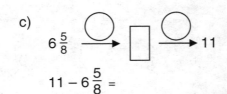

Nearest whole number ↓

$5\frac{4}{5}$ →($\frac{1}{5}$)→ $\boxed{6}$ →(2)→ $\boxed{8}$ →($\frac{3}{5}$)→ $8\frac{3}{5}$

$$8\frac{3}{5} - 5\frac{4}{5} = \frac{1}{5} + 2 + \frac{3}{5} = 2\frac{4}{5}$$

b) $3\frac{5}{8}$ → ◯ → ☐ → ◯ → ☐ → ◯ → $8\frac{1}{8}$

5. Find the differences mentally:

a) $6\frac{2}{5} - 5\frac{4}{5} =$

b) $9\frac{1}{7} - 3\frac{4}{7} =$

c) $17\frac{1}{8} - 13\frac{3}{8} =$

d) $13\frac{1}{6} - 6\frac{5}{6} =$

Answer the questions below in your notebook.

1. Write six fractions equivalent to 1.

2. Anne just turned 19 years old. How old was she $4\frac{3}{4}$ years ago?

3. Rita raises money for three charities. She gives $\frac{1}{4}$ to a homeless shelter, $\frac{1}{2}$ to an environmental group and the rest to a food bank. What fraction of her money did she give to each organization?

4. The chart shows the times of day when the Eyed Lizard is active.

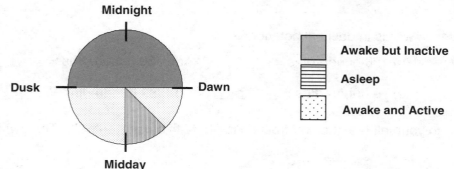

Awake but Inactive

Asleep

Awake and Active

a) What fraction of the day is the lizard...
    i)   awake but Inactive
    ii) asleep
    iii) awake and Active

b) How many hours a day is the lizard...
    i)   awake but Inactive
    ii) asleep
    iii) awake and Active

5. Find the sum:

    HINT: you can add the fractions quickly by grouping them in a clever way.

    $$\frac{1}{2} + \frac{2}{3} + \frac{1}{4} + \frac{2}{5} + \frac{5}{6} + \frac{1}{6} + \frac{3}{5} + \frac{3}{4} + \frac{1}{3} + \frac{1}{2}$$

6. a) Find:

    i) $1 - \frac{1}{2}$ ii) $\frac{1}{2} - \frac{1}{3}$ iii) $\frac{1}{3} - \frac{1}{4}$ iv) $\frac{1}{4} - \frac{1}{5}$ v) $\frac{1}{99} - \frac{1}{100}$

    b) Look at your answers to part a). Find: $\frac{1}{2} + \frac{1}{6} + \frac{1}{12} + \frac{1}{20}$

7. Write each fraction as a sum of exactly three fractions, each with numerator 1.

    Example: $\frac{5}{6} = \frac{1}{2} + \frac{1}{6} + \frac{1}{6}$ **HINT: how does finding the factors of the denominator help?**

    a) $\frac{7}{8}$ b) $\frac{13}{15}$ c) $\frac{17}{18}$ d) $\frac{3}{7}$ e) $\frac{4}{3}$

8. Decide whether each statement is true or false. Explain your answer:
    a) If the numerator and denominator are both even, the fraction is never in lowest terms.
    b) If the numerator and denominator are both odd, the fraction is always in lowest terms.
    c) If the numerator is prime, the fraction is always in lowest terms.

NS8-27: Decimal Tenths and Hundredths

Fractions with denominators that are powers of ten
(tenths, hundredths) commonly appear in units of measurement:

- A millimetre is a tenth of a centimetre (10 mm = 1 cm)
- A centimetre is a tenth of a decimetre (10 cm = 1 dm)
- A decimetre is a tenth of a metre (10 dm = 1 m)
- A centimetre is a hundredth of a metre (100 cm = 1 m)

REMEMBER:

3. 7 5

ones tenths hundredths

The first digit to the right of a decimal tells you the number of tenths: .<u>7</u>3 (7 tenths). The second digit tells you the number of hundredths: .7<u>3</u> (3 hundredths).

1. Write the decimal that is given in words in decimal notation:

   a) 27 hundredths = ___.27___   b) 26 hundredths = _____   c) 30 hundredths = _____

   d) 73 hundredths = _____   e) 9 hundredths = _____   f) 89 hundredths = _____

2. Say the name of the fraction to yourself (i.e. the first fraction is "thirty-five hundredths"). Then write a decimal for the fraction:

   a) $\frac{35}{100}$ = .35   b) $\frac{21}{100}$ =   c) $\frac{1}{100}$ =   d) $\frac{36}{100}$ =

   e) $\frac{40}{100}$ =   f) $\frac{99}{100}$ =   g) $\frac{72}{100}$ =   h) $\frac{5}{100}$ =

3. Count the number of shaded squares. Write a fraction for the shaded part of the hundreds square. Then write the fraction as a decimal:

   HINT: Count by 10s for each column or row that is shaded.

   a) 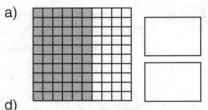   b) 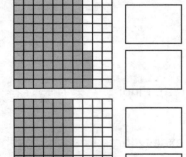   c)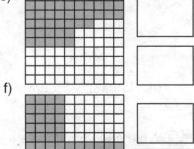

   d)   e)   f)

   g) 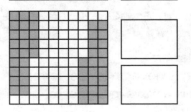   h) 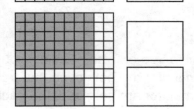   i)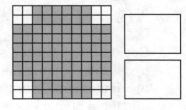

jump math
E   Number Sense 1

4. Write a fraction for the number of <u>hundredths</u>. Then draw a heavy line around each column and write a fraction for the number of <u>tenths</u>:

a)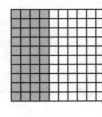

$$\overline{100} = \overline{10}$$

b)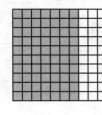

$$\overline{100} = \overline{10}$$

c)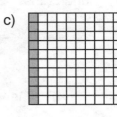

$$\overline{100} = \overline{10}$$

d)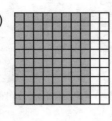

$$\overline{100} = \overline{10}$$

5. Fill in the chart below. The first one has been done for you:

Drawing	Fraction	Decimal	Equivalent Decimal	Equivalent Fraction	Drawing
	$\frac{5}{10}$	0.5	0.50	$\frac{50}{100}$	

6. Fill in the missing numbers:

REMEMBER: $\frac{10}{100} = \frac{1}{10}$

a) $.6 = \frac{6}{10} = \overline{100} = \cdot \_\_$ b) $\cdot \_ = \frac{4}{10} = \overline{100} = .40$ c) $\cdot \_ = \frac{7}{10} = \overline{100} = .70$

d) $\cdot \_ = \frac{5}{10} = \overline{100} = \cdot \_\_$ e) $\cdot \_ = \overline{10} = \frac{80}{100} = \cdot \_\_$ f) $\cdot \_ = \overline{10} = \frac{30}{100} = \cdot \_\_$

g) $\cdot \_ = \frac{8}{10} = \overline{100} = \cdot \_\_$ h) $\cdot \_ = \frac{9}{10} = \overline{100} = \cdot \_\_$ i) $.2 = \overline{10} = \overline{100} = \cdot \_\_$

7. Circle the greater number by first changing the fraction in tenths to hundredths:

a) $\frac{80}{100}$ $\frac{3}{10} = \boxed{}$ b) $\frac{90}{100}$ $\frac{5}{10} = \boxed{}$ c) $\frac{60}{100}$ $\frac{1}{10} = \boxed{}$

NS8-28: Fractions and Decimals

1. Fill in the missing numbers:

    a) .56 = _____ tenths _____ hundredths   b) .75 = _____ tenths _____ hundredths

    c) .07 = _____   d) .14 = _____

2. Write as a decimal:

    a) 1 tenths 8 hundredths =   b) 0 tenths 7 hundredths =   c) 5 tenths 4 hundredths =

3. Write the following decimals as fractions:

    a) .45 =   b) .7 =   c) .01 =   d) .83 =   e) .3 =

4. Change the following fractions to decimals by filling in the blanks:

    a) $\frac{4}{10}$ = . ___   b) $\frac{20}{100}$ = . __ __   c) $\frac{41}{100}$ = . __ __   d) $\frac{2}{100}$ = . __ __

5. Change the following decimals to fractions:

    a) .15 =   b) .63 =   c) .06 =   d) .6 =

6. Circle the equalities that are <u>incorrect</u>:

    HINT: Count the number of digits in the decimal and compare it to the number of zeros in the denominator of the fraction.

    .34 = $\frac{34}{100}$ .7 = $\frac{7}{10}$ .05 = $\frac{5}{10}$ $\frac{18}{10}$ = .18 $\frac{6}{100}$ = .006

    .02 = $\frac{2}{100}$ .26 = $\frac{26}{100}$ 6.7 = $\frac{67}{100}$ .05 = $\frac{5}{100}$ .08 = $\frac{8}{10}$

7. State the place value ("tenths" or "hundredths") of the digit 7 in the following decimals:

    a) .27 = _____   b) .07 = _____   c) .75 = _____

8. Write words for the following decimals:

    a) .25 = _____   b) .06 = _____   c) .3 = _____

9. Write a decimal for each description:

    a) Between .79 and .89 . ☐ ☐   b) Between .65 and .75 . ☐ ☐

    c) Between .29 and .31 . ☐ ☐   d) Between .5 and .6 . ☐ ☐

10. Put a decimal in each number so the digit **4** has the value $\frac{4}{10}$:

    a) 8 4 3   b) 1 0 4   c) 6 8 5 4 1   d) 4   e) 7 4 3

A hundreds block may be used to represent a whole. 10 is a tenth of 100, so a tens block represents a tenth of the whole. 1 is a hundredth of 100, so a ones block represents a hundredth of the whole:

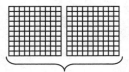   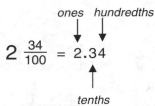

      2 wholes   3 tenths   4 hundredths

$$2 \frac{34}{100} = 2.34$$

ones hundredths

tenths

NOTE: A mixed fraction can be written as a decimal.

---

1. Write a mixed fraction and a decimal for the base ten models below:

    a)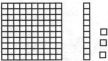

    b)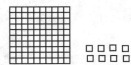

    c)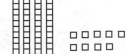

    d)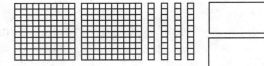

    e)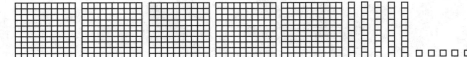

2. Draw a base ten model for the following decimals:

    a) 3.8   b) 2.52

3. Write a decimal and a mixed fraction for each of the pictures below:

    a)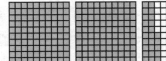

    b)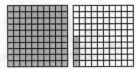

4. Write a decimal for each of the mixed fractions below:

    a) $8\frac{23}{100} =$ b) $11\frac{60}{100} =$ c) $7\frac{7}{10} =$ d) $9\frac{15}{100} =$

    e) $30\frac{1}{100} =$ f) $17\frac{8}{10} =$ g) $61\frac{1}{10} =$ h) $14\frac{3}{100} =$

5. Which decimal represents a greater number?
    Explain your answer in your notebook with a picture:

    a) 5 tenths or 5 hundredths?   b) .7 or .07?   c) 2.05 or 2.50?

This number line is divided into tenths. The number represented by point **A** is $2\frac{3}{10}$ or 2.3:

1. Write a fraction or a mixed fraction for each point:

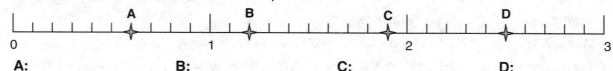

   A: _____ **B:** _____ **C:** _____ **D:** _____

2. Write a decimal and a mixed fraction for each of the points below.

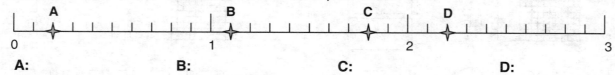

   A: _____ **B:** _____ **C:** _____ **D:** _____

3. Mark each point with an 'X' and label the point with the correct letter:

   A. .2   **B.** 1.7   **C.** .80   **D.** 1.1   **E.** $2\frac{9}{10}$ **F.** $\frac{1}{10}$

4. Mark each point with an 'X' and label the point with the correct letter:

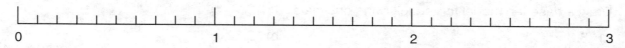

   A. two and one tenths   **B.** nine tenths   **C.** two and four tenth   **D.** two decimal nine

5. Write a fraction and a decimal for each point:

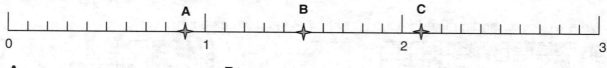

   A. _____   **B.** _____   **C.** _____

6. Mark the decimals on the number lines.

   a) **0.6** 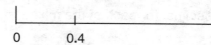   b) **1.2**

BONUS:

7. Mark the following fractions and decimals on the number line:

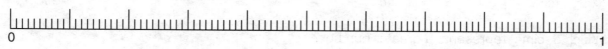

   A. .84   **B.** $\frac{62}{100}$ **C.** .07   **D.** $\frac{28}{100}$

1.

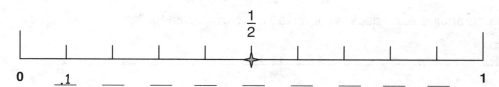

   a)   Write a decimal for each point marked on the number line. The first decimal is written for you.

   b)   Which decimal is equal to one half? $\frac{1}{2}$ = _____

2.   Use the number line in Question 1 to say whether each decimal is closer to "zero", "a half" or "one":

   a)   .2 is closer to _____   b)   .4 is closer to _____   c)   .9 is closer to _____

   d)   .8 is closer to _____   e)   .6 is closer to _____   f)   .3 is closer to _____

3.

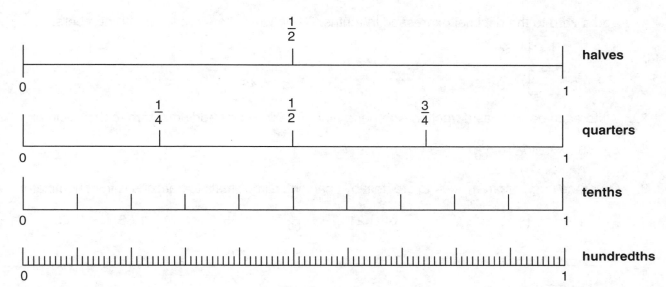

Use the number lines above to compare the numbers given. Write < (less than) or > (greater than) between each pair of numbers:

   a)   0.4 ☐ $\frac{1}{2}$ b)   0.7 ☐ $\frac{3}{4}$ c)   0.2 ☐ $\frac{1}{4}$ d)   0.4 ☐ $\frac{1}{4}$

   e)   0.55 ☐ $\frac{1}{2}$ f)   0.45 ☐ $\frac{1}{2}$ g)   0.69 ☐ $\frac{3}{4}$ h) $\frac{1}{4}$ ☐ .35

4.   Write the numbers in order first changing each decimal to a fraction with a denominator of 10:
   NOTE: Show your work beside each number.

   a)   0.5   0.7   0.4   b)   0.5 $\frac{9}{10}$ 0.7   c)   0.2 $\frac{3}{10}$ 0.15

   _____   _____   _____

   d)   1.5   1.8   1.3   e)   2.4   2.9 $2\frac{7}{10}$ f)   3.3 $3\frac{40}{100}$ $3\frac{2}{10}$

   _____   _____   _____

5. Which whole number is each decimal or mixed fraction closest to: "zero", "one", "two," or "three"?

0   1   2   3

a) 1.2 is closest to _____

b) 0.3 is closest to _____

c) $1\frac{7}{10}$ is closest to _____

d) $2\frac{8}{10}$ is closest to _____

e) 2.1 is closest to _____

f) $2\frac{6}{10}$ is closest to _____

6. Ali says:

"To compare .6 and .42, I first add a zero to .6.":   *.6 = 6 tenths = 60 hundredths = .60*
     And 60 (hundredths) is greater than 42 (hundredths), so .6 is greater than .42."

Add a zero to the decimal expressed in tenths. Then write > or < between the numbers:

a) .4 ☐ .39

c) .71 ☐ .7

b) .89 ☐ .9

d) .48 ☐ .5

7. Write each decimal as a fraction with denominator 100 by first adding a zero to the decimal:

a) .3 = .30 = $\frac{30}{100}$

b) .9 =

c) .4 =

8. Order the numbers from least to greatest by changing all decimals to fractions with denominator 100:

a) .1   .11   .13

b) .21 $\frac{23}{100}$ .25

c) 1.56   1.65 $1\frac{50}{100}$

_____   _____   _____

9. Change $\frac{23}{10}$ to a mixed fraction by shading the correct number of pieces:

Mixed Fraction _____

Answer the following questions in your notebook.

10. Change the following improper fractions to mixed fractions:

a) $\frac{18}{10}$

b) $\frac{72}{10}$

c) $\frac{70}{10}$

d) $\frac{95}{10}$

e) $\frac{146}{100}$

f) $\frac{275}{100}$

11. Change the following improper fractions to decimals by first writing them as mixed fractions:

a) $\frac{35}{10} = 3\frac{5}{10} = 3.5$

b) $\frac{86}{10}$

c) $\frac{37}{10}$

d) $\frac{12}{10}$

e) $\frac{159}{100}$

f) $\frac{316}{100}$

12. Which is greater, $\frac{231}{100}$ or 2.3?
     Explain.

13. Write five decimals greater than 2.45 and less than 2.53.

NS8-32: Thousandths

If a thousands cube is used to represent a whole number, then a hundreds block represents a tenth, a tens block represents a hundredth, and a unit block represents a thousandth of a whole:

  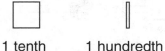

1 whole   1 tenth   1 hundredth   1 thousandth

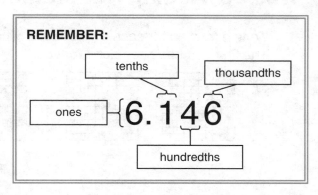

REMEMBER:

tenths   thousandths

ones — {6.146

hundredths

---

1. Beside each number, write the place value of the underlined digit:

   a) 3.<u>8</u>19

   b) 9.78<u>2</u>

   c) 4.<u>5</u>14

   d) 7.15<u>9</u>

   e) <u>2</u>.541

   f) 3.8<u>98</u>

2. Write the following numbers into the place value chart. The first one has been done for you:

	ones	tenths	hundredths	thousandths
a) 6.512	6	5	1	2
c) 2.96				
e) 3.063				
g) 10.02				
i) 7.009				

	ones	tenths	hundredths	thousandths
b) .081				
d) 1.306				
f) .53				
h) 8				
j) 3.01				

3. Write the following decimals as fractions:

   a) .925 =

   b) .274 =

   c) .049 =

   d) .003 =

4. Write each decimal in expanded form:

   a) .237 = 2 tenths + 3 hundredths + 7 thousandths

   b) .483 =

   c) 5.263 =

5. Write the following fractions as decimals:

   a) $\frac{94}{100}$ =

   b) $\frac{5}{100}$ =

   c) $\frac{875}{1000}$ =

   d) $\frac{25}{1000}$ =

6. Compare each pair of decimals by writing < or > in the circle:
   HINT: Add zeros wherever necessary to give each number the same number of digits.

   a) .275 ⬤< .277

   b) .392 ◯ .39

   c) .596 ◯ .695

   d) .27 ◯ .237

   e) .7 ◯ .82

   f) .6 ◯ .526

1. Write a fraction for each shaded part. Then add the fractions, and shade your answer. The first one has been done for you:

   a)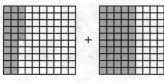

   $$\frac{25}{100} + \frac{50}{100} = \frac{75}{100}$$

   b)

   c)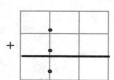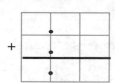

   d)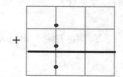

2. Write the decimals that correspond to the fractions in Question 1 above:

a) .25 + .50 = .75	b)
c)	d)

3. Add the decimals by lining up the digits. Be sure that your final answer is expressed as a decimal:

   a) 0.32 + 0.57   b) 0.91 + 0.08   c) 0.54 + 0.72   d) 0.31 + 0.65

   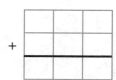  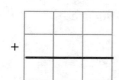 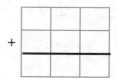

   e) 0.3 + 0.56   f) 0.5 + 0.48   g) 0.71 + 0.57   h) 0.63 + 0.22

Answer the following questions in your notebook.

4. Line up the decimals and add the following numbers:

   a) 0.41 + 0.17   b) 0.64 + 0.35   c) 0.46 + 0.1   d) 0.87 + 0.02   e) 0.56 + 0.21

5. Three geckos measure 0.18, 0.15, and 0.11 metres long. What fraction of a metre is each gecko? What fraction of a metre would all 3 be if they were laid end to end?

6. Demitra made a snack mix by mixing 0.48 kg of peanuts and 0.39 kg of raisins. How many kg of mix did she make?

NS8-34: Adding and Subtracting Decimals

1. Subtract by crossing out the correct number of boxes:

a)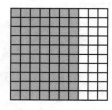

$$\frac{70}{100} - \frac{20}{100} =$$

b)

$$\frac{45}{100} - \frac{19}{100} =$$

c)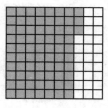

$$\frac{73}{100} - \frac{37}{100} =$$

2. Write the decimals that correspond to the fractions in Question 1 above:

a) .70 - .20 =	b)	c)

3. Subtract the decimals by lining up the digits:

a) 0.53 − 0.21

	0	5	3
−	0	2	1
	0	3	2

b) 0.76 − 0.24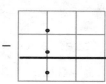

c) 0.47 − 0.22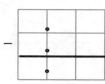

d) 0.91 − 0.21

e) 0.42 − .17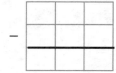

f) 0.53 − 0.37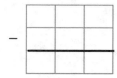

g) 0.95 − 0.59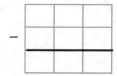

h) 0.61 − 0.26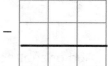

i) 1.00 − .38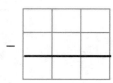

j) 1.00 − 0.49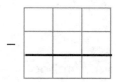

k) 1.00 − 0.71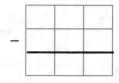

l) 1.00 − 0.93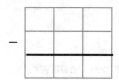

4. In your notebook, subtract the following decimals:

a) .73 − .29   b) .96 − .27   c) .61 − .59   d) .15 − .04

e) .86 − .7   f) .51 − .3   g) 1.00 − .03   h) 1.00 − .51

5. Find the missing decimal in each of the following:

a) 1 = .46 + ☐   b) 1 = .52 + ☐   c) 1 = .09 + ☐

1. Add by drawing a base ten model. Then, using the chart provided, line up the decimal points and add:
   NOTE: Use a hundreds square for a whole and a tens rod for one tenth.

   a) 1.23 + 1.12

   b) 1.37 + 1.43

   = ▢ ||| ⁚⁚ + ▢ || ⁚

   = ▢ ▢ ||| ⁚⁚

	ones	tenths	hundredths
+			

	ones	tenths	hundredths
+			

2. Draw a model of the greater number. Then subtract by crossing out blocks, as shown in part a):

   a) 2.35 − 1.12 = 1.23

   b) 3.68 − 1.37

   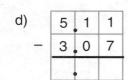 = 1.23

3. Add or subtract:

   a)
	3 . 6	7
+	2 . 0	2

   b)
	2 . 3	4
+	5 . 4	7

   c)
	4 . 5	8
−	2 . 6	2

   d)
	5 . 1	1
−	3 . 0	7

   e)
	1 3 . 0	4
−	1 0 . 3	7

Show your work for the remaining questions in your notebook.

4. Subtract each pair of numbers by lining up the decimal points:

   a) 6.49 − 2.18   b) 7.54 − 3.28   c) 5.71 − .38   d) 19.31 − 12.6   e) 16.7 − 9.59

5. Bamboo can grow up to 0.3 m in a single day in ideal conditions.
   How high could it grow in 3 days?

6. The largest axe in the world is 18.28 m long and can be found in Nackawic, New Brunswick.
   If a regular axe is 1.45 metres long, how much longer is the world's largest axe?

7. Continue the patterns: a) .5, 1, 1.5, _____, _____, _____   b) .02, .04, .08, _____, _____, _____

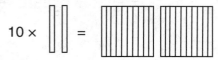

If a hundreds block represents 1 whole,
then a tens block represents 1 tenth (or 0.1).

10 tenths make 1 whole:
10 × 0.1 = 1.0

----

1. Multiply the number of tens blocks by 10. Then show how many hundreds blocks you would have.
   The first one is done for you:

   a)
   10 ×   =

   10 × 0.2 = ___2___

   b)
   10 ×   =

   10 × 0.4 = _____

   c)
   10 ×   =

   10 × 0.8 = _____

2. Multiply:

   a) 10 × .6 = ____   b) 10 × .1 = ____   c) 10 × 1.2 = ____   d) 10 × .9 = ____

   e) 10 × 1.7 = ____   f) 2.4 × 10 = ____   g) 10.2 × 10 = ____   h) 16.1 × 10 = ____

   i) 10 × 28.3 = ____   j) 10 × 10.98 = ____   k) 10 × 80.6 = ____   l) 73.48 × 10 = ____

3. To change from dm to cm, you multiply
   by 10 (there are 10 cm in 1 dm):

   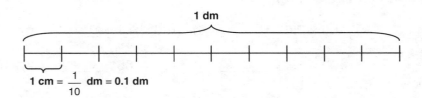

   1 dm

   $1 \text{ cm} = \frac{1}{10} \text{ dm} = 0.1 \text{ dm}$

   Find the answers:

   a) .3 dm = _____ cm   b) .8 dm = _____ cm   c) 1.2 dm = _____ cm

Answer the remaining questions in your notebook.

4. 10 × 3 can be written as a sum: 3 + 3 + 3 + 3 + 3 + 3 + 3 + 3 + 3 + 3.
   Write 10 × .6 as a sum and skip count by .6 to find the answer.

5. A dime is a tenth of a dollar (10¢ = $0.10).
   Draw a picture or use play money to show that 10 × $0.30 = $3.00.

= 1.0   □ = 0.01   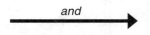 *and* $100 \times$ □ =

If a hundreds block   ... a ones block represents   100 hundredths makes
represents 1 whole then...   1 hundredth (or .01).   1 whole: $100 \times .01 = 1.00$

----

1. Write a multiplication statement for each picture:

   a)
   $100 \times$ ▤ =

   $\underline{\quad 100 \times .02 \quad}$ = $\underline{\hspace{2cm}}$

   b)
   $100 \times$ ▤ =

   $\underline{\hspace{2cm}}$ = $\underline{\hspace{2cm}}$

2. The picture shows why the decimal shifts two places to the right when multiplying by 100:

      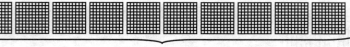

   $100 \times 0.12 = \underline{\quad 12 \quad}$ $100 \times 0.1 = \underline{\quad 10 \quad}$ $100 \times 0.02 = \underline{\quad 2 \quad}$

   In each case, shift the decimal two places to the right:

   a) $100 \times .7 = \underline{\quad 70 \quad}$ b) $100 \times .3 \quad = \underline{\hspace{1.5cm}}$ c) $100 \times 5.6 \quad = \underline{\hspace{1.5cm}}$

   d) $100 \times 6.9 \quad = \underline{\hspace{1.5cm}}$ e) $100 \times 3.36 \quad = \underline{\hspace{1.5cm}}$ f) $100 \times 6.0 \quad = \underline{\hspace{1.5cm}}$

   g) $100 \times 0.31 \quad = \underline{\hspace{1.5cm}}$ h) $100 \times 0.28 \quad = \underline{\hspace{1.5cm}}$ i) $100 \times 0.06 \quad = \underline{\hspace{1.5cm}}$

3. Multiply:

   a) $100 \times .07 = \underline{\quad 7 \quad}$ b) $100 \times .03 = \underline{\hspace{1.5cm}}$ c) $100 \times .54 = \underline{\hspace{1.5cm}}$ d) $.91 \times 100 = \underline{\hspace{1.5cm}}$

   e) $100 \times 2.67 = \underline{\hspace{1.5cm}}$ f) $100 \times 4.1 = \underline{\hspace{1.5cm}}$ g) $100 \times .20 = \underline{\hspace{1.5cm}}$ h) $100 \times .8 = \underline{\hspace{1.5cm}}$

   i) $100 \times 1.4 = \underline{\hspace{1.5cm}}$ j) $100 \times .65 = \underline{\hspace{1.5cm}}$ k) $100 \times .84 = \underline{\hspace{1.5cm}}$ l) $.27 \times 100 = \underline{\hspace{1.5cm}}$

4. a) What do 1000 thousandths add up to? $\underline{\hspace{2cm}}$ b) What is $1000 \times .001$? $\underline{\hspace{2cm}}$

5. Look at your answer to Question 4 b).
   How many places right does the decimal shift when you multiply by 1000? $\underline{\hspace{3cm}}$

6. Multiply the numbers by shifting the decimal:

   a) $1000 \times .02 = \underline{\hspace{2cm}}$ b) $1000 \times .873 = \underline{\hspace{2cm}}$ c) $1000 \times 6.147 = \underline{\hspace{2cm}}$

   d) $1000 \times .034 = \underline{\hspace{2cm}}$ e) $1000 \times 5.205 = \underline{\hspace{2cm}}$ f) $1000 \times 2.8 = \underline{\hspace{2cm}}$

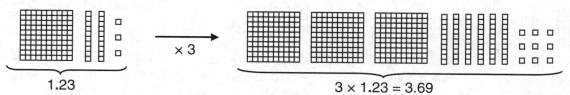
The picture shows how to multiply a decimal by a whole number:

1.23   × 3   →   3 × 1.23 = 3.69

HINT: Simply multiply each digit separately.

---

1. Multiply mentally:

    a) $2 \times 1.4 =$ _____   b) $2 \times 2.43 =$ _____   c) $4 \times 3.01 =$ _____   d) $3 \times 2.1 =$ _____

    e) $3 \times 4.12 =$ _____   f) $5 \times 1.1 =$ _____   g) $3 \times 1.32 =$ _____   h) $2 \times 4.43 =$ _____

2. Multiply by exchanging tenths for ones (the first one is done for you):

    a) $6 \times 1.4 =$ __6__ ones + __24__ tenths = __8__ ones + __4__ tenths = __8.4__

    b) $2 \times 3.8 =$ _____ ones + _____ tenths = _____ ones + _____ tenths = _____

    c) $5 \times 2.4 =$ _____ ones + _____ tenths = _____ ones + _____ tenths = _____

    d) $4 \times 5.9 =$ _____

3. Multiply by exchanging tenths for ones or hundredths for tenths:

    a) $3 \times 2.62 =$ _____ ones + _____ tenths + _____ hundredths

    = _____ ones + _____ tenths + _____ hundredths = _____

    b) $4 \times 3.45 =$ _____ ones + _____ tenths + _____ hundredths

    = _____ ones + _____ tenths + _____ hundredths = _____

    c) $5 \times 2.79 =$ _____ ones + _____ tenths + _____ hundredths

    = _____ ones + _____ tenths + _____ hundredths = _____

4. Multiply. In some questions you will have to regroup twice:

    a) 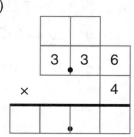   b) 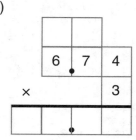   c) 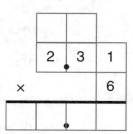   d)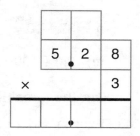

5. In your notebook, find the products:

    a) 3×3.1 b) 5×0.4 c) 6×5.7 d) 8×2.06 e) 9×3.25 f) 7×5.21

    g) 3×4.9 h) 4×6.78 i) 7×2.56 j) 8×3.23 k) 2×25.25 l) 9×11.12

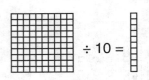 ÷ 10 =   ÷ 10 = □   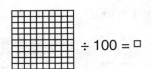 ÷ 100 = □

When you divide a decimal by 10 the decimal shifts <u>one place to the left</u>:

0 , 7 ÷ 10 = .07   7 , 0 ÷ 10 = .7

When you divide a decimal by 100 the decimal shifts <u>two places to the left</u>.

7 . 0 ÷ 100 = .07

Divide 1 whole into 10 equal part;: each part is 1 tenth: 1.0 ÷ 10 = 0.1

Divide 1 tenth into 10 equal parts; each part is 1 hundredth: 0.1 ÷ 10 = 0.01

Divide 1 whole into 100 equal parts; each part is 1 hundredth: 1.0 ÷ 100 = 0.01

1. Complete the picture and write a division statement for each picture:

a) 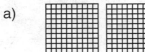 ÷ 10 =

b)   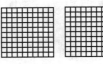 ÷ 10 =

    2.0 ÷ 10 = .2   _____ = _____

c) ÷ 10 = □□□

d) ÷ 10 =

e) ÷ 10 =

    .3 ÷ 10 = _____   _____ = _____   _____ = _____

2. Complete the picture and write a division statement. The first one is done for you:

a) 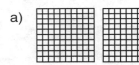 ÷ 10 =

b)   ÷ 10 =

    2.3 ÷ 10 = .23   _____ = _____

3. Shift the decimal one or two places to the left by drawing an arrow, as shown in part a):
    HINT: If there is no decimal, add one to the right of the number first.

a) 0.9 ÷ 10 = _____   b) 0.8 ÷ 10 = _____   c) 0.5 ÷ 10 = _____   d) 1.9 ÷ 10 = _____

e) 6.8 ÷ 10 = _____   f) 15.0 ÷ 10 = _____   g) 6 ÷ 10 = _____   h) 7.61 ÷ 10 = _____

i) 37 ÷ 10 = _____   j) 21 ÷ 10 = _____   k) .1 ÷ 10 = _____   l) 20.4 ÷ 10 = _____

m) 2.0 ÷ 100 = _____   n) 3.6 ÷ 100 = _____   o) .2 ÷ 100 = _____   p) 23.4 ÷ 100 = _____

Answer the remaining questions in your notebook.

4. Explain why 1.00 ÷ 100 = .01, using dollar coins as a whole.

5. A wall 3.5 m wide is painted with 100 stripes of equal width. How wide is each stripe?

6. 5 × 3 = 15 and 15 ÷ 5 = 3 are in the same fact family.
    Write a division statement in the same fact family as 10 × 0.9 = 9.0.

Linda is preparing snacks for four classes. She needs to divide 95 crackers into 4 groups.

She will use long division and a model to solve the problem:

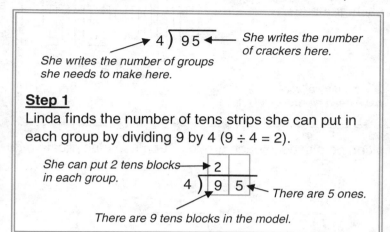

She writes the number of groups she needs to make here.

She writes the number of crackers here.

Step 1

Linda finds the number of tens strips she can put in each group by dividing 9 by 4 (9 ÷ 4 = 2).

She can put 2 tens blocks in each group.

There are 9 tens blocks in the model.

There are 5 ones.

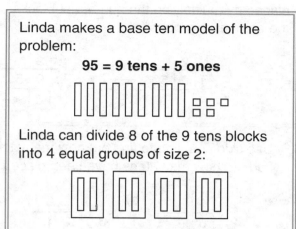

Linda makes a base ten model of the problem:

95 = 9 tens + 5 ones

Linda can divide 8 of the 9 tens blocks into 4 equal groups of size 2:

1. Linda has written a division statement to solve a problem. How many groups does she want to make? How many tens blocks and how many ones would she need to model the problem?

a) 2 ⟌ 37

groups _____

tens blocks _____

ones _____

b) 4 ⟌ 62

groups _____

tens blocks _____

ones _____

c) 3 ⟌ 76

groups _____

tens blocks _____

ones _____

d) 5 ⟌ 96

groups _____

tens blocks _____

ones _____

2. How many tens blocks can be put in each group? (Use skip counting to find the answers.) Write your answer in the box above the tens digit of the dividend:

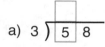 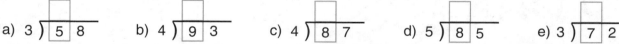

a) 3 ⟌ 5 8   b) 4 ⟌ 9 3   c) 4 ⟌ 8 7   d) 5 ⟌ 8 5   e) 3 ⟌ 7 2

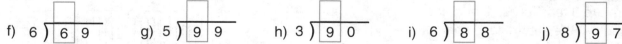

f) 6 ⟌ 6 9   g) 5 ⟌ 9 9   h) 3 ⟌ 9 0   i) 6 ⟌ 8 8   j) 8 ⟌ 9 7

3. For each division statement, write how many groups have been made and how many tens blocks are in each group:

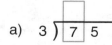

a) 3 ⟌ 7 5

groups _____

number of tens in
each group _____

b) 5 ⟌ 9 1

groups _____

number of tens in
each group _____

c) 7 ⟌ 8 3

groups _____

number of tens in
each group _____

d) 2 ⟌ 9 2

groups _____

number of tens in
each group _____

Step 2

Linda calculates the total number of tens blocks that have been placed by multiplying the number of blocks in each group (2) by the number of groups (4).

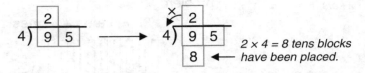

2 × 4 = 8 tens blocks
have been placed.

In the model:

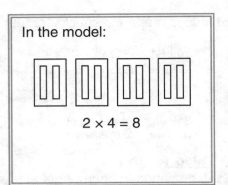

2 × 4 = 8

5. Use skip counting to find out how many tens can be placed in each group. Then use multiplication to find out how many tens have been placed:

a)   2) 6 5

b)   3) 5 1

c)   4) 7 7

d)   5) 6 7

e)   9) 9 4

f)   8) 8 5

g)   4) 9 2

h)   6) 7 2

i)   7) 9 1

j)   8) 9 5

k)   2) 8 7

l)   6) 8 5

m)   4) 5 2

n)   5) 6 8

o)   8) 9 4

Step 3

There are 9 tens locks. Linda has placed 8. She subtracts to find out how many are left over (9 − 8 = 1).

In the model:

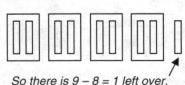

So there is 9 − 8 = 1 left over.

6. For each question, carry out the first three steps of the long division:

a)   7) 9 8

b)   3) 7 8

c)   2) 7 3

d)   4) 7 8

e) 6) 9 9

Step 4

There is one tens block left over and 5 ones.
So there are 15 ones left over. Linda writes the
5 beside the 1 to show this.

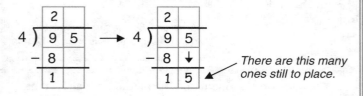

There are this many
ones still to place.

In the model:

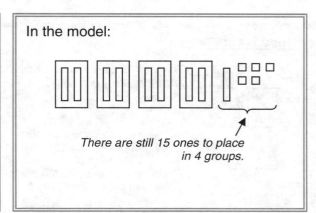

There are still 15 ones to place
in 4 groups.

7. Carry out the first <u>four</u> steps of long division:

a) 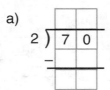   b) 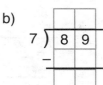   c) 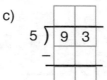   d) 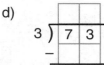   e)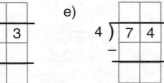

f) 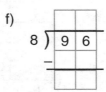   g) 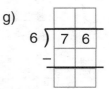   h) 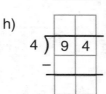   i) 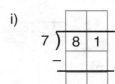   j)

Step 5

Linda finds the number of ones she can put
in each group by dividing 15 by 4.

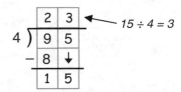

$15 \div 4 = 3$

In the model:

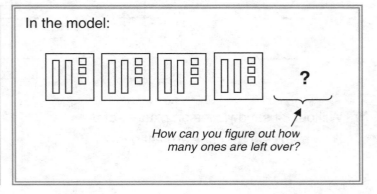

How can you figure out how
many ones are left over?

8. Carry out the first <u>five</u> steps of long division:

a) 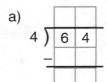   b)   c) 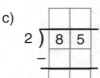   d) 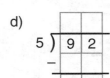   e)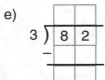

f) 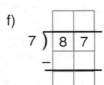   g) 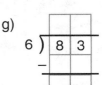   h) 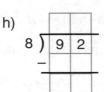   i)   j)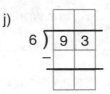

Steps 6 and 7

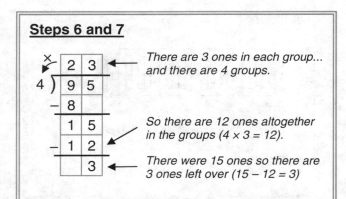

There are 3 ones in each group... and there are 4 groups.

So there are 12 ones altogether in the groups (4 × 3 = 12).

There were 15 ones so there are 3 ones left over (15 – 12 = 3)

In the model:

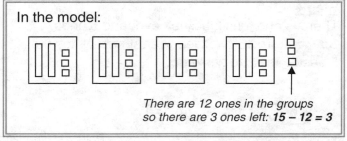

There are 12 ones in the groups so there are 3 ones left: **15 – 12 = 3**

The division statement and the model both show that Linda can give each class 23 crackers with 3 left over.

9. Carry out <u>all seven</u> steps of long division:

a) 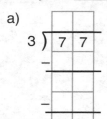   b)   c) 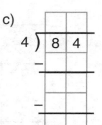   d) 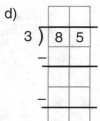   e)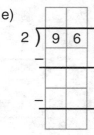

f) 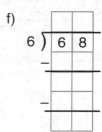   g) 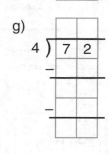   h) 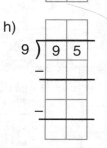   i) 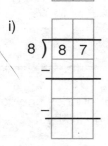   j)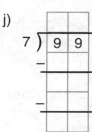

10. Will put 84 sandwiches on platters of 6. How many sandwiches are left over?

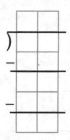

11. How many weeks are in 84 days?

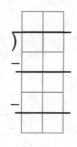

Show your work for the remaining questions in your notebook.

12. Mita spends $91 per week. How much money does she spend daily?

13. Saran divides 59 candies equally among 4 friends and Wendy divides 74 candies equally among 5 friends.

    Who will have more candies leftover?

NS8-41: Long Division — 3- and 4-Digit by 1-Digit

1. Find **313 ÷ 2** by drawing a base ten model and by long division:

   Step 1   Draw a base ten model of 313.

Draw your model here:

   Step 2   Divide the hundreds blocks into 2 equal groups.

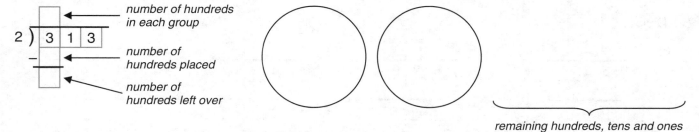

remaining hundreds, tens and ones

   Step 3   Regroup the left over hundreds block for 10 tens.

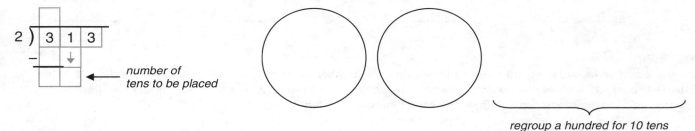

regroup a hundred for 10 tens

   Step 4   Divide the tens blocks into 2 equal groups.

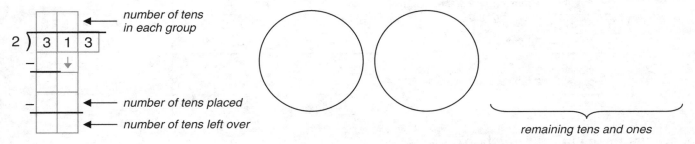

remaining tens and ones

   Step 5   Regroup the left over tens blocks for 10 ones.

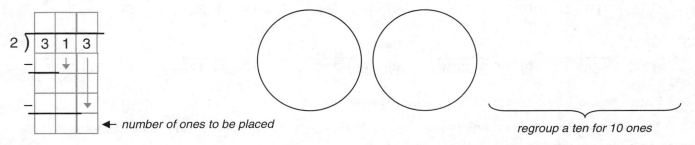

regroup a ten for 10 ones

Steps 6 and 7   Divide the ones into 2 equal groups.

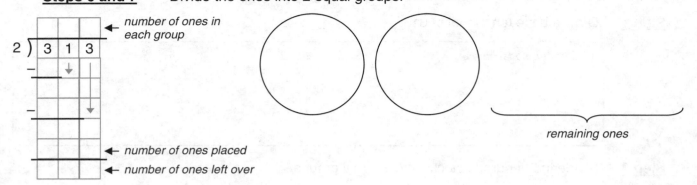

2.   Divide:

a)

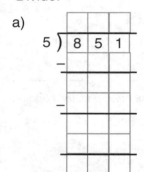

b)

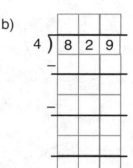

c)

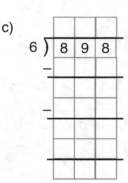

d)

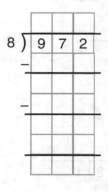

TEACHER:

In each question below, there are fewer hundreds than the number of groups. Tell your students to write a '0' in the hundreds position to show that no hundreds can be placed in equal groups. Your students should then perform the division as if the hundreds had automatically been regrouped for tens.

3.   Divide. The first one has been done for you:

a)

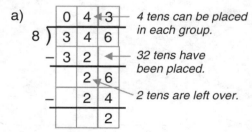

b)

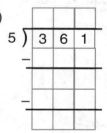

c)

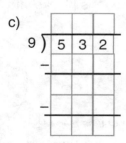

d)

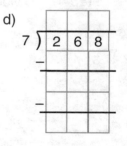

Show your work in your notebook.

4.   Divide:

a) $3 \overline{) 168}$ b) $4 \overline{) 216}$ c) $6 \overline{) 439}$ d) $7 \overline{) 523}$ e) $9 \overline{) 891}$

5.   Divide:

a) $2 \overline{) 2567}$ b) $5 \overline{) 2394}$ c) $6 \overline{) 7241}$ d) $4 \overline{) 1978}$ e) $7 \overline{) 2135}$

6.   Karen swims 4 laps of a pool. Altogether she swims 144 metres. How long is the pool?

7.   The perimeter of a regular hexagonal park is 732 km. How long is each side of the park?

jump math
MULTIPLYING POTENTIAL.

Number Sense 1

You can divide a decimal by a whole number by making a base ten model. Keep track of your work using long division.

Use the hundreds block to represent 1 whole, the tens block to represent 1 tenth and a unit block to represent 1 hundredth:

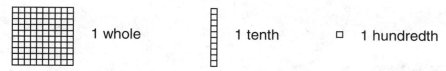

1 whole   1 tenth   □   1 hundredth

---

1. Find **5.12 ÷ 2** by drawing a base ten model and by long division:

Step 1   Draw a base ten model of 5.12.

> *Draw your model here.*

Step 2   Divide the (large) units blocks into 2 equal groups.

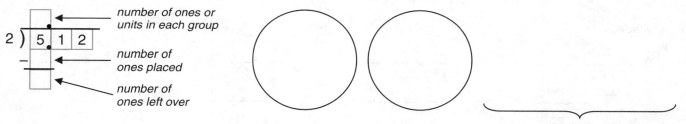

number of ones or units in each group

number of ones placed

number of ones left over

remaining ones, tenths and hundredths

Step 3   Exchange the left over units blocks for 10 tens.

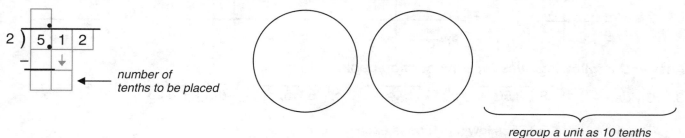

number of tenths to be placed

regroup a unit as 10 tenths

REMEMBER: A unit is represented by a hundreds block.

Step 4   Divide the tenths blocks into 2 equal groups.

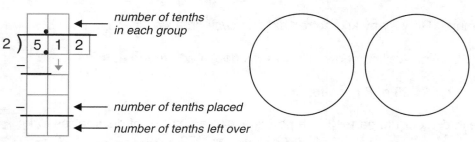

number of tenths in each group

number of tenths placed

number of tenths left over

remaining tenths and hundredths

Step 5   Regroup the left over tenth block as 10 hundredths.

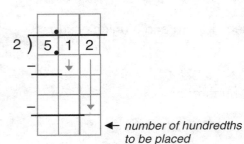

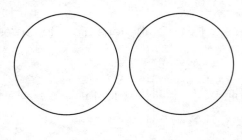

← number of hundredths
   to be placed

exchange a tenth for 10 hundredths

Steps 6 and 7   Divide the hundredths into 2 equal groups.

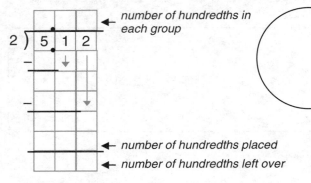

← number of hundredths in
   each group

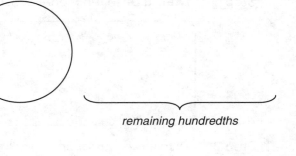

remaining hundredths

← number of hundredths placed

← number of hundredths left over

2. Divide:

a) 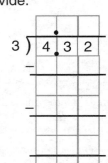   b) 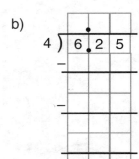   c) 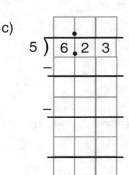   d)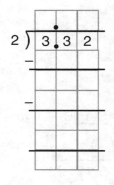

Answer the following questions in your notebook.

3. Divide: a) $8\overline{)\,2.56}$ b) $7\overline{)\,9.4}$ c) $6\overline{)\,5.79}$ d) $9\overline{)\,8.24}$ e) $5\overline{)\,45.8}$

4. Five apples cost $2.75. How much does each apple cost?

5. An equilateral triangle has a perimeter of 2.85 m. How long is each side?

6. Karen cycled 62.4 km in 4 hours. How many kilometres did she cycle in an hour?

7. Four friends earn a total of $29.16 shovelling snow. How much does each friend earn?

8. Which is a better deal: 6 pens for $4.99 or 8 pens for $6.99?

9. James divides 3.4 m of rope into six equal parts. Each part is a whole number of decimetres long:
   a) How long is each part?   b) How many decimetres of rope are left over?

1. Practice the first two steps in rounding:

| **Step 1**
 Underline the digit you wish to round to.

 hundreds
 [5][2][<u>3</u>][7][5] round up / **round down** | **Step 2**
 Put your pencil on the digit to the **right** of the one you underlined.

 ↓
 [5][2][<u>3</u>][7][5] round up / **round down** | • If the digit under your pencil is 5 or greater, circle "round up"
 • Otherwise circle "round down"

 ↓
 [5][2][<u>3</u>][7][5] (round up) / **round down** |

a) *thousands*

[5][7][8][4][1]   round up / round down

b) *ten thousands*

[8][4][3][3][2]   round up / round down

c) *hundreds*

[2][8][5][4][5]   round up / round down

2. Complete the first two steps of rounding. Then follow steps 3 and 4 below:

| **Step 1**   *thousands*
 [2][<u>7</u>][3][2][5] ru / rd

 Step 2   *thousands*
 [2][<u>7</u>][3][2][5] ru / (rd) | **Step 3**
 Round the digit underlined up or down.
 • To round up add 1 to the digit.
 • To round down keep the digit the same

 [2][<u>7</u>][3][2][5] ru /(rd)
 [ ][7][ ][ ][ ] | **Step 4**
 The digits to the right of the rounded digit become zeros.
 The digits to the left remain the same.

 [2][<u>7</u>][3][2][5] ru /(rd)
 [2][7][0][0][0] |

a) *tens*

[5][1][2][7][2][9] ru / rd

b) *thousands*

[4][1][6][2][4][8] ru / rd

c) *thousands*

[8][4][0][1][5][4] ru / rd

d) *thousands*

[6][2][0][8][1][4] ru / rd

e) *ten thousands*

[6][8][4][6][2][7] ru / rd

f) *ten thousands*

[2][9][7][3][5] ru / rd

g) *hundred thousands*

[3][1][5][3][9][7][4] ru / rd

h) *ten thousands*

[4][9][5][8][3][0][5] ru / rd

i) *hundred thousands*

[3][6][4][2][7][8][9] ru / rd

3. Sometimes in rounding, you have to regroup:

| *Example:*
 Round 37 952 to the nearest hundred. | [3][7][<u>9</u>][5][2]
 [ ][ ][10][ ][ ]
 900 rounds to 1000. | [3][7][<u>9</u>][5][2]
 [ ][8][0][ ][ ]
 Regroup the 10 hundreds as 1 (thousand) and add it to the 7 (thousand). | [3][7][<u>9</u>][5][2]
 [3][8][0][0][0]
 Complete the rounding. |

In your notebook, round each number to the digit given (regroup if necessary):

a) 595 481   *ten thousands*

b) 517 874   *thousands*

c) 39 754   *ten thousands*

d) 637 486   *tens*

e) 86 103   *hundreds*

f) 9 765 322   *hundred thousands*

g) 94 537   *ten thousands*

h) 8 951 735   *hundred thousands*

1. Follow the steps you used in the previous section to round the decimals:
    HINT: Don't forget to write the decimal point in your answer.

a) 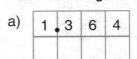 *tenths*

b)  *hundredths*

c)  *tenths*

d)  *ones*

e) 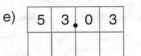 *tens*

f) 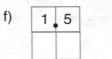 *ones*

g) 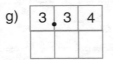 *tenths*

h)  *hundredths*

i) 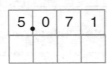 *hundredths*

j) 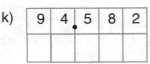 *tenths*

k) 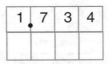 *hundredths*

l)  *ones*

m) 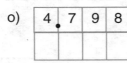 *ones*

n) 4 6 0 8 *tens*

o) 4 7 9 8 *hundredths*

Answer the remaining questions in your notebook.

2. Multiply and round your answer to the nearest whole numbers:

    a) .56 × 10   b) .34 × .8   c) .29 × 12   d) 3.09 × 5.6

3. Divide and round your answers to the nearest whole numbers:

    a) 206 ÷ 10   b) 568.9 ÷ 100   c) 324 ÷ 5   d) 500 ÷ 40

4. Add, then round your answers to the nearest tenth:

    a) 5.01 + 2.4   b) 4.89 + 6.67   c) 24.61 + 6.468   d) 97.56 + 24.18

5. Estimate whether each sum is greater than or less than 100. Then check by adding:

    a) 58.89 + 49.04   b) 48.91 + 39.79   c) 61.78 + 50.14

6. Estimate each amount. Then calculate the exact amount:

    a) 1.2 × 4.9   b) 8.5 × .5   c) .2 × .6   d) .09 × 25   e) 30.06 × .6

7. Use estimation to put the decimal place in the right place (without calculating). Then check the answers with a calculator:

    a) .88 × 21 = 1 8 4 8   b) .98 × .9 = 8 8 2   c) 6.26 × 11 = 6 8 8 6   d) 12.19 × 50 = 6 0 9 5

8. Sam earned $33.22 on Friday and $60.73 on Saturday:

    a) Find Sam's average earnings for the two days.

    b) What digit should you round your answer to so that it makes sense as a money amount?

NS8-45: Scientific Notation

A number is in **Scientific Notation** when it written as (i) a decimal between 1 and 10, and (ii) multiplied by a power of 10.

Example:

These numbers *are* in Scientific Notation: 6×10^5 3.35×10^3 7 9.05×10

These numbers *are not* in Scientific Notation:

The leading numbers are not between 1 and 10.

1000 is not written as a power of 10.

---

1. Rewrite each product in standard form and then find the product. Show your work, as in a):

   a) 7.2×10^3 = $7.2 \times 1\,000$

   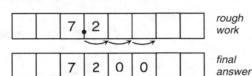

   b) 5.35×10^2

   c) 3.51×10^4

   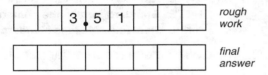

   d) 7.6×10^3

   e) 2×10^5

   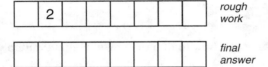

   f) 2.75×10

   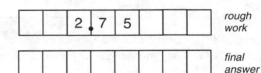

2. Rewrite each number in Scientific Notation, as shown in a):

   a) [6 7 0 0]   *rough work*

   6.7×10^3

   b) [2 5 3 0 0 0]   *rough work*

   c) [3 8 7.2]   *rough work*

   d) [9 5 0 0 0 0]   *rough work*

   e) [2 0 2.1]   *rough work*

   f) [3 0 0 0 0 0 0 0 0]   *rough work*

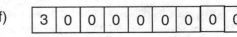

g)

| | | 5 | 7 | 0 | 0 | | |

rough work

_____

h)

| | | 0 | 2 | 0 | | | |

rough work

_____

i)

| | | 3 | 2 | . | 8 | 5 | 7 | |

rough work

_____

j)

| | | 7 | . | 0 | 5 | | |

rough work

_____

3.   Fill in the missing numbers:

a) $8\,000 = 8 \times 10^{\square}$

b) $270 = 2.7 \times 10^{\square}$

c) $50\,000 = 5 \times 10^{\square}$

d) $60\,000 = 6 \times 10^{\square}$

e) $250 = 2.5 \times 10^{\square}$

f) $920\,000 = 9.2 \times 10^{\square}$

4.   Rewrite the number in Scientific Notation or standard form.   Then write < or > between the numbers:

a) 6.14×10^4 6 123

b) 9×10^2 1 000

c)   30 000 2.3×10^4

_____ $\square$ _____   _____ $\square$ _____   _____ $\square$ _____

5.

Great Lake	Area	Area in Standard Form
Ontario	$1.9 \times 10^4 \, \text{km}^2$	
Erie	$25\,000 \, \text{km}^2$	
Michigan	$5.7 \times 10^4 \, \text{km}^2$	
Superior	$8.1 \times 10^4 \, \text{km}^2$	
Huron	$60\,000 \, \text{km}^2$	

a)   Write each lake's area in standard form.
   NOTE: Standard form is the numerical form for numbers (e.g. 342 is in standard form).

b)   Write the areas in order from least to greatest:

6.   Rewrite each product as a single power:
   CHALLENGE: Can you write a rule in your notebook that tells you how to find the power without multiplying?

a) $10^2 \times 10^3$

= _____100 × 1 000_____

= _____100 000_____

= _____10^5_____

b) $10^3 \times 10^4$

= _____

= _____

= _____

c) $10^5 \times 10^2$

= _____

= _____

= _____

Answer the following questions in your notebook.

7.   Rewrite each number in Scientific Notation:
   a) $3 \times 10^2 \times 2 \times 10^5$ b) $2 \times 10^3 \times 4 \times 10^7$

8.   Which number is largest:
   1.4×10^3 or   1 414   or 4.1×10^2?

9.   The Andromeda constellation is 22 000 000 000 000 000 km from Earth.
   a)   Write this distance in Scientific Notation.
   b)   How long would it take light from Andromeda to reach Earth?
      HINT: Light travels at 300 000 km per second.

10.   The total area of land on Earth is $1.5 \times 10^8 \, \text{km}^2$ and the total area of ocean is $3.6 \times 10^8 \, \text{km}^2$.
   How much greater is the area of the ocean than the area of the land?

Answer the following questions in your notebook.

1. Write a decimal for each description:
   IMPORTANT: Some questions have more than one answer.

   a) Between 5.63 and 5.68: ☐.☐☐

   b) Between 2.70 and 2.80: ☐.☐☐

   c) Between 21.75 and 21.8: ☐☐.☐☐

   d) Between 0.6 and 0.7: ☐.☐☐

   e) One tenth greater than 4.54: ☐.☐☐

   f) One hundredth less than 6.00: ☐.☐☐

2. Put a decimal in each number so that the digit **4** has the value $\frac{4}{10}$:

   a) 3 4 8   b) 5 0 4   c) 1 5 4 7 9   d) 4

3. Under which deal do you pay less for 1 pen: 3 pens for $2.99 or 5 pens for $4.99?

4. On a map, 1 cm represents 15 km. Two towns are 2.3 cm apart on the map.
   How far apart are the towns?

5. $0.68 means 6 dimes and 8 pennies. Why do we use the decimal notation for money?
   a) What is a dime a tenth of?
   b) What is a penny a hundredth of?

6. Here are the greatest lengths of sea creatures ever recorded:

   a) Order the lengths from the least to the greatest.

   b) How much longer than the great white shark is the blue whale?

   c) About how many times longer than the turtle is the great white shark?

   d) About how long would 3 Blue Whales be if they swam in a row?
      Write a decimal for each description:

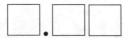

Animal	Length (m)
Blue Whale	33.58
Great White Shark	7.92
Pacific Leather Back Turtle	2.13
Ocean Sun Fish	2.95

7. The wind speed in Vancouver was 26.7 km/h on Monday, 16.0 km/h
   on Tuesday and 2.4 km/h on Wednesday.
   What was the average wind speed over the 3 days?

8. Encke's Comet appears in our sky every 3.3 years. It was first seen in 1786.
   When was the last time the comet was seen in the 1700s (i.e. before 1800)?
   Show your work.

E

ME8-1: Measuring Lengths

The standard unit for measuring length in the metric system is the **metre** (m).

Other units for measuring length, based on the metre, include the **millimetre** (mm), **centimetre** (cm), **decimetre** (dm) and **kilometre** (km):

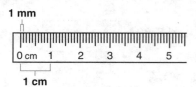

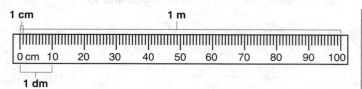

1 cm = 10 mm
1 dm = 10 cm
1 m = 100 cm
1 km = 1000 m

NOTE: Rulers are not drawn to scale.

---

1. Guess which line is longer by estimating. Then measure each length in millimetres (mm):

Guess A or B   **Guess A or B**

a) 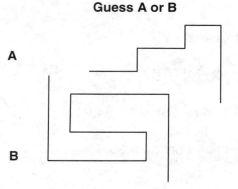   b)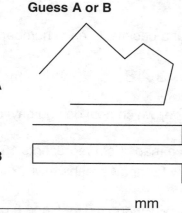

A: _____ mm   A: _____ mm

B: _____ mm   B: _____ mm

2. Find the diameter of each circle:

a)   b) 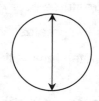   c)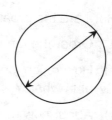

_____ cm = _____ mm   _____ cm = _____ mm   _____ cm = _____ mm

3. This line segment is 1 dm 2 cm 3 mm long:

Measure the line segments to the nearest millimetre:

a) _____   _____ dm _____ cm _____ mm

b) _____   _____ dm _____ cm _____ mm

c) _____   _____ dm _____ cm _____ mm

Answer the questions below in your notebook.

4. Use a ruler to draw a line segment of length:

   a)   2 dm   b)   5 cm 3 mm   c)   2 dm 1 cm 7 mm   d)   2 dm 0 cm 5 mm

ME8-2: Appropriate Units

1. Match the object with the appropriate unit of measurement:

a) mm   height of a cat

    cm   width of a swimming pool

    m   distance of a marathon

    km   length of a bee's antenna

b) km   thickness of a noodle

    cm   height of a dandelion

    m   distance between cities

    mm   length of a soccer field

2. Which unit of measurement (mm, cm, m or km) would make the statement correct?

a) A fast runner can run 1 _____ in 3 minutes.

b) The length of your arm is about 60 _____.

c) A juggler likes ceilings to be 4 _____ high.

d) A birthday card is about 150 _____ wide.

3. Nicholas measured some objects, but forgot to include the units. Add the appropriate unit:

a) television: 60 _____

b) $20 dollar bill: 151 _____

c) classroom floor: 11 _____

d) pencil: 16 _____

e) CD: 12 _____

f) tree: 13 _____

4. Choose which unit (km, m, or cm) belongs to complete each sentence. Read carefully!

a) Canada's entire coastline is about 200 000 _____ long.

b) Mount Logan, in the Yukon Territory, is almost 6000 _____ high.

c) A house sparrow is 16 _____ long.

d) Lake Erie is more than 60 _____ deep.

e) A cod can grow up to 2 _____ long.

f) A maple leaf is 10 _____ wide.

5. Put the numbers in the correct places below (select from the box): | .5   133   35 000 |

According to the Guinness Book of World Records...

a) ...the tallest tree ever measured was a eucalyptus tree more than _____ **m** tall.

b) ...the longest round-trip migration by a bird is _____ **km**, by the Arctic tern.

c) ...the smallest spider, the Samoan moss spider, is _____ **mm** long.

ME8-3: Converting Units: From Larger to Smaller

1. Complete the table to show the equivalent measurements:
   HINT: Follow the pattern.

m	1	2	3	4	5	6
dm	10	20				
cm	100	200				
mm	1000	2000				

2. Circle the **larger** unit in each pair:
   HINT: Which unit is higher on the stairs?

   a) cm   mm   b) cm   dm   c) dm   mm

   d) m   cm   e) dm   m   f) mm   m

3. Looking at the definition box to the right, circle the correct word in each case:

   a) When you use a smaller unit to measure, you need (more / fewer) units than when you use a larger unit.

   b) To change a measurement from a larger unit to a smaller one, I will (multiply / divide) the measurement.

> Units **increase** in size when you go up the stairs:
>
>
> ➢ 1 step up = 10 × larger
> ➢ 2 steps up = 100 × larger
> ➢ 3 steps up = 1000 × larger
>
> How to change *larger* units to *smaller* units:
>
> **Step 1**
> Metres are 2 steps up from centimetres so m are 100 × larger than cm.
>
> **Step 2**
> Multiply by 100 to change m to cm.

4. Count the steps going up the stairs.

   What do you multiply by to change a measurement from...

   a) cm to mm ____   b) dm to cm ____   c) m to cm ____   d) m to mm ____   e) dm to mm ____

5. How many zeros do you add to a whole number when you multiply by...

   a) 10? You add ____ zero.   b) 100? You add ____ zeros.   c) 1000? You add ____ zeros.

6. Fill in the missing numbers:

   a) 1 cm = _____ mm   b) 1 dm = _____ cm   c) 1 m = _____ dm

   d) 1 dm = _____ mm   e) 1 m = _____ cm   f) 1 m = _____ mm

7. Fill in the missing numbers:

   a)
mm	cm
	27
940	

   b)
cm	dm
	62
	74

   c)
cm	m
	5
	70

   d)
mm	m
	8
	32

8. 1 km = _____ m, so you would multiply by _____ to change a length from kilometres to metres.

9. Change the measurements from kilometres to metres:

   a) 17 km = _____ m   b) 4 km = _____ m   c) 390 km = _____ m

1. Circle the **smaller** unit in each pair:
   HINT: Which unit is lower on the stairs?

   a) dm   cm   b) mm   m   c) dm   mm

   d) m   cm   e) dm   m   f) cm   mm

2. Looking at the definition box to the right, circle the correct word in each case:

   a) When you use a larger unit to measure, you need (more / fewer) units than when you use a smaller unit.

   b) To change a measurement from a smaller to a larger unit, I will (multiply / divide) the measurement.

3. Count the steps going down the stairs.

   What do you divide by to change a measurement from…

   a) mm to cm ____   b) cm to dm ____   c) cm to m ____   d) mm to m ____   e) mm to dm ____

> Units **decrease** in size when you <u>go down</u> the stairs:
>
> ➢ 1 step down = 10 × smaller
> ➢ 2 steps down = 100 × smaller
> ➢ 3 steps down = 1000 × smaller
>
> How to change *smaller* units to *larger* units:
>
> **Step 1**
> Centimetres are 2 steps down from metres so cm are 100 × smaller than m.
>
> **Step 2**
> Divide by 100 to change cm to m.

4. How many zeros do you remove from a whole number when you divide by…

   a) 10? Remove ____ zero.   b) 100? Remove ____ zeros.   c) 1000? Remove ____ zeros.

5. Divide:

   a) $600 \div 10 =$ ____   b) $6500 \div 100 =$ ____   c) $7000 \div 1000 =$ ____   d) $18000 \div 10 =$ ____

   d) $5300 \div 10 =$ ____   e) $400 \div 100 =$ ____   f) $87000 \div 100 =$ ____   g) $9000 \div 100 =$ ____

6. Fill in the missing units:

   a) 10 mm = 1 ____   b) 100 cm = 1 ____   c) 10 cm = 1 ____   d) 1 000 mm = 1 ____

7. Fill in the missing numbers:

   a)
mm	cm
20	
520	

   b)
cm	dm
90	
5400	

   c)
cm	m
700	
32000	

   d)
mm	m
13000	
4000	

8. 1 km = _____ m, so you would divide by _____ to change a length from metres to kilometres.

9. Fill in the missing numbers:
   HINT: First decide if you will multiply or divide.

   a) 350 mm = ____ cm   b) 84 dm = ____ mm   c) 24 km = _____ m   d) 5 000 mm = ____ m

   e) 3 500 dm = ____ m   f) 17 m = _____ mm   g) 48 000 m = ____ km   h) 70 000 m = ____ km

There are 10 mm in 1 cm.

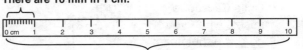

There are 10 cm in 1 dm.

NOTE: Rulers are not drawn to scale.

There are 100 cm in 1 m.

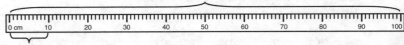

1 dm: there are 10 dm in 1 m.

There are 1 000 m in a km.

---

1. State the number of...   a)   mm in a dm: _____

                              b)   cm in a km: _____

                              c)   dm in a km: _____

2. Complete each statement below. The first two are done for you:

   a)   There are ___10___ cm in 1 dm. So 1 cm = $\boxed{\frac{1}{10}}$ dm = ___0.1___ dm.

   b)   There are ___100___ cm in 1 m. So 1 cm = $\boxed{\frac{1}{100}}$ m = ___0.01___ m.

   c)   There are _____ mm in 1 cm. So 1 mm = $\boxed{}$ cm = _____ cm.

   d)   There are _____ mm in 1 dm. So 1 mm = $\boxed{}$ dm = _____ dm.

   e)   There are _____ dm in 1 m. So 1 dm = $\boxed{}$ m = _____ m.

3. Complete the statements below:

   a)   1 cm = $\frac{1}{10}$ of a __dm__   b)   1 mm = $\frac{1}{10}$ of a _____   c)   1 dm = $\frac{1}{10}$ of a _____

        1 cm = 0.1 __dm__   1 mm = 0.1 _____   1 dm = 0.1 _____

   d)   1 cm = $\frac{1}{100}$ of a _____   e)   1 mm = $\frac{1}{100}$ of a _____   f)   1 mm = $\frac{1}{1000}$ of a _____

        1 cm = 0.01 _____   1 mm = 0.01 _____   1 mm = 0.001 _____

   BONUS:
   To answer parts g) to i), first form a mental picture of the amount given. Then ask yourself: "What larger unit is the amount a <u>tenth</u> of?" (i.e. what unit would the amount fit into ten times?):

   g)   10 cm = $\frac{1}{10}$ of a _____   h)   10 mm = $\frac{1}{10}$ of a _____   i)   100 m = $\frac{1}{10}$ of a _____

        10 cm = 0.1 _____   10 mm = 0.1 _____   100 m = 0.1 _____

Answer the remaining questions in your notebook.

4.   a)   How many pennies make 4 dollars and 23 cents?   b)   How many cm are in 4 m 23 cm?
     c)   Write 4 dollars 23 cents in decimal notation for dollars.
     d)   Write 4 m 23 cm in decimal notation for metres.
     e)   How are the questions above the same?

5. Is 5 m 28 cm equal to 5.28 m or 5.28 cm? Explain.

1. Change each measurement to the smaller unit:

    a) 12 m = _____ cm   b) 7 m = _____ dm   c) 4 cm = _____ mm

    d) 31 dm = _____ cm   e) 22 m = _____ cm   f) 15 m = _____ dm

    g) 99 dm = _____ mm   h) 80 cm = _____ mm   i) 700 m = _____ dm

    j) 75 cm = _____ mm   k) 450 dm = _____ mm   l) 120 m = _____ cm

2. Change each measurement to the smaller unit:

    a) 5 m 3 cm = __500__ cm + __3__ cm = __503__ cm   b) 7 m 89 cm = _____ cm + _____ cm = _____ cm

    c) 6 m 1 dm = _____ dm + _____ dm = _____ dm   d) 3 m 8 cm = _____ cm + _____ cm = _____ cm

    e) 8 m 3 mm = _____ mm + _____ mm = _____ mm   f) 16 dm 5 mm = _____ mm + _____ mm = _____ mm

    g) 2 km 352 m = _____ m + _____ m = _____ m   h) 4 km 27 m = _____ m + _____ m = _____ m

3. Fill in the missing numbers to make the equivalent fractions:

    a) .5 m = $\dfrac{}{10}$ m = $\dfrac{}{100}$ m = $\dfrac{}{1000}$ m   b) .83 m = $\dfrac{}{100}$ m = $\dfrac{}{1000}$ m

    c) .8 dm = $\dfrac{}{100}$ dm   d) .74 m = $\dfrac{}{1000}$ m   e) .9 km = $\dfrac{}{100}$ km

4. What unit will fit into…

    a) a metre 100 times? ___a centimetre___   b) a centimetre 10 times? _____

    c) a decimetre 100 times? _____   d) a metre 10 times? _____

5. Express each measurement in a whole number of units:

    HINT: To express $\frac{57}{100}$ m in a whole number of units, think: "What unit will fit into a metre 100 times?
    There are 100 cm in a m. So $\frac{57}{100}$ m = 57 cm."

    a) $\dfrac{7}{10}$ m = ___7 dm___   b) $\dfrac{4}{10}$ m = _____   c) $\dfrac{93}{100}$ m = _____

    d) $\dfrac{2}{10}$ dm = _____   e) $\dfrac{37}{100}$ dm = _____   f) $\dfrac{56}{1000}$ m = _____

    g) $\dfrac{72}{100}$ dm = _____   h) $\dfrac{8}{10}$ cm = _____   i) $\dfrac{75}{1000}$ km = _____

6. Change each measurement to the unit given in the box, as in a):

    HINT: To change .7 dm to mm, think: "There are 100 mm in a dm, so I should change .7 to a fraction with
    denominator 100. .7 dm = $\frac{70}{100}$ dm = 70 mm."

    a) $\boxed{\text{mm}}$ .3 cm = $\frac{3}{10}$ cm = 3 mm   b) $\boxed{\text{cm}}$ .37 m =

    c) $\boxed{\text{cm}}$ .6 dm =   d) $\boxed{\text{mm}}$ .37 m =

    e) $\boxed{\text{dm}}$ .21 m =   f) $\boxed{\text{mm}}$ .4 dm =

7.   Change each measurement to the unit given in the box. Show your work, as done in part a):

   a) $\boxed{cm}$ $3.5 \text{ m} = 3 \text{ m} + \frac{5}{10} \text{ m} = 3 \text{ m} + \frac{50}{100} \text{ m} = 300 \text{ cm} + 50 \text{ cm} = 350 \text{ cm}$

   b) $\boxed{cm}$ 5.4 m =

   c) $\boxed{dm}$ 4.6 m =

   d) $\boxed{cm}$ 7.9 dm =

   e) $\boxed{mm}$ 8.43 dm =

   f) $\boxed{mm}$ 3.2 cm =

8.   Write each measurement in mixed units:

   a)   2.357 m = _____ m _____ dm _____ cm _____ mm   b)   3.52 dm = _____ dm _____ cm _____ mm

   c)   5.006 m = _____ m _____ dm _____ cm _____ mm   d)   8.04 dm = _____ dm _____ cm _____ mm

   e)   3.5 cm = _____ cm _____ mm   f)   20.54 dm = _____ dm _____ cm _____ mm

9.   Underline the digit that stands for the unit given in the box:

   a)   3.7 2 3 m $\boxed{cm}$ b)   1 7 . 5 2 dm $\boxed{mm}$ c)   1 0 . 7 9 cm $\boxed{dm}$

   d)   2 3 . 4 5 9 m $\boxed{dm}$ e)   5 8 . 4 1 dm $\boxed{m}$ f)   1 2 1 mm $\boxed{dm}$

10. In the measurement 2.375 km, underline the digit that represents metres.

Answer the remaining questions in your notebook.

11. $1.72 stands for 1 dollar 7 dimes 2 pennies. In the measurement 1.72 m, are cm like dimes or like pennies? Explain.

12. Rita wants to plant 4 rows of trees in her yard: trees that will grow taller at the back and those that will grow shorter in the front.

   a) How should she order the trees?

   b) How much taller will the poplar grow than the yucca?

Tree	Height
Creeping Juniper	7.31 m
White Poplar	15.24 m
Weeping Willow	1 291 cm
Yucca	121 cm

13. Sally has a stack of dimes 5 dm high. Tina has a row of toonies 54 cm long. If each dime is 1 mm thick and each toonie is 27 mm wide, who has more money?

14. Carl has a set of sticks: some are 3 dm long, some are 4 cm long, and some are 5 mm long.

   Using the least number of sticks possible, show how Carl can make a stick which is:

   a) 42 dm long   b) 73 dm long   c) 14 cm long   d) 140 cm long   e) 2 dm long   f) 385 mm long

ME8-7: Mixed Units (Advanced)

1. Change each measurement to the larger unit:

   a) 7 m 53 cm = 7 m + $\frac{53}{100}$ m = 7.53 m

   b) 7 m 3 cm =

   c) 9 dm 4 mm =

   d) 12 m 6 dm =

2. Change each improper fraction to a mixed fraction, and then to a decimal:

	a) $\frac{140}{100}$	b) $\frac{2713}{100}$	c) $\frac{84}{10}$	d) $\frac{5476}{1000}$	e) $\frac{430}{100}$	f) $\frac{2006}{1000}$	g) $\frac{735}{100}$
Mixed Fraction	$1\frac{40}{100}$						
Decimal	1.40						

3. Write each measurement as an improper fraction of the <u>larger</u> unit:

   a) 274 cm = ☐ m

   b) 389 dm = ☐ m

   c) 13 dm = ☐ m

   d) 27 cm = ☐ dm

   e) 98 mm = ☐ cm

   f) 2 597 mm = ☐ m

   g) 861 cm = ☐ dm

   h) 461 mm = ☐ cm

   i) 63 cm = ☐ dm

   j) 6 739 mm = ☐ m

   k) 789 dm = ☐ m

   l) 8 905 cm = ☐ m

4. Change each measurement into the unit given in the box:

   a) ☐m 247 cm = $\frac{247}{100}$ m = 2.47 m

   b) ☐dm 850 mm =

   c) ☐cm 39 mm =

   d) ☐dm 507 mm =

   e) ☐m 1563 mm =

   f) ☐km 75 m =

   g) ☐m 61 dm =

   h) ☐m 653 mm =

5. a) $\frac{1}{10}$ of 1 000 = _____

   b) $\frac{1}{100}$ of 1 000 = _____

   c) $\frac{1}{10}$ of 100 = _____

   d) $\frac{1}{100}$ of 100 = _____

6. a) $\frac{1}{10}$ of a km = $\frac{1}{10}$ of _____ m = _____ m

   b) $\frac{1}{10}$ of a m = $\frac{1}{10}$ of _____ cm = _____ cm

   c) $\frac{1}{10}$ of a dm = $\frac{1}{10}$ of _____ mm = _____ mm

   d) $\frac{1}{100}$ of a km = $\frac{1}{100}$ of _____ m = _____ m

7. The line represents 1 km. It is divided into 10 parts. How many **m** are in $\frac{1}{10}$ **km** (or .1 km)? _____
   Fill in the missing measurements in metres:

0 km	.1 km	.2 km	.3 km	.4 km	.5 km	.6 km	.7 km	.8 km	.9 km	1 km

   0 m _____ m _____ m _____ m _____ m _____ m _____ m _____ m _____ m _____ m _____ m

8. Mark the approximate position of the following measurements on the number line above:

   A 750 m   **B** 638 m   **C** 95 m   **D** 944 m   **E** 593 m

1. a) To multiply by 10, I move the decimal __1__ place(s) to the __right__.

   b) To multiply by 1 000, I move the decimal ____ place(s) to the _____.

   c) To divide by 100, I move the decimal ____ place(s) to the _____.

   d) To divide by 10, I move the decimal ____ place(s) to the _____.

   e) To _____ by 1 000, I move the decimal ____ places to the left.

   f) To _____ by 10, I move the decimal ____ place to the left.

   g) To _____ by 100, I move the decimal ____ places to the right.

   h) To divide by 10 000 000, I move the decimal ____ places to the _____.

   i) To multiply by 100 000, I move the decimal ____ places to the _____.

2. Fill in the blanks. Next draw arrows to show how you would shift the decimal. Then write your answers in the grid. The first two have been done for you:

   a) 7.325 × 100

   I move the decimal __2__ places __right__.

   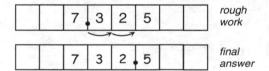

   b) 5.3 ÷ 1 000

   I move the decimal __3__ places __left__.

   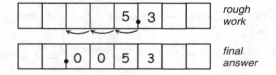

   c) 572.499 × 1 000

   I move the decimal ____ places _____.

   d) 300.94 ÷ 100

   I move the decimal ____ places _____.

   e) 123.67 ÷ 10 000

   I move the decimal ____ places _____.

   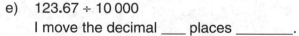

   f) .067 × 100 000

   I move the decimal ____ places _____.

   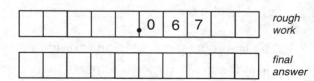

3. Copy the questions below onto grid paper. Show how you would shift the decimal in each case:

   a) 5.6 × 1 000   b) 34.007 × 100   c) 0.072 × 10   d) 39.85 × 1 000   e) 0.07 × 10 000

   f) 0.475 ÷ 10   g) 820.78 ÷ 100   h) 62.09 ÷ 1 000   i) 95.57 ÷ 10 000   j) 0.08 ÷ 1 000

ME8-9: Changing Units

1. Fill in the missing numbers:

    a) 1 cm = _____ mm   b) 1 dm = _____ cm

    c) 1 dm = _____ mm   d) 1 m = _____ dm

    e) 1 m = _____ cm   f) 1 m = _____ mm

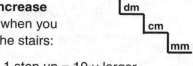

RECALL:

Units **increase**
in size when you
<u>go up</u> the stairs:

➢ 1 step up = 10 × larger
➢ 2 steps up = 100 × larger
➢ 3 steps up = 1000 × larger

2. Fill in the blanks. The first one is done for you:

    a) I wish to change mm to cm.

        The new units are __10__ times ___larger___ .

        I need _10_ times ___fewer___ cm than mm.

    b) I wish to change cm to dm.

        The new units are _____ times _____ .

        I need _____ times _____ dm than cm.

    c) I wish to change m to mm.

        The new units are _____ times _____ .

        I need _____ times _____ mm than m.

    d) I wish to change m to cm.

        The new units are _____ times _____ .

        I need _____ times _____ cm than m.

3. Change the measurements below by following the steps. The first one has been done for you:

    a) Change 3.5 mm to cm

        i)   The new units are 10 times ___larger__ .

        ii) So I need 10 times __fewer__ units.

        iii) So I ___divide___ by 10.

        3.5 mm = __.35__ cm

    b) Change 37.6 cm to m

        i)   The new units are 100 times _____ .

        ii) So I need 100 times _____ units.

        iii) So I _____ by 100.

        37.6 cm = _____ m

    c) Change 2.9 m to dm

        i)   The new units are 10 times _____ .

        ii) So I need 10 times _____ units.

        iii) So I _____ by 10.

        2.9 m = _____ dm

    d) Change 45 mm to m

        i)   The new units are 1000 times _____ .

        ii) So I need 1000 times _____ units.

        iii) So I _____ by 1000.

        45 mm = _____ m

    e) Change 70 mm to dm

        i)   The new units are 100 times _____ .

        ii) So I need 100 times _____ units.

        iii) So I _____ by 100.

        70 mm = _____ dm

    f) Change 65.4 m to cm

        i)   The new units are 100 times _____ .

        ii) So I need 100 times _____ units.

        iii) So I _____ by 100.

        65.4 m = _____ cm

ME8-9: Changing Units (continued)

4. In the questions below, you will need to multiply or divide by 10, 100 or 1 000:

a) Change 70.09 m to cm

    i) The new units are _____ times _____

    ii) So I need _____ times _____units

    iii) So I _____ by _____

    70.09 m = _____ cm

b) Change 74 cm to m

    i) The new units are _____ times _____

    ii) So I need _____ times _____units

    iii) So I _____ by _____

    74 cm = _____ m

c) Change 63 m to dm

    i) The new units are _____ times _____

    ii) So I need _____ times _____units

    iii) So I _____ by _____

    63 m = _____ dm

d) Change 84 mm to dm

    i) The new units are _____ times _____

    ii) So I need _____ times _____units

    iii) So I _____ by _____

    84 mm = _____ m

e) Change 47 mm to m

    i) The new units are _____ times _____

    ii) So I need _____ times _____units

    iii) So I _____ by _____

    47 mm = _____ m

f) Change 9.2 m to mm

    i) The new units are _____ times _____

    ii) So I need _____ times _____units

    iii) So I _____ by _____

    9.2 m = _____ mm

5. Change the units by following the steps in Question 4 <u>in your head</u>:

a) 10 dm = _____ m   b) 4.2 m = _____ dm   c) 71 m = _____ cm

d) .72 mm = _____ dm   e) 38.1 cm = _____dm   f) 63 cm = _____ m

Show your work for the remaining questions in your notebook.

6. The tallest human skeleton is 2.7 m high and the shortest is 60 cm high.
What is the difference between the heights of the skeletons?

7. Katie can buy 4 m of ribbon for $2.00 or 3 dm of ribbon for 12 ¢.
Which is the better buy?

8. Jack ran a 100 m race in 12 seconds and then ran a 5 km race in 30 minutes.
How much faster was he in the shorter race than in the longer race (in km/hour)?

9. Write the following prices in order from least to greatest.
What is the difference between the highest and the lowest price?
HINT: Change all the prices to dollars per kilogram.

A: Cherries – 59¢/100 g   **B:** Watermelon – $3.90/kg

C: Strawberries – $0.32/100 g   **D:** Blueberries – $3.99/500 g

ME8-10: Changing Units (Advanced)

Krista wants to change 2.5 m to cm.

She thinks:

Step 1	**Step 2**	**Step 3**
"The new unit is 100 times smaller…	…so I will need 100 times more of the unit: this means shifting the decimal 2 right…	… so I will draw arrows to shift the decimal."
_100_ times _smaller_	_100_ times _smaller_	_100_ times _smaller_
2.5 m = _____ cm	2.5 m = _____ cm	2.5 m = _250_ cm

----

1. Draw arrows to shift the decimal in the direction indicated:

a) 8 . 2 m = _____ mm

b) 7 . 4 dm = _____ cm

c) 6 . 3 mm = _____ dm

> **RECALL:**
>
> Units **increase** in size when you <u>go up</u> the stairs:
>
>
> km
> increase in size as you go up
> m
> dm
> cm
> mm
>
> ➢ 1 step up = 10 × larger
> ➢ 2 steps up = 100 × larger
> ➢ 3 steps up = 1000 × larger

d) 5 . 4 m = _____ cm

e) 7 . 0 6 m = _____ mm

f) 7 cm = _____ dm

g) 51 . 4 dm = _____ cm

h) 36 . 04 mm = _____ dm

i) 19.2 m = _____ dm

j) 42.7 m = _____ km

k) . 5 dm = _____ mm

l) 9423 cm = _____ km

2. How many times larger or smaller are the new units?
   HINT: Write "S" if the new unit is smaller and "L" if it is larger. Use the chart to help you.

   a) mm are ____10 times S____ than cm

   b) dm are _____ than m

   c) cm are _____ than dm

   d) m are _____ than mm

   e) km are _____ than m

   f) m are _____ than cm

   g) km are _____ than dm

   h) dm are _____ than km

   i) cm are _____ than m

   j) mm are _____ than km

ME8-10: Changing Units (Advanced) *(continued)*

3. Change the following units using Krista's method. The first one is done for you:
   REMEMBER: If the new unit is larger, you need less of the unit so you shift the decimal left.

a) ____10____ times ____L____

   (←1)
   3.5 mm = __.35__ cm

b) _____ times _____
   ( )
   4.83 km = _____ m

c) _____ times _____
   ( )
   5 cm = _____ m

d) _____
   ( )
   2 mm = _____ cm

e) _____
   ( )
   4.7 m = _____ km

f) _____
   ( )
   .056 cm = _____ m

g) _____
   ( )
   8.243 dm = _____ mm

h) _____
   ( )
   83.4 cm = _____ dm

i) _____
   ( )
   5.27 cm = _____ mm

j) _____
   ( )
   7 000 m = _____ km

k) _____
   ( )
   430 mm = _____ dm

l) _____
   ( )
   .043 m = _____ cm

m) _____
   ( )
   0.286 dm = _____ m

n) _____
   ( )
   5.47 cm = _____ dm

o) _____
   ( )
   7.46 m = _____ km

4. Compare the measurements by writing > or < in the box. The first one is done for you:
   HINT: Change the larger unit into the smaller unit.

a) 2.5 m   175 cm

   __250 cm__ [>] __175 cm__

b) 3 m   2 752 mm

   _____ [ ] _____

c) 2.7 km   2 683 m

   _____ [ ] _____

Show your work for the following questions in your notebook.

5. Write the measurements in order from smallest to largest:
   a) 21 dm   3 m   2 752 mm   2 930 cm   43 dm
   b) 675 mm   .6 mm   582 dm   632 cm   65 983 mm

6. Food moves through the esophagus at a rate of 72 km per hour. How many metres per hour is this?

7. A mm of gold wire costs 8¢. How much would...   a) 1 cm cost?   b) 1 dm cost?   c) 2 m cost?

8. How is the relation between millimetres and metres similar to the relation between metres and kilometres?

ME8-11: Area and Perimeter

1. Each edge is 1 cm long. Write the total length of each side in cm as shown in the first figure.
   (i) Write an addition statement and find the perimeter. Don't miss any edges!
   (ii) Find the area (in cm^2).

a)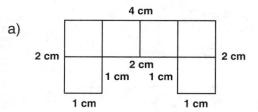

b)

   Perimeter: _____

   Area: _____

   Perimeter: _____

   Area: _____

2. Each edge is 1 unit long. Write the length of each side beside the figure (don't miss any edges!).
   Then use the side lengths to find the perimeter:

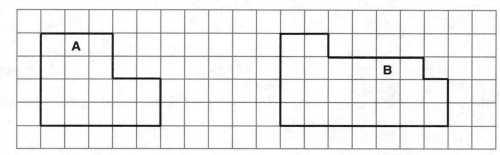

   Perimeter of **A**: _____ units

   Perimeter of **B**: _____ units

3. Draw two shapes that have the same area but different perimeter.

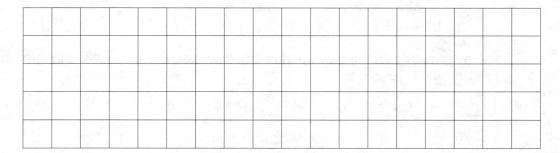

4. Draw three different (non-congruent) rectangles with perimeter 12. Which one has the least area?

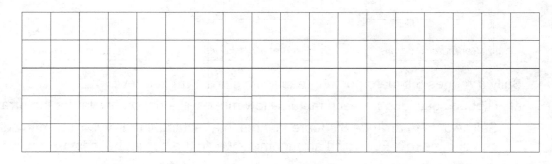

5. On grid paper, find all rectangles with area 12. Do all of the rectangles have the same perimeter?

ME8-12: Perimeter

1. Find the perimeter of each shape. Be sure to include the units in your answer:

    a)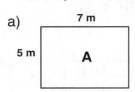

    b)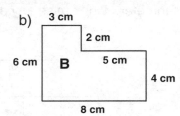

    c)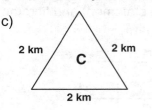

    d)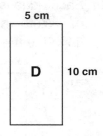

    Perimeter: _____   Perimeter: _____   Perimeter: _____   Perimeter: _____

    e) Write the letters of the shapes in order from <u>greatest</u> perimeter to <u>least</u> perimeter:
        HINT: Make sure you look at the units!

    _____

2. Find the missing lengths or widths in each figure. (Note that the pictures are not drawn to scale.)

    a) Perimeter = 14 m

    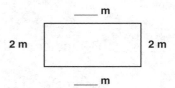

    b) Perimeter = 14 cm

    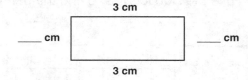

    c) Perimeter = 18 cm

    d) Perimeter = 100 m

    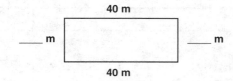

3. Find all rectangles with the given perimeters (with lengths and widths that are whole numbers). Show your work in your notebook:

    a)

Width	Length
Perimeter = 6 units	

    b)

Width	Length
Perimeter = 12 units	

    c)

Width	Length
Perimeter = 16 units	

    d)

Width	Length
Perimeter = 18 units	

4. Sally arranges 5 square posters (each with sides 1 m) in a row:

    a) Ribbon costs 35¢ for each meter. How much will a ribbon border for the arrangement cost?

    b) Sally wants to arrange 8 square posters in a rectangular array. How many different rectangles can she make? For which arrangement would the border be <u>least</u> expensive?

5. Write a rule for finding the perimeter of a rectangle using its width and length: _____

    _____

1. Mark makes a sequence of figures with toothpicks:

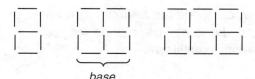

base

a) Count the number of toothpicks in the base and perimeter of each figure. Write the numbers in the chart:

b) Complete the rule that tells how to make the OUTPUT numbers from the INPUT numbers:

Multiply the INPUT by _____ and add _____.

c) Use the rule to predict the perimeter of a figure with a base of 10 toothpicks: _____

INPUT Number of Toothpicks in Base	OUTPUT Perimeter
1	6

2. Find the perimeter of each figure. Then add one square to the figure so that the perimeter of the new figure is 10 units:

NOTE: Assume all edges are 1 unit.

a)

Original Perimeter = ____ units

New Perimeter = 10 units

b)

Original Perimeter = ____ units

New Perimeter = 10 units

c)

Original Perimeter = ____ units

New Perimeter = 10 units

3. Add 2 squares so that the perimeter stays the same. (Can you find several ways for each question?)

a)

b)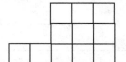

c)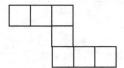

Answer the remaining questions in your notebook.

4. Repeat steps a) to c) of Question 1 for the following patterns:

a)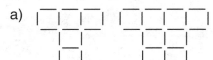

b)

5. On cm grid paper, the distance shown is approximately 1.4 cm:

 ← 1.4 cm

If these shapes were drawn on cm grid paper, what would their approximate perimeters be?

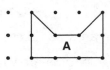

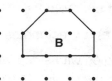

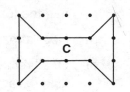

ME8-14: Comparing Area and Perimeter

1. For each shape below, calculate the perimeter and area of each shape, and write your answers in the chart below. The first one has been done for you:

NOTE: Each edge represents a centimetre.

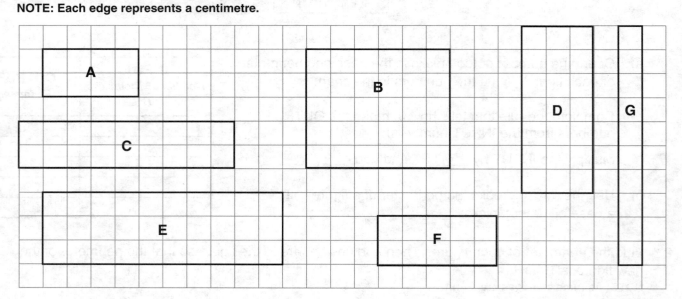

Shape	Perimeter	Area
A	2 + 4 + 4 + 2 = 12 cm	2 x 4 = 8 cm²
B		
C		
D		
E		
F		
G		

2. Name two shapes where one has a greater perimeter and the other, a greater area: _____

3. Write the shapes in order from:

   a) Greatest to least area: _____   b) Greatest to least perimeter: _____

4. Name two shapes that have the same area and different perimeter: _____

Answer the remaining questions in your notebook.

5. a) Find all rectangles (with sides whose length are whole numbers) that have area 16 cm². (Remember a square is also a rectangle.) Record the perimeter of your shapes. Which shape has the least perimeter?

   b) Repeat part a) for rectangles with an area 25 cm².

   c) Of all rectangles with sides whose lengths are whole numbers and that have area 36 cm², what kind of rectangle do you think would have the least perimeter? Explain.

ME8-15: Area of Rectangles

1. Write a multiplication statement for each array:

   a)

   b)

   c)

   d)

   _____   _____   _____   _____

2. Draw a dot in each box.
   Then write a multiplication statement that tells you the number of boxes in the rectangle.

   a)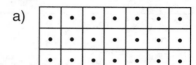

   b)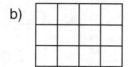

   c)

   d)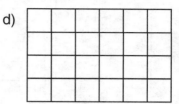

   <u>__3 × 7 = 21__</u>   _____   _____   _____

3. Write the number of boxes along the width and length of each rectangle.
   Then write a multiplication statement for the area of the rectangle (in square units):

   a) 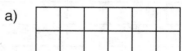 Width = ___

   Length = _____

   b)  Width = ___

   Length = _____

   c)   Width = ___

   Length = _____

   _____   _____   _____

4. The sides of the rectangles have been marked in centimetres. Using a ruler, draw lines to divide each rectangle into squares. Write a multiplication statement for the area of the boxes in cm².
   NOTE: You will have to mark the last row of boxes yourself using a ruler.

   a)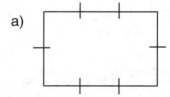

   b)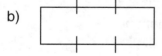

   c)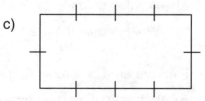

   d)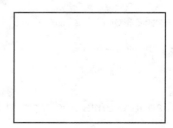

   e)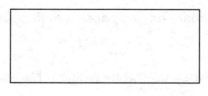

5. If you know the length and width of a rectangle, how can you find its area?

   _____

1. Measure the length and width of each rectangle, and then record your answers in the chart below:

5 cm

A

2 cm

B   C   D

F   G   E

Rectangle	Estimated Perimeter	Estimated Area	Length	Width	Actual Perimeter	Actual Area
A	cm	cm²	cm	cm	cm	cm²
B						
C						
D						
E						
F						
G						

2. A table measures 50 by 90 cm. Alan would like to buy a table cloth that hangs down 30 cm on each side:

    a) What should the perimeter of the table cloth be?

    b) What should the area of the table cloth be?

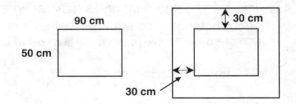

90 cm   **30 cm**

50 cm

30 cm

3. Find the area of the rectangle using the clues. Show your work in your notebook:

    a) Width = 2 cm   Perimeter = 10 cm   Area = ?   b) Width = 4 cm   Perimeter = 18 cm   Area = ?

4. Draw a square on grid paper with the given perimeter. Then find the area of the square:

    a) Perimeter = 12 cm   Area = ?   b) Perimeter = 20 cm   Area = ?

5. On grid paper, draw a rectangle with:

    a) an area of 10 square units and a perimeter of 14 units.

    b) an area of 8 square units and a perimeter of 12 units.

6. Draw two rectangles on grid paper, so that the length and width of one rectangle are twice as long as the length and width of the other. Compare the area and perimeter of the two rectangles. Try this several times. What do you notice?

1. The rectangle was made by moving the shaded triangle from one end of the parallelogram to the other:

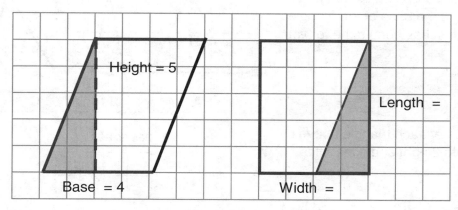

a) Is the area of the rectangle the same as the area of the parallelogram? _____

   How do you know?_____

b) Fill in the width of the rectangle.

   What do you notice about the base of the parallelogram and the width of the rectangle?

   _____

c) Fill in the length of the rectangle.

   What do you notice about the height of the parallelogram and the length of the rectangle?

   _____

d) Recall that, for a rectangle: Area = length × width

   Can you write a formula for the area of a parallelogram using the base and height?

   _____

2. Measure the height of the parallelograms using a protractor and a ruler. Measure the base using a ruler. Find the area of the parallelogram using your formula from Question 1 d):

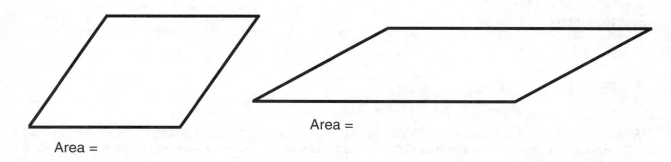

Area =

Area =

3. Find the area of the following parallelograms:

   a) Base = 5 cm
       Height = 7 cm
       Area =

   b) Base = 4 cm
       Height = 3 cm
       Area =

   c) Base = 8 cm
       Height = 6 cm
       Area =

   d) Base = 3.7 cm
       Height = 6 cm
       Area =

ME8-18: Area of Triangles

1. a) Draw a dotted line to show the height of the triangle. Then find the length of the height and the base of the triangles in cm. The first has been done for you:

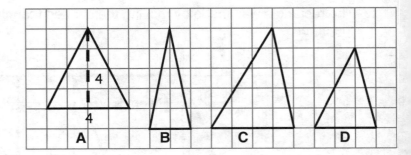

   b) Find the area of each triangle above by dividing it into 2 right angle triangles:

   Area of A: _____   Area of B: _____

   Area of C: _____   Area of D: _____

   REMEMBER:

   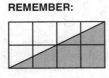 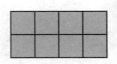

   Area of Triangle = Area of Rectangle divided by 2

2. Parallelogram B was made by joining two copies of triangle A together. How can you find the area of triangle A?

   HINT: Use what you know about the area of parallelograms.

   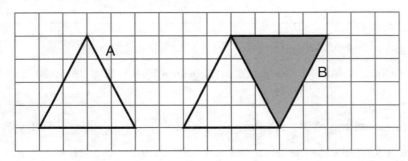

   _____

3. Find the area of the triangle by joining two copies of the triangle together to form a parallelogram as in Question 2:

   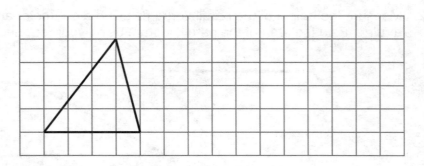

4. Write a formula for the area of a triangle using the base and the height of the triangle:

   HINT: How are the areas of the triangles in Questions 2 and 3 related to the areas of the parallelograms?

   _____

5. Show how you would calculate the area of triangle A in Question 1 using your formula:

   _____

1. On the previous page, you discovered the formula: **Area of Triangle = (base × height) ÷ 2**
    Find the area of a triangle with the dimensions:

    a) Base = 6 cm   b) Base = 4 cm   c) Base = 6 cm   d) Base = 3.2 cm
        Height = 2 cm   Height = 3 cm   Height = 4 cm   Height = 8 cm
        Area =   Area =   Area =   Area =

2. Using the formula: **Area of a parallelogram = base × height**
    Find the area of a parallelogram with the dimensions:

    a) Base = 5 cm   b) Base = 10 cm   c) Base = 3.5 cm   d) Base = 2.75 cm
        Height = 7 cm   Height = 17 cm   Height = 9 cm   Height = 8 cm
        Area =   Area =   Area =   Area =

3. Measure the base and height of the triangle using a ruler. Then find the area of the triangle:

    a)   b)   c)

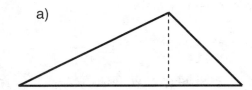
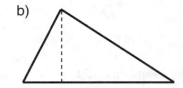
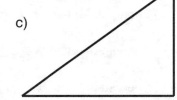

4.

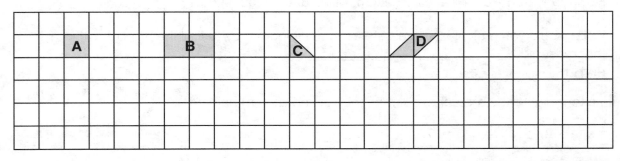

    a) Two polygons are similar if they are the same shape. Draw a shape <u>similar</u> to the original.
        Make the base 2 times as long. How high should you make the new shape?

    b) Find the area (in square units) of each original shape, then the area of each new shape:

    Area of A: _____   Area of B: _____   Area of C: _____   Area of D: _____

    Area of the new shape: Area of the new shape: Area of the new shape: Area of the new shape:

    _____   _____   _____   _____

    c) When the base and the height of a shape are doubled, what happens to the area of the shape?

5. On centimetre grid paper draw:

    a) a triangle with area 13 cm^2 b) a parallelogram with area 32 cm^2

Recall that a trapezoid is a quadrilateral with exactly one pair of parallel sides.

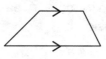
trapezoid

trapezoid

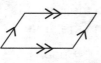
not a trapezoid

1. Draw an upside down copy of each trapezoid as shown in a) to create a parallelogram:

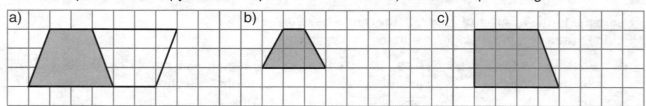

2. Find the length of the base and the height of each parallelogram in Question 1. Then find the area using the formula: Area of Parallelogram = (height) × (length of base):

   a) length of base = 4 + 2 height of parallelogram = _____ Area of parallelogram = _____

   b) length of base = _____ height of parallelogram = _____ Area of parallelogram = _____

   c) length of base = _____ height of parallelogram = _____ Area of parallelogram = _____

3. a) How many trapezoids make up each parallelogram in question 1? _____

   b) What would you multiply the area of each parallelogram by to find the area of the trapezoid? _____
      HINT: The answer is a fraction.

4. Write a formula for the area of each trapezoid as shown in a) below:

   a) $\frac{1}{2} \times \underbrace{(4 + 2)}_{\text{sum of bases}} \times \underbrace{3}_{\text{height}}$

   b)

   c)

5. Write a formula for the area of the trapezoid using a, b and h:

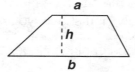

Answer the remaining questions in your notebook.

6. Draw a trapezoid with one base 5 cm, the other base 3 cm and height 4 cm.
   Find the area of the trapezoid:
   i) using the formula you developed ii) by subdividing the trapezoids into triangles and rectangles

7. Estimate, then find the area of the trapezoids:

   a)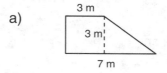

   b)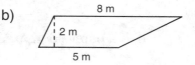

   c)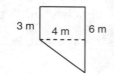

1. Two half squares  cover the same area as a whole square  .

    Count each <u>pair</u> of half squares as a whole square to find the area shaded:

    a)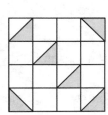

    = _____ whole squares

    b)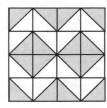

    = _____ whole squares

    c)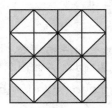

    = _____ whole squares

    d)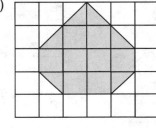

    = _____ whole squares

    e)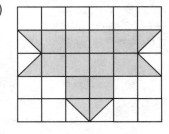

    = _____ whole squares

    f)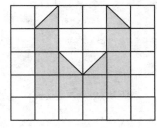

    = _____ whole squares

    g)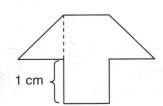

    = _____ whole squares

    h)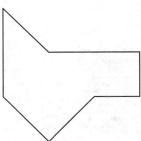

    = _____ whole squares

    i)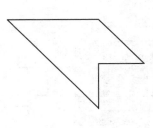

    = _____ whole squares

2. Draw lines to divide the shape into squares and triangles that are half-squares.
    Determine the area of the shape in square units.

    a)   b)   c)

    1 cm {

3. On grid paper, draw three different shapes with an area of 12 ½ square units.
    Use at least three half-squares in each shape.

BONUS:

4. The area of the half square is 8 m². What is the perimeter of the square?
    HINT: Find the area of the square.

5. Since the length and width of a square are equal, we can write this formula for the area of
    a square: $A = l \times l = l^2$ *(Area = length squared).* Write a formula for the area of half a square. _____

ME8-22: Area of Composite Shapes

1. Calculate the area of each shape by counting squares and half squares or by using formulas:

    a)   A   B   C

    Area of A = _____ Area of B = _____

    Area of C = _____

    Draw a line to show how C can be divided
    into shapes A and B.

    Write a formula for the area of C using Area

    of A and B: Area of C = _____

    b)   A   B   C

    Area of A = _____ Area of B = _____

    Area of C = _____

    Draw a line to show how C can be divided
    into shapes A and B.

    Write a formula for the area of C using Area

    of A and B: Area of C = _____

    c)   A
                             C
          B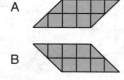

    Area of A = _____ Area of B = _____

    Area of C = _____

    Draw a line to show how C can be divided
    into shapes A and B.

    Write a formula for the area of C using Area

    of A and B: Area of C = _____

    d)   A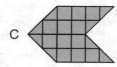
                             C
          B

    Area of A = _____ Area of B = _____

    Area of C = _____

    Draw a line to show how C can be divided
    into shapes A and B.

    Write a formula for the area of C using Area

    of A and B: Area of C = _____

2. a)   A   C
                    B
    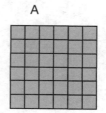 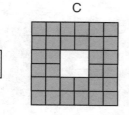

    Area of A = _____ Area of B = _____

    Write a formula for the area of C using Area

    of A and B: Area of C = _____

    b)   A   B   C
      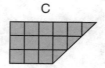

    Copy the shape onto grid paper. Show 3
    different ways of calculating the area of the
    shaded trapezoid:
    i)   by dividing the trapezoid into a rectangle
         and a triangle;
    ii) by using the area of the large rectangle
         and the unshaded triangle;
    iii) using the formula for the area of a
         trapezoid.

1. Draw a line to cut each figure into 2 rectangles. Calculate the are of the two rectangles and then the area of the figure:

a)
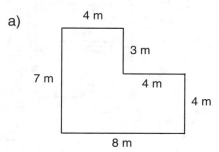

Area = _____

b)
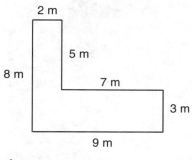

Area = _____

c)

Area = _____

2. a)

The tower is _____ stories high

A building is 8 stories high. The wing is 5 stories high. How many stories is the tower?

b)

The wing is _____ m wide

The tower of a building is 10 m wide. The base is 50 m wide. How wide is the wing?

3. Find the measurements of the sides that have not been labelled. Then divide the figure into smaller rectangles and find the area:

a)
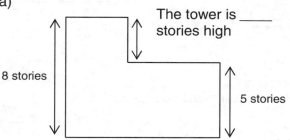

Area _____

b)
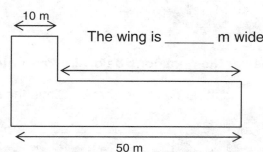

Area _____

c)

Area _____

4. Find the area of each figure. Show your work in your notebook:

a)
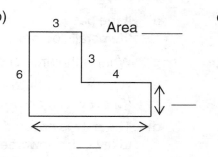

b)
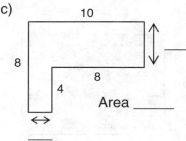

c)

1.　Find the area of each shaded shape:

a)

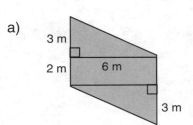

b)

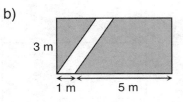

c)

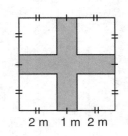

d)

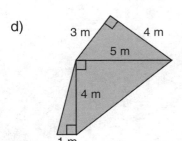

e)

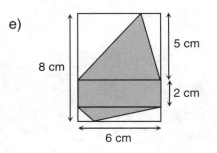

f)

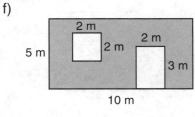

Answer the questions below in your notebook.

2.　Find the area of the shape. Circle the measurements that you didn't need to use:

a)

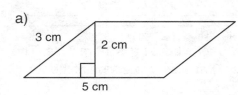

b)

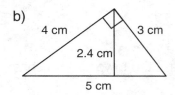

c)

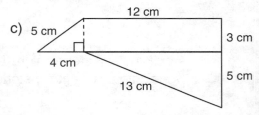

3.

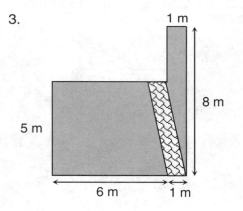

A garden (the shaded area) has a path in the shape of a parallelogram:

a)　If the base of the parallelogram is 1 m long. how high is the parallelogram?

b)　What is the area of the path?

c)　What is the total area of the flower beds?
(Show your work.)

d)　The path is covered in tiles with cost $3 per square metre to lay. The flowerbeds cost $5 per square metre to plant. How much did it cost to create the garden?

4.　What is the area of shaded part?

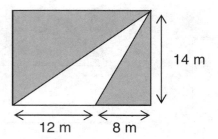

M N

A **bar graph** has four parts: a vertical and horizontal **axis**, a **scale**, **labels** (including a title) and **data** (given by the bars). Bar graphs tend to be drawn on square **grids**.

The bars in a bar graph can either be vertical or horizontal. The scale tells how much each square on the axis represents. The labels indicate what the data in the bars is.

1.

Transportation Used to Get to Bambury PS	Number of Students
Bike	51
Subway	46
Walk	145
Bus	118
Car	28

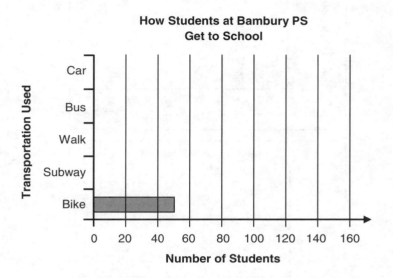

a)   Complete the bar graph.

b)   What scale was used in the bar graph? Do you think it was a good choice? Why or why not?

_____

_____

c)   Think of the students at your own school. How do they get to school? Would you predict similar or different results from those found at Bambury PS? Explain.

_____

_____

Answer the remaining question in your notebook.

2.   Bobby made a tally chart and bar graph of all the wildlife he saw at his cottage:

a)   Based on the information in the bar graph, recreate Bobby's original tally chart.

b)   Which bars were the most difficult to read? What strategy did you use to read them?

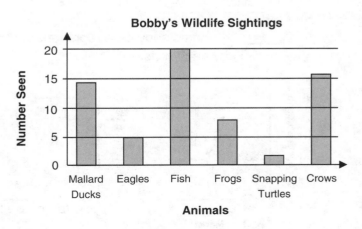

1. A teacher tallied the marks on a science test and then made a bar graph (Figure 1) to show the distribution of marks:

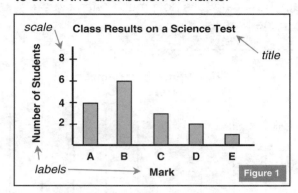

Figure 1

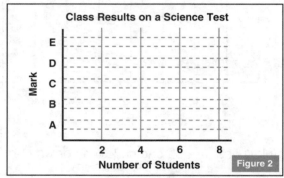

Figure 2

a) Fill in the table for the test:

Mark	Tally	Frequency
A		
B		
C		
D		
E		

b) How many students received an A on the test? _____

c) How many students received a C? _____

d) How many students took the test? _____

e) Circle the most common mark: A, B, C, D, E

f) Use the axes provided in Figure 2 to show the same data, but make the bars horizontal instead of vertical.

2. Draw a bar graph for each frequency table (use the grids below). For each graph you will first need to decide the scale. For instance, you might use the scale 5, 10, 15, 20, 25 for part b):

a)
Mark	A	B	C	D	E
Frequency	2	9	6	1	0

___2___ students should be represented by each division

b)
Mark	A	B	C	D	E
Frequency	16	23	17	5	2

_____ students should be represented by each division

c)
Mark	A	B	C	D	E
Frequency	19	24	13	3	2

_____ students should be represented by each division

d)
Mark	A	B	C	D	E
Frequency	10	46	30	8	3

_____ students should be represented by each division

a)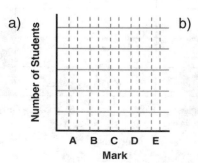

b)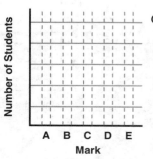

c)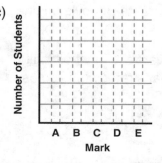

d)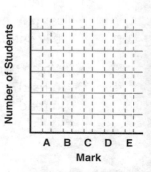

1. Two sporting goods companies compare sales for January through June:

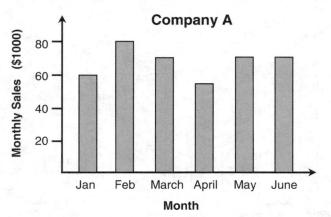
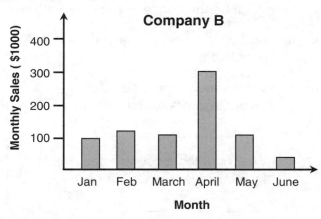

a) When you glance quickly at the two graphs, which company appears to have higher monthly sales? _____ Why? _____

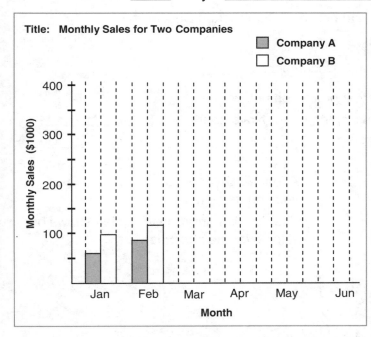

b) When you look closely at the scales, which company actually has higher sales? _____

c) Why are most of Company B's data so low on the graph? _____

_____

_____

_____

d) The two companies decide to put their graphs on the <u>same axes</u>. The key shows you which company is represented by which kind of bar. Complete the graph on the left.

> A **double bar graph** compares two categories.
>
> The graph you drew in Question 1 d) is a double bar graph.

e) In which month(s) did Company A sell more than Company B? _____

_____

f) During one month in this period, Company B had several items in their store autographed by a famous athlete.

Which month do you think that was? _____

2. Leslie tracked the height of two seedlings. Draw a double bar graph in your notebook or on a computer to show her data:

Day	1	2	3	4	5	6
Height of plant in full sun (cm)	2.0	4.2	6.5	8.8	11.0	14.1
Height of plant in the shade (cm)	1.9	3.6	5.1	6.4	7.9	9.3

3. Students in a Grade 8 class were asked "What is your favourite snack?" at two different times: once in early October and once in early December.

    a) Add your choice of title to the double bar graph.

    b) What was the most-selected favourite snack in October?

        _____

    c) What was the most-selected favourite snack in December?

        _____

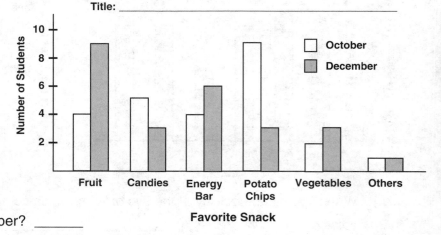

    d) How many students chose fruit in October? _____ In December? _____

    e) For which snack was there the biggest change between October and December? _____

    f) How many students responded to the survey question in:

        i)   October? _____   ii) December? _____

    g) Sometime before Christmas the students did a project on nutrition.
        Do you think they completed their project in September or November? _____
        Explain: _____

4.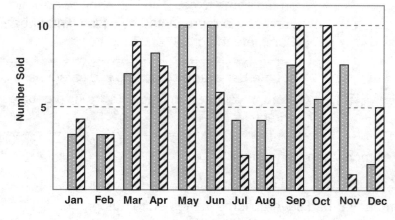

    A real estate agent sells both houses and condominiums.

    The double bar graph to the left shows her sales over the past year.

    a) In what month(s) did the agent sell the most houses? _____

    b) In what month(s) did the agent sell the most condominiums? _____

    c) In what month did the agent sell the most total units (houses *and* condominiums)? _____

    d) The agent wants to take a month of vacation next year.
        In which month would you suggest she take her holiday? _____
        Why? _____

The bar graph and the line graph below both show the price of CDs on sale:

Using a ruler, you could draw an arrow across from the '5 CD' bar to show 5 CDs cost $25.

Similarly you could draw a line up from the '5 CD' mark and then across to the $25 mark.

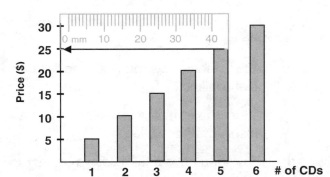
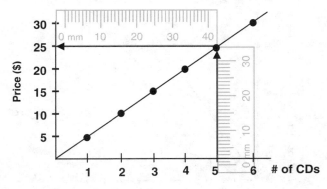

1. Draw arrows (using a ruler) on the <u>line graph</u> above to find the cost of:

    a) 3 CDs: $ _____   b) 4 CDs: $ _____   b) 6 CDs: $ _____

2. To find out how many CDs you can buy for $20, you could draw arrows as shown:

    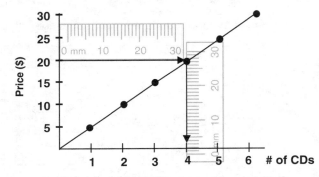

    Draw arrows (using a ruler!) on the line graph to find how many CDs you can buy for:

    i) $15: _____ CDs

    ii) $25: _____ CDs

    iii) $30: _____ CDs

These graphs show how much money Sally will earn painting houses in the summer:

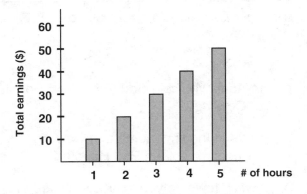
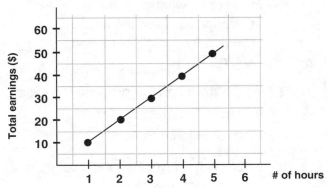

a) On both graphs, show how much Sally would make for working: i) 3 hours   ii) 4 hours

b) If Sally works $3\frac{1}{2}$ hours, she will make between $ _____ and $ _____.

d) Draw arrows on the line graph to show how much Sally will earn in $3\frac{1}{2}$ hours.

e) Extend the line graph to show how much Sally could make in: i) 6 hours   ii) $\frac{1}{2}$ hour

f) In your notebook, explain an advantage of a line graph over a bar graph.

Two line graphs on the same grid can show a **comparison**. A **legend** shows what the two graphs mean.

1. Josh and his younger brother walked 10 km in a charity walk:

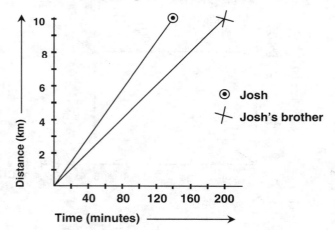

a) How long does it take Josh to complete the walk? _____

b) After 1 hour, how many kilometres has Josh walked? _____

c) After 1 hour, how many kilometres has Josh's brother walked? _____

d) How long does it take Josh's brother to complete the walk? _____

Answer the questions below in your notebook.

2. Two neighbouring towns began a recycling program in the same year.

    Here are the results after the first year:

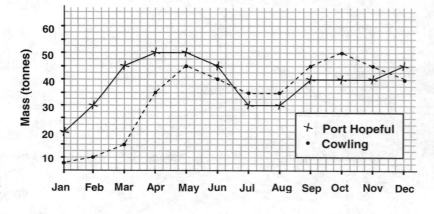

a) How much did Port Hopeful collect in January?

b) In January, what was the difference between the amount collected by Port Hopeful and Cowling?

c) Which town had the greatest increase:
    i)   from February to March?
    ii) from March to April?

d) In Cowling, in which month was there the greatest increase?

e) In which month was there the greatest difference between the two towns in the amount collected?

f) For Cowling, in which month was there no change from the previous month?

g) In April, who collected more: Port Hopeful or Cowling?

h) What is the first month that Cowling collects more than Port Hopeful?

i) Which town do you think conducted the better information campaign before the recycling program started? Why?

j) Can you predict which town's recycling program will be most successful in the next six months? Explain.

1. Terri walks 1 km to school everyday.

   She records her distance from home after 10 minutes and again after 20 minutes:

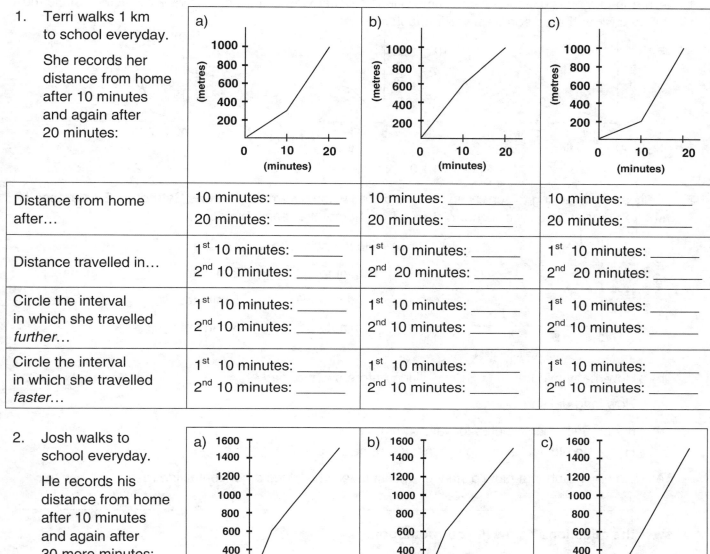

Distance from home after…	10 minutes: _____ 20 minutes: _____	10 minutes: _____ 20 minutes: _____	10 minutes: _____ 20 minutes: _____
Distance travelled in…	1st 10 minutes: _____ 2nd 10 minutes: _____	1st 10 minutes: _____ 2nd 20 minutes: _____	1st 10 minutes: _____ 2nd 20 minutes: _____
Circle the interval in which she travelled *further*…	1st 10 minutes: _____ 2nd 10 minutes: _____	1st 10 minutes: _____ 2nd 10 minutes: _____	1st 10 minutes: _____ 2nd 10 minutes: _____
Circle the interval in which she travelled *faster*…	1st 10 minutes: _____ 2nd 10 minutes: _____	1st 10 minutes: _____ 2nd 10 minutes: _____	1st 10 minutes: _____ 2nd 10 minutes: _____

2. Josh walks to school everyday.

   He records his distance from home after 10 minutes and again after 30 more minutes:

Distance travelled in…	first 10 minutes: _____ last 30 minutes: _____	first 10 minutes: _____ last 30 minutes: _____	first 10 minutes: _____ last 30 minutes: _____
Speed in…	first 10 minutes: _____ last 30 minutes: _____	first 10 minutes: _____ last 30 minutes: _____	first 10 minutes: _____ last 30 minutes: _____
Is the graph steeper in the first 10 minutes or in the last 30 minutes?	_____	_____	_____

3. Look at your answers to Questions 1 and 2. When is one part of the graph steeper than another?

jump math
MULTIPLYING POTENTIAL

Probability & Data Management 1

1. A graph that plots distance versus time will be steeper when the person is walking faster. Circle the interval when the person was walking fastest:

a)
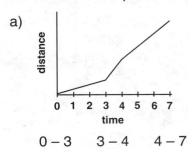

$0 - 3 \qquad 3 - 4 \qquad 4 - 7$

b)
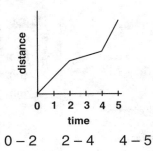

$0 - 2 \qquad 2 - 4 \qquad 4 - 5$

c)
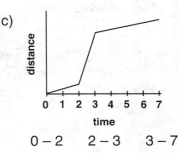

$0 - 2 \qquad 2 - 3 \qquad 3 - 7$

2. Sally started walking to school and then stopped when she realized it was Saturday. Embarrassed, she ran home. She records her distance from home after each minute:

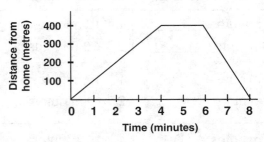

a) How far from home was she after:

1 minute: _____ 2 minutes: _____ 3 minutes: _____

4 minutes: _____ 5 minutes: _____ 6 minutes: _____

7 minutes: _____ 8 minutes: _____

b) How many minutes was Sally walking before she stopped? _____

c) How long did she stop for? _____

d) It took Sally four minutes to walk 400 m.
How long did it take her to run the 400 m back home? _____

e) On any graph that plots distance against time, what does a horizontal line mean?

_____

Answer the questions below in your notebook.

2. a) Match the stories to the graphs: which is Graph A and which is Graph B?

(i) Jeff started _walking to school_, then _ran back_ home to get his homework, and then _ran to school_.

(ii) Jane started _walking to school_, then _stopped_ to play with a kitten, and _ran the rest of the way_.

A
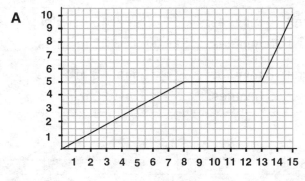

B
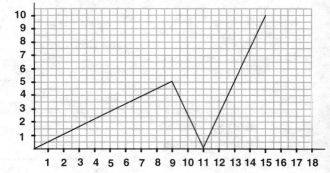

b) On the graph, what kind of line shows that the person is standing still?

c) How can you tell which line shows walking and which shows running?

d) What would a vertical line mean? Why is this impossible?

PDM8-8: Drawing Line Graphs

Answer any parts of questions below that require a written answer in your notebook.

1. The chart shows the number of snow shovels the store sells between September and April. Complete the accompanying line graph. Explain any trends you notice:

Month	# of Snow Shovels Sold
September	4
October	8
November	11
December	17
January	18
February	16
March	3
April	1

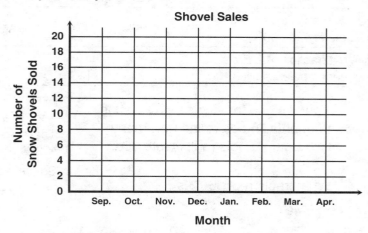

2. The data shows minimum wage increases in Ontario (data from the Ontario Ministry of Labour).

   Graph the data using the grids below:

Year	1995	2004	2005	2006	2007
Minimum Wage ($/hour)	6.85	7.15	7.45	7.75	8.0

   a) Which graph makes it look as if the minimum wage increased at the same rate from 1995 to 2007?

   b) Which graph shows that the minimum wage started increasing more quickly in 2004?

   c) Which graph best represents the data? What is wrong with the other graph?

3. The following data shows when the world's population first reached 1 billion, 2 billion, and so on.

   Data from U.S. Census Bureau's global profit: 2002

Population in Billions	1	2	3	4	5	6
Year first reached	1804	1922	1959	1974	1987	1999

   a) Look the data on the graph. Is it possible to join the data points with a straight line? Why or why not?

   b) In what year do you think we will reach 7 billion people?

   c) The United Nations predicts that it will take longer to change from 6 to 7 billion than it did to change from 5 to 6 billion. Why might this be?

1.

	45°	60°	90°	120°	180°
How many times does the angle fit into 360°?	_____ times	_____ times	_____ times	_____ times	_____ times
What fraction of a circle is each angle?					

2. You can use the angles in Question 1 to (mentally) determine how many times other angles will fit into 360°:

   Example:
   There are <u>two</u> 30° angles in <u>60°</u>. There are <u>six 60°</u> angles in 360°.
   So there are <u>2 × 6° = 12</u> 30° angles in 360°: 30° = $\frac{1}{12}$ of 360°

   What fraction of 360° is …

   a) **40°**
   There are _____ 40° angles in <u>120°</u>.
   There are _____ <u>120°</u> angles in 360°.
   So there are _____ 40° angles in 360°.
   40° = ☐ of 360°

   b) **20°**
   There are _____ 20° angles in _____.
   There are _____ angles in 360°.
   So there are _____ 20° angles in 360°.
   20° = ☐ of 360°.

   c) **15°**
   There are _____ 15° angles in _____.
   There are _____ angles in 360°.
   So there are _____ 15° angles in 360°.
   15° = ☐ of 360°.

   d) **12°**
   There are _____ 12° angles in _____.
   There are _____ angles in 360°.
   So there are _____ 12° angles in 360°.
   12° = ☐ of 360°.

Answer the remaining questions in your notebook.

3. Answer each question below by forming a fraction and then reducing it to lowest terms:

   Example:
   What fraction of 360° is 80°? $\frac{80}{360}$ →*reduce*→ $\frac{80 ÷ 10}{360 ÷ 10} = \frac{8}{36}$ →*reduce*→ $\frac{8 ÷ 4}{36 ÷ 4} = \frac{2}{9}$ So 80° is $\frac{2}{9}$ of 360°.

   What fraction of 360° is…   a) 140°   b) 160°   c) 270°   d) 300°

4. a) Using a protractor, determine what fraction of each company's staff works part-time:
   HINT: Write the angle you measure over 360° and reduce.

   ☐ **Full time staff**

   ▥ **Part time staff**

   Company A 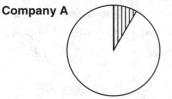   **Company B**   **Company C**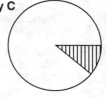

   b) Company A has 60 employees, Company B has 18 employees and Company C has 54 employees. How many employees in each firm work part-time?

1. Find the fraction of the circle that is shaded:

a)

fraction
shaded = _____

b)

fraction
shaded = _____

c)

fraction
shaded = _____

d)

fraction
shaded = _____

e)

fraction
shaded = _____

2. Find what fraction of the circle is each colour and then add to find the total:

a)

red: $\frac{3}{8}$

blue: $\frac{1}{4}$

yellow: $\frac{3}{8}$

total: $\frac{1}{4} + \frac{3}{8} + \frac{3}{8} = 1$

b)

red:

blue:

yellow:

total:

c)

red:

blue:

yellow:

total:

d)

red:

blue:

yellow:

total:

3. Look at the circle graph below. Sally filled in the answers as shown:

red: $\frac{3}{8}$

blue: $\frac{3}{8}$

yellow: $\frac{1}{8}$

total: $\frac{7}{8}$

a) How can she know that she made a mistake?

_____

b) Find her mistake(s) and put in the correct numbers.

c) Why is it useful to find the total? _____

_____

4. Crystal makes a circle graph to show how she spends her lunch money:

a) What fraction of her lunch money was spent on:

fruit: _____ drink: _____

dessert: _____ sandwich: _____

b) If Crystal spent $8 on lunch, how much did her dessert cost? _____

5. The graph shows the goals scored by each line of a hockey team in 10 games:

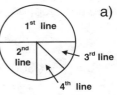

a) What fraction of goals was scored by the...

1st line: _____ 2nd line: _____

3rd line: _____ 4th line: _____

b) During the first 10 games, the team scored a total of 40 goals. How many goals did the 4th line score? _____

1. Find what fraction of the circle is each colour, and then add to find the total:

a)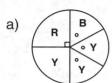

red: $\frac{1}{4}$

blue: $\frac{1}{6}$

yellow: $\frac{1}{4} + \frac{1}{6} + \frac{1}{6} = \frac{7}{12}$

total: $\frac{1}{4} + \frac{1}{6} + \frac{7}{12} = \frac{12}{12} = 1$

b)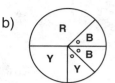

red:

blue:

yellow:

total:

c)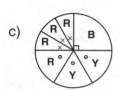

red:

blue:

yellow:

total:

d)

red:

blue:

yellow:

total:

2. In each survey, what fraction of people chose each sport as their favourite?

a)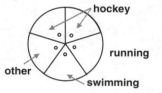

Hockey: Swimming:

Running: Other:

If 50 people were surveyed, how many chose hockey? _____

b)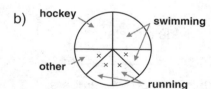

Hockey: Swimming:

Running: Other:

If 120 people were surveyed, how many chose swimming? _____

Answer the remaining questions in your notebook.

3. Fern wants to know what fraction of students will vote for her in the student elections. She asked 40 students. 30 said yes they would vote for her, and 10 said no.

a) What fraction of the students said yes?

b) Fern displayed her results on a circle graph. Which colour shows the yes vote?

c) If 600 students vote in the election, how many votes should she expect to get?

4. Find …

a) $\frac{1}{3}$ of 360   b) $\frac{2}{5}$ of 360   c) $\frac{3}{4}$ of 360   d) $\frac{3}{10}$ of 360

5. In your notebook or on a computer draw a circle graph to represent the following data:

a) $\frac{3}{4}$ of the students at a school live within 1 km of the school; $\frac{1}{4}$ live more than 1 km away.

b) A soil sample taken near a beach is…

$\frac{1}{2}$ sand $\frac{1}{3}$ clay $\frac{1}{6}$ silt

Scatter plots are used to show whether there is a relationship between two sets of data. Each dot represents one piece of data.

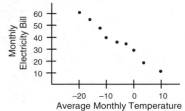

As the average temperature increases in the later winter, the electricity used decreases.

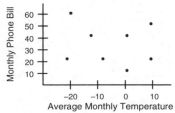

The increase in temperature does not affect the phone bill. There is no relationship.

- -

1. Does each scatter plot show a relationship? If so, explain the relationship in your notebook. If not, write "no":

a)
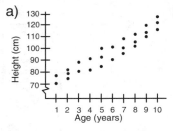

b)
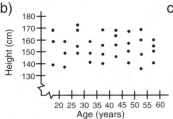

c)
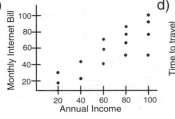

d)
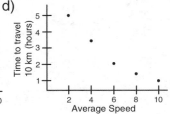

2. Match each scatter plot with the information it's comparing:
   NOTE: The scales have not been included. The first quanatity mentioned is on the horizontal axis.

a) i) Annual income and years of education: ____

ii) Age (1 – 20) and number of hours of sleep needed each night: ____

iii) Height and number of pets owned: ____

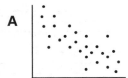

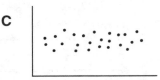

b) i) Monthly temperature and monthly cable bill: ____

ii) Number of books read each month and vocabulary learned: ____

iii) Test score and number of questions left unanswered: ____

3. In your notebook, sketch what you think a scatter plot of each of the following might look like. Include titles and labels, but not scales.

a) shoe size against monthly cable bill

b) a person's mass against the mass one person can lift

c) height against number of hours of sleep needed each night

d) number of sides in a regular polygon against size of each angle in the polygon

e) number of sides in a regular polygon against side length of that polygon

f) circumference of a circle against radius of that circle

1. Draw three scatter plots based on the following data about a soccer team:

Age	12	13	14	14	15	15	13	14	15	12	15	14
Height	141	162	174	154	166	174	150	168	182	156	160	152
Gender	F	M	M	F	F	M	F	M	M	M	F	F

Which of the following statements do you agree with?

a) Males on the soccer team are likely to be taller.

b) Taller people on the soccer team are likely to be older.

c) Males on the soccer team are likely to be older.

2.

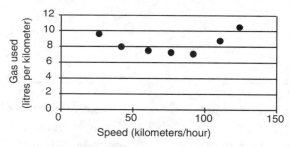

Relationship between speed and fuel efficiency

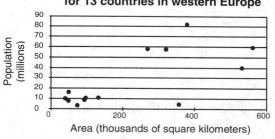

Relationship between population and area for 13 countries in western Europe

a) For each graph say whether the data show a trend. If there is a trend can you explain it?

b) Are there any data points on either graph you find surprising?

c) The chart below goes with the second graph above. On the graph, put a circle around the data point for Finland:

Country in Area	Thousands of km²	Population (millions)	Country in Area	Thousands of km²	Population (millions)	Country in Area	Thousands of km²	Population (millions)
Austria	84	8.1	Greece	132	10.5	Portugal	89	9.8
Belgium	31	10.2	Ireland	70	3.6	Spain	505	39.7
Finland	338	5.1	Italy	301	57.2	Switzerland	41	7.2
France	543	58.3	Netherland	42	15.6	United Kingdom	243	58.1
Germany	357	81.9						

A **histogram** is used when the data set consists of continuous numerical data, put into groups of the same size. There are no spaces between the bars because the data is continuous.

Answer the question below in your notebook.

1. a)   Which of the following graphs are histograms and which are bar graphs:

    b)   One of the graphs is drawn as a histogram but more properly should have been drawn as a bar graph. Which is it?

i)
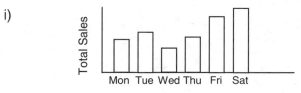

ii)
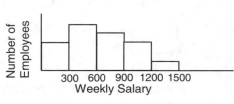

iii)
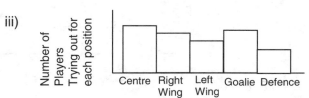

iv)
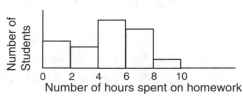

A number on the **border** of an interval is always put in the higher interval, so an interval of 2 – 4 hours per week spent on homework actually means any time between 2 hours and 3 hours and 59 minutes.

2.
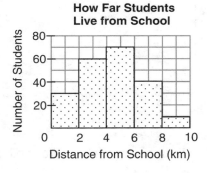

a)   How many students live:
 i)   between 4 km and 6 km from school?
 ii)   6 km or more from school?

b)   Can you tell:
 i)   How many students live between 3 km and 5 km from school?
 ii)   How far from school the closest student lives?
 iii)   How many students live within 2 km of school?

3.
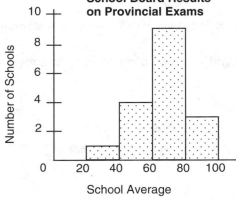

a)   Use the graph to complete the frequency table:

Average Mark	Frequency
20 – 39	
40 – 59	
60 – 79	
80 – 100	

b)   How many schools were included in this analysis?

c)   A passing mark is 60. How many schools' averages were below the passing marks?

4. The data gives the time (in seconds) for students competing in the 100 m backstroke:

    121 118 135 149 145 133 99 123 108 117 103 137 146 114 100
    142 120 139 126 114 132 122 139 124 116 111 90 148 96 102

    What's wrong with each group of intervals for the data?

    a) 100 – 110   110 – 120   120 – 130   130 – 140   140 – 150

    b) 90 – 100   100 – 110   100 – 120   120 – 140   140 – 160

    c) 90 – 95   95 – 100   100 – 105   105 – 110   110 – 115   115 – 120

        120 – 125   125 – 130   130 – 135   135 – 140   140 – 145   145 – 150

    d) 90 – 140   140 – 190

5. In your notebook, divide the data from Question 4 into intervals and make a histogram:

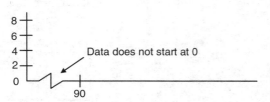

6. Here are the class results from a test:

    56 68 70 95 75 41 66 82 89 77 73 60 79 81

    a) Complete the table. The first three have been done for you:

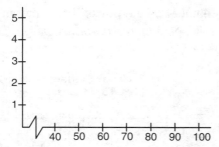

Grouping of Marks	Tally	Frequency
40 – 50	|	
50 – 60	|	
60 – 70	|||	
70 – 80		
80 – 90		
90 – 100		

    b) Why was the mark 70 placed in the 70 – 80 group instead of the 60 – 70 group?

    c) Copy and complete the histogram in your notebook.

7. An organization wants to know the ages of people who respond to their survey. Here are their data:

    29 37 41 40 38 42 49 54 57 42 61 28 34 44 44 58 63 88 64 59

    a) Organize the data into intervals and make a frequency table.

    b) Make a histogram using your intervals.
        REMEMBER: if the data does not start at 0, you will need a jagged line to show this. Title your histogram and label both axes.

    c) Find a classmate with a different histogram to yours. What are the differences? Do they highlight different information?

BONUS:
8. A track-and-field coach records the time for 20 practices of the 50 m dash:

    7.9 7.5 9.7 8.4 6.8 10.2 7.7 6.4 10.5 8.6 7.1 6.9 7.8 7.5 9.6 7.0 8.2 6.9 8.3 7.5

    Make a frequency table and histogram for the result.

Answer the question below in your notebook.

1. Sally wants to donate money to a charity that sends medical supplies to developing countries. She compares how the two charities spend their money by using a double bar graph:

   a) How much does each charity spend on fundraising, salaries, administration and medical supplies?

   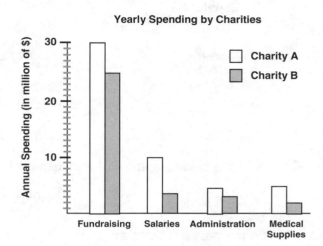

   b) In your notebook, draw two circle graphs showing the fraction of each charity's money spent on each area.

      i) Which charity spends more on medical supplies?

      ii) Which charity spends more money altogether?

      iii) What fraction of Charity A's money is spent on medical supplies?

      iv) What fraction of Charity B's money is spent on medical supplies?

   c) If Sally donates $100 to Charity A, how much of her money would go toward medical supplies?

   d) If Sally donates $100 to Charity B, how much of her money would go toward medical supplies?

   e) If you were Sally, which charity would you give your $100 to? Why?

   f) Which type of graph gave you the most relevant information to help you decide which charity to donate money to? Explain your answer.

2. Draw two bar graphs (using the scales provided) to show the data given below:

Province	Percent of households reporting "gifts of money and contributions"
British Columbia	74
Alberta	76
Saskatchewan	83
Manitoba	80
Ontario	80

   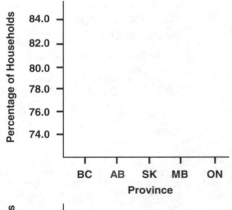

   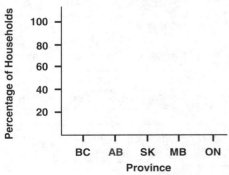

   a) Which graph makes it look as though the percentage of households giving money in Saskatchewan is almost 10 times the percentage of households giving money in BC?

   b) In which graph is it harder to see the difference between the households in each province?

   c) Which graph is the best representation of the data?

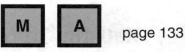
1. Match each type of graph with its purpose. The first one has been done for you:

   a. Line Graph   Compares two sets of data.

   b. Circle Graph   Shows a trend in data or makes prediction (usually used when graphing change over time).

   c. Histogram   Visually displays the frequency of results.

   d. Double Bar Graph   Shows whether one type of data increases, decreases or neither when another type of data increases.

   e. Bar Graph   Compares trends on two different data sets.

   f. Double Line Graph   Shows how data is divided into fractions of a whole.

   g) Scatter plot   Visually displays the frequency of results for continuous data.

2. Match the data with its graph:

   i)

Favourite Sport	Frequency	Fraction of Total
Hockey	42	$\frac{3}{10}$
Soccer	35	$\frac{1}{4}$
Baseball	28	$\frac{1}{5}$
Volleyball	28	$\frac{1}{5}$
Other	7	$\frac{1}{20}$

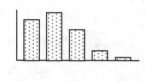

   ii)

Time to get to school (minutes)	0 – 10	10 – 20	20 – 30	30 – 40	40 – 50	50 – 60
Number of students	6	7	7	4	2	1

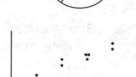

   iii) Martha's math test scores this school year (out of 10):

Test #	1	2	3	4	5	6	7	8	9	10
Score	3	4	6	5	6	6	7	7	8	8

   iv)

Month	Jan	Feb	Mar	Apr	May	Jun
Home Sales: *Company A*	3	4	5	6	5	5
Home Sales: *Company B*	10	8	6	7	6	6

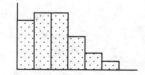

   v) Families are surveyed about how many cars they have:

Number of cars	0	1	2	3	4
Frequency	12	15	11	5	2

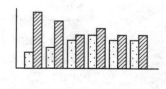

   vi)

Number of hours studies	1	4	2	4	3	2	3	3
Score on math test	3	9	6	8	7	5	7	6

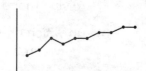

3. Using each type of graph (line, bar, double bar, circle, histogram, scatter plot) only once, select which type of graph you would use if you wanted to…

    a)   … know how many hours a night people in your class
         study (0 hours each night, 1 hour, 2 hours, etc.):   _____

    b)   … compare the number of ticket sales at a
         hockey arena and a movie theatre each month: _____

    c)   … know whether vocabulary increases with age: _____

    d)   … know how much of your $100 donation a charity
         will spend on building a shelter for homeless people: _____

    e)   … know how the temperature of a glass of ice water
         changes over time: _____

    f)   … group students in the school according to their height: _____

4. In your notebook or on a computer, choose and draw an appropriate type of graph to represent each set of data and then explain your choice. Use each type of graph (line graph, circle graph, bar graph, double bar graph, histogram, scatter plot) only once. Be sure to title, label and scale your graph:

    a)   Ages of people at a tennis club:

Age	10 – 20	20 – 30	30 – 40	40 – 50	50 – 60	60 – 70	70 – 80
Frequency	14	56	48	35	36	20	3

    b)   Fraction of votes given to each candidate in a school election:

Candidate	Katie	John	Rita	Melanie	Paul
Fraction of Votes	$\frac{2}{5}$	$\frac{1}{4}$	$\frac{1}{5}$	$\frac{1}{10}$	$\frac{1}{20}$

    c)   Jessica's marks on her first five Science and Math tests of the year (each out of 100):

Test	1	2	3	4	5
Science Marks	70	84	85	80	82
Math Marks	68	78	81	72	76

    d)   Age and weekly allowance of different people:

Age	10	12	11	8	12	9	8	10	13	13	9	12	11	8	13
Weekly Allowance ($)	40	80	50	10	100	75	20	30	60	70	30	20	60	30	90

    e)   A class survey showing how many pets the students have:

Number of Pets	0	1	2	3	4	5 +
Frequency	8	7	6	1	2	3

    f)   Number of times Friday the 13th occurred (or will occur) in each year:

Year	1990	1991	1992	1993	1994	1995	1996	1997	1998	1999	2000	2001
# of Occurrences	2	2	2	1	1	2	2	1	3	1	1	2
Year	2002	2003	2004	2005	2006	2007	2008	2009	2010	2011	2012	2013
# of Occurrences	2	1	2	1	2	2	1	3	1	1	3	2

To measure an angle, you use a **protractor**. A protractor has 180 subdivisions around its curved edge. These subdivisions are called **degrees**. 45° is a short form for "forty-five degrees."

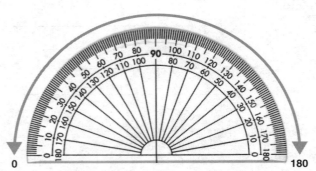

There are 180 subdivisions (180°) around the outside of a protractor.

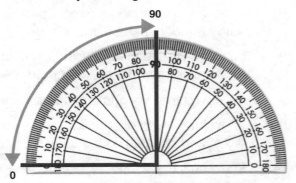

There are 90° in a right angle (or a square corner).

Angles that are *less* than 90° are called **acute** angles.

 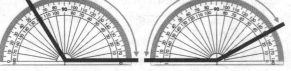

Angles that are *more* than 90° and *less* than 180° are called **obtuse** angles.

- -

1. Without using a protractor, identify each angle as <u>acute</u> or <u>obtuse</u>:

a)

_____

b)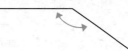

_____

c)

_____

d)

_____

e)

_____

f)

_____

g)

_____

h)

_____

i)

_____

A protractor has two scales. The exercise below will help you decide which scale to use:

2.　a)　Identify the angle as acute or obtuse.

　　b)　Next, circle the <u>two</u> numbers that the arm of the angle passes through.

　　c)　Then pick the correct measure of the angle (i.e. if you said the angle is acute, pick the number that is <u>less</u> than 90).

(i)

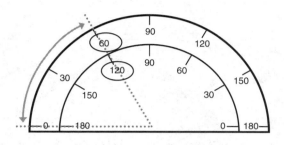

The angle is: _____

The angle measures: _____

(ii)

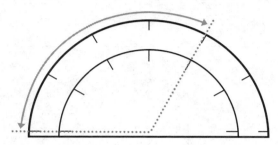

The angle is: _____

The angle measures: _____

(iii)

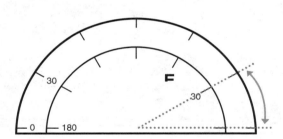

The angle is: _____

The angle measures: _____

(iv)

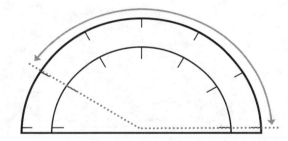

The angle is: _____

The angle measures: _____

3.　Again, identify the angle as acute or obtuse. Then write the measure of the angle:

a)

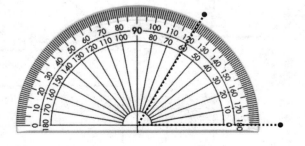

_____　_____

b)

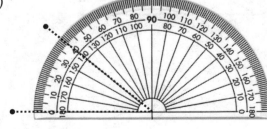

_____　_____

c)

d)

e)

f)

g)

h)

4. Measure the angles using a protractor. Write your answers in the boxes provided – don't forget units!
   HINT: For one question, you will have to turn the page (or the protractor!) upside down.

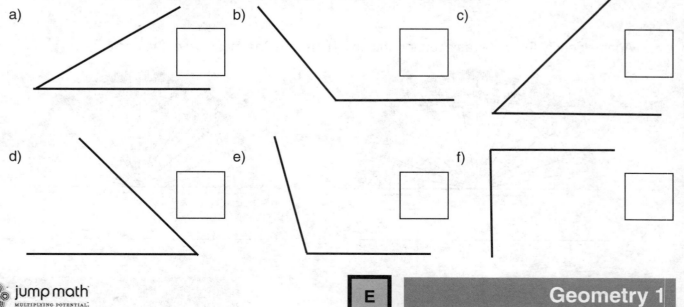

a)

b)

c)

d)

e)

f)

G8-2: Naming Angles

To **name an angle**, follow these steps:

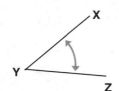

(i) Write an angle sign, i.e. ∠

(ii) Write the letter of a point that lies on one of the arms of the angle, i.e. ∠X̲ (or ∠Z̲)

(iii) Write the letter of the vertex that lies at the centre of the angle, i.e. ∠XY̲ (or ∠ZY̲)

(iv) Write the letter of the point on the other arm of the angle, i.e. ∠XYZ̲ (or ∠ZYX̲)

----

1. In each triangle, circle ∠ABC. Then measure the angle:

a)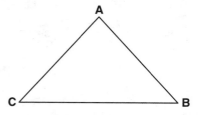

Measure of ∠ABC: _____

b)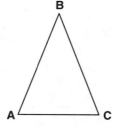

Measure of ∠ABC: _____

c)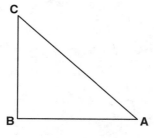

Measure of ∠ABC: _____

2. In each polygon, circle angle ∠XYZ. Then measure the angle:

a)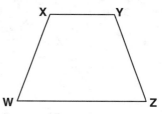

Measure of ∠XYZ: _____

b)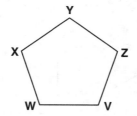

Measure of ∠XYZ: _____

c)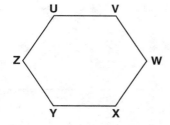

Measure of ∠XYZ: _____

3.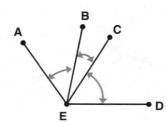

Name each of the angles marked. Then measure the angles:

measure of ___∠AEB___ = _____

measure of _____ = _____

measure of _____ = _____

Write the names of the angles in order, from least to greatest: _____

4.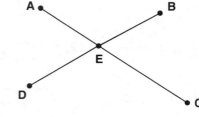

Write the names of two acute angles and two obtuse angles:

acute angles: _____ _____

obtuse angles: _____ _____

RECALL:
An <u>acute</u> angle is less than 90°, an <u>obtuse</u> angle is greater than 90° (and less than 180°) and a <u>right</u> angle is exactly 90°.

Triangles can be classified by **the size of their angles**:

(i) An **acute-angled triangle** has *all* acute angles.

(ii) An **obtuse-angled triangle** has *one* obtuse angle.

(iii) A **right-angled triangle** has *one* 90° angle.

If you measure the angles in a triangle accurately, you will find that they always add up to 180°.

----

1. Classify each triangle as <u>acute</u>, <u>obtuse</u> or <u>right</u>:

a) 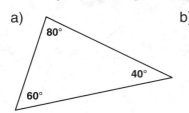   b) 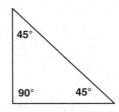   c) 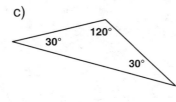   d)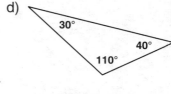

_____   _____   _____   _____

2. Measure all of the angles in each triangle and write your measurements in the triangle. Then say what type of triangle it is:

a) 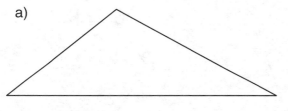   b) 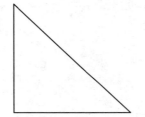   c)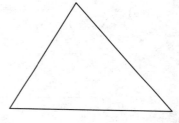

_____   _____   _____

3. Measure all the angles in each shape (write your answers in the polygons).
    Then use the Venn diagram to classify the shapes:

a)   b)   c)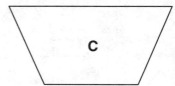

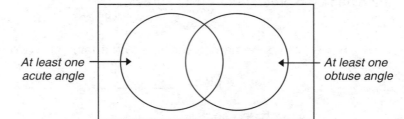

At least one acute angle   At least one obtuse angle

d) Give the mathematical name of the shape above that has all obtuse angles: _____

G8-4: Classifying Triangles

Triangles can be classified by the size of their angles, but they can also be classified by **the length of their sides**:

(i) In an **equilateral triangle**, all three sides are of equal length.

(ii) In an **isosceles triangle**, two sides are of equal length.

(iii) In a **scalene triangle**, no two sides are of equal length.

---

1. Measure the <u>angles</u> and <u>sides</u> (in mm if necessary) of each triangle and then write your measurements on the triangles.

   Use the charts to in parts a) and b) to classify the triangles:

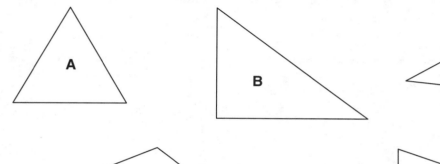

   a) Classify the triangles by their angles:

Property	Triangles with Property
Acute	
Obtuse	
Right	

   b) Classify the triangles by their sides:

Property	Triangles with Property
Equilateral	
Isosceles	
Scalene	

2. Sort the triangles using the properties given. Be sure to include <u>all 5 triangles</u> in each Venn diagram:

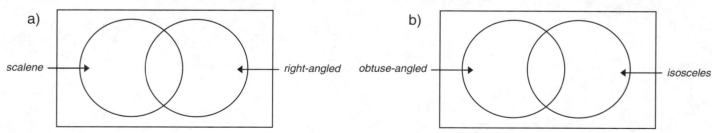

a)

scalene ——→   ←—— right-angled

b)

obtuse-angled ——→   ←—— isosceles

Answer the following questions in your notebook.

3. Pick one property from each list below. Draw a rough sketch of a triangle that has both properties. If you can't sketch the triangle, write "impossible":

   List 1: acute-angled, obtuse-angled, right-angled   **List 2:** equilateral, isosceles, scalene

E   Geometry 1

Clare makes a 60° angle as follows:

Step 1
She draws a base line and places the protractor on the base line as shown:

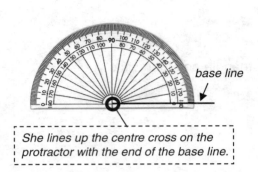

base line

She lines up the centre cross on the protractor with the end of the base line.

Step 2
She makes a mark at 60°:

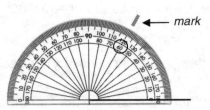

← *mark*

Step 3
Using a ruler, Clare joins the end point of the base line to her mark:

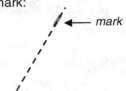

← *mark*

1. Use a protractor to make the given angles:

   a)

   b)

   30°

   120°

2. Use a protractor to make the two given angles. Then extend the lines to create a triangle:

   a)

   b)

   40°   **60°**

   25°   **110°**

3. In your notebook, use a protractor to construct the following angles:

   a) 45°   b) 80°   c) 50°   d) 35°   e) 62°

   f) 90°   g) 125°   h) 75°   i) 145°   j) 168°

	Line	Ray	Line Segment
Picture	A B	A B	A B
Number of ends	Zero (0) ends	One (1) end	Two (2) ends
In words or mathematical symbols	$\overleftrightarrow{AB}$, line AB, or line ℓ	$\overrightarrow{AB}$ or ray AB	$\overline{AB}$ or line segment AB

Example: Construct two lines intersecting at 45°.

Step 1   **Step 2**   **Step 3**

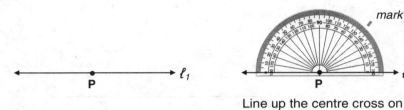

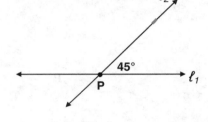

Line up the centre cross on the protractor with point P.

---

1.   Follow the steps in the example above to construct two lines intersecting at:

   a)   30°   b)   60°

2.   Using a ruler and protractor, measure all line segments and angles in the shapes below. Then draw identical shapes in your notebook:

   a)   b)

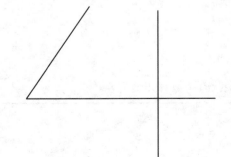

Using a **protractor**, construct a line segment through point P, perpendicular to $\overleftrightarrow{AB}$:

Example 1:

P <u>on</u> $\overleftrightarrow{AB}$:

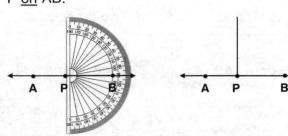

Example 2:

P <u>outside</u> $\overleftrightarrow{AB}$:

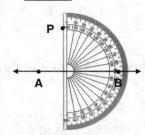

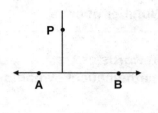

1. Use a protractor to construct a line segment through point P, perpendicular to $\overleftrightarrow{AB}$:

a)

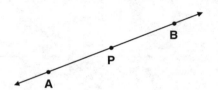

b)

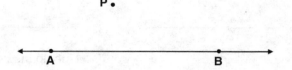

The **altitude** of a triangle is a perpendicular line from a vertex to the side opposite the vertex.

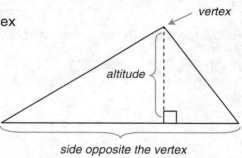

2. a) Construct *three* altitudes for the triangle:

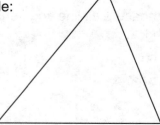

b) What do you notice?

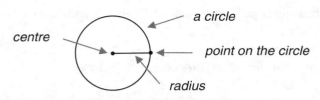

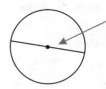

The diameter is twice the length of the radius.

You can use a compass to draw a circle.

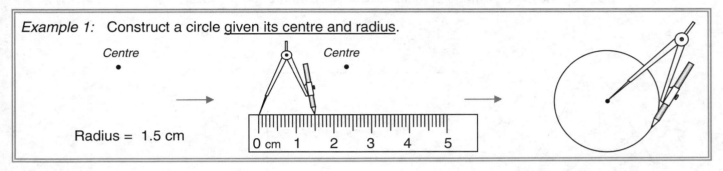

Example 1: Construct a circle <u>given its centre and radius</u>.

Centre

Radius = 1.5 cm

1. In your notebook, construct a circle for each radius on diameter:
   a) radius = 3 cm   b) radius = 1.5 cm   c) radius = 4.5 cm   d) diameter 6 cm   e) diameter 9 cm

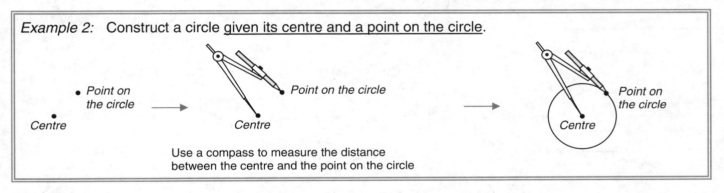

Example 2: Construct a circle <u>given its centre and a point on the circle</u>.

Use a compass to measure the distance between the centre and the point on the circle

2. In your notebook, draw a centre and a point you would like to be on a circle, then draw the circle. Repeat this twice.

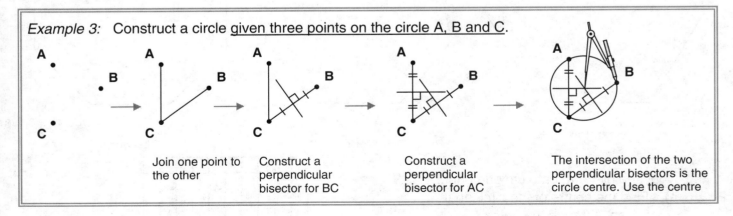

Example 3: Construct a circle <u>given three points on the circle A, B and C</u>.

Join one point to the other

Construct a perpendicular bisector for BC

Construct a perpendicular bisector for AC

The intersection of the two perpendicular bisectors is the circle centre. Use the centre

3. In your notebook, draw three points that form the vertices of a triangle (as in Example 3 above). Then construct a circle through the points.

G8-8: Circles (continued)

4. Follow the steps below to draw a circle for each regular polygon, such that all the vertices of the polygon are on the circle.

   Step 1 Construct perpendicular bisectors for any two sides of the regular polygon.

   Step 2 The intersection of the two perpendicular bisectors is the circle centre. Take any vertex as a point on the circle, and construct the circle following Example 2.

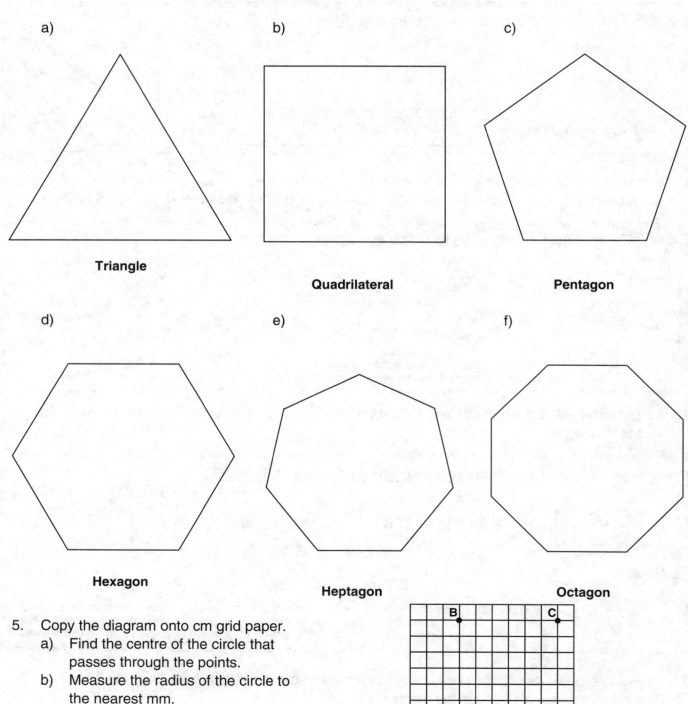

a)

Triangle

b)

Quadrilateral

c)

Pentagon

d)

Hexagon

e)

Heptagon

f)

Octagon

5. Copy the diagram onto cm grid paper.
   a) Find the centre of the circle that passes through the points.
   b) Measure the radius of the circle to the nearest mm.

Parallel lines are like railway tracks (on a straight section of the track) – that is, they are:

- ✓ Straight
- ✓ Always the same distance apart

No matter how long they are, parallel lines will *never* meet.

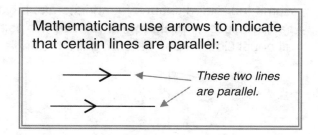

Mathematicians use arrows to indicate that certain lines are parallel:

These two lines are parallel.

NOTE:
Lines of different lengths can still be parallel (as long as they are both straight and are always the same distance apart).

- -

1. Each of the shapes below has <u>one pair</u> of parallel sides. Put an 'X' through the sides that *are not parallel*. The first one has been done for you:

a)    b) 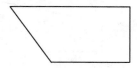   c) 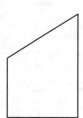   d)

e)    f)   g)    h)

IMPORTANT:

If a figure contains <u>more than one pair of parallel lines</u>, you can avoid confusion by using a different number of arrows on each pair:

Example:

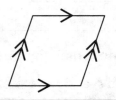

---

2. Use arrows to mark any pairs of parallel lines in the figures below:
    HINT: One figure has three pairs – you will need three different sets of arrows.

a)    b)    c) 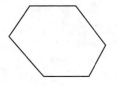   d)

_____ pairs   _____ pairs   _____ pairs   _____ pairs

Some four-sided shapes (quadrilaterals) have *no* pairs of parallel lines. A **trapezoid** has exactly *one* pair of parallel sides. **Parallelograms** have *two* pairs of parallel lines. A **rhombus** – which is a parallelogram with all equal sides – also has *two* pairs of parallel lines:

 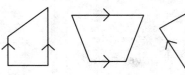 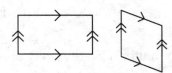

NO *pairs of parallel lines*   **ONE** *pair of parallel lines*   **TWO** *pairs of parallel lines*

3. For each of the shapes below, mark the parallel lines with arrows. Mark any pairs of sides that are not parallel with Xs. Under each quadrilateral, write how many <u>pairs</u> of sides are parallel:

A _____   B _____   C _____   D _____

  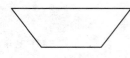

E _____   F _____   G _____   H _____

4. Sort the shapes **A** through **H** (above) into the chart by writing the letter in the correct column:

No pairs of parallel sides	One pair of parallel sides	Two pairs of parallel sides

Answer the remaining questions in your notebook.

5. If lines ℓ_1 and ℓ_2 were extended, would they ever meet? Explain in each case:
    HINT: Notice that the angles change from a) to b).

a)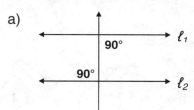

b)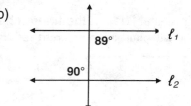

c)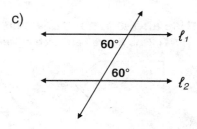

6. On grid paper, draw:

    a) a pair of horizontal lines that are parallel and 3 units apart.

    b) a figure with 1 pair of parallel sides.

    c) a trapezoid with 2 right angles.

    d) a parallelogram with no right angles.

    e) a rhombus.

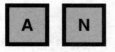
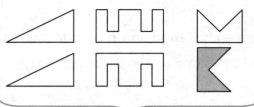

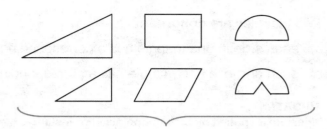

*These pairs of shapes are **congruent**.*   *These pairs of shapes <u>are not</u> **congruent**.*

---

1. What does it mean to say two shapes are congruent? _____

2. Write the same letter of the alphabet in any parts of the following shapes that appear congruent:

a)
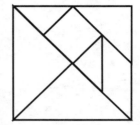

b)
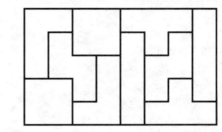

c)
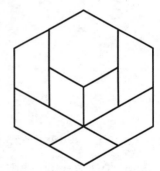

d)
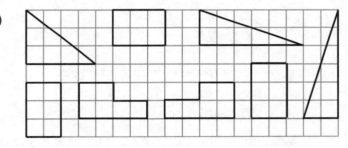

3. Divide each figure into <u>four</u> smaller, congruent shapes – each having the same shape as the original figure:

a)
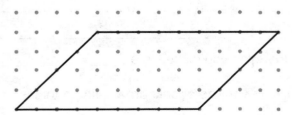

b)
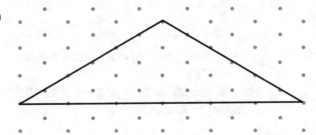

Answer the remaining questions in your notebook.

4. Find the area of each shape in Question 1 d). Are shapes with the same area always congruent?

5. This picture shows one way to cut a 3 by 4 grid into two congruent shapes. Show how many other ways you can cut a 3 by 4 grid into two congruent shapes.

G8-11: Exploring Congruency

Two triangles are **congruent** if:

a) each **side** in one triangle has a corresponding side **of the same length** in the other triangle, and...

b) each **angle** in one triangle has a corresponding **angle of the same size** in the other triangle.

IMPORTANT:
Sides are identified by their endpoints. For instance, the side marked by an 'X' in △ABC below is side AB.

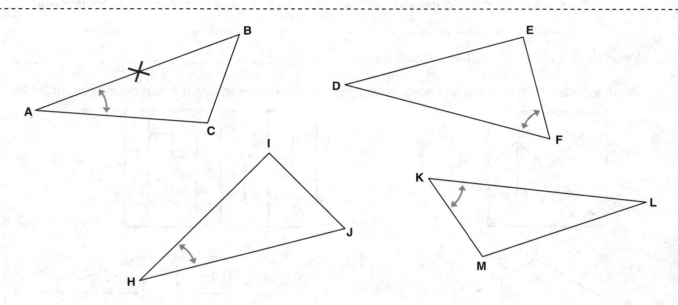

1. Name the angle marked in each triangle:

   a) in △ABC: __∠BAC__   b) in △DEF: _____   c) in △HIJ: _____   d) in △KLM: _____
      (or ∠CAB)

2. a) Measure all the sides of each triangle to the nearest cm. Write the lengths on the triangles.

   b) Measure all of the angles in each triangle. Write the size of the angles inside each vertex.

3. a) Name a pair of congruent triangles: _____

   b) Name all pairs of equal sides for the triangles you picked in a): _____

   _____

   c) Name one pair of congruent angles from the triangles you picked in a): _____

4. Measure the sides and angles of each figure below. In your notebook, draw a figure that is congruent to each original:

   a) 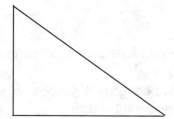   b)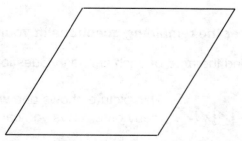

Answer the questions below in your notebook. You will need a ruler and a protractor.

1. a) You must draw a triangle that is congruent to the one shown
   but you are only allowed to make <u>two</u> measurements
   (for instance a side and an angle, or two sides).

   Can you do it? Explain.

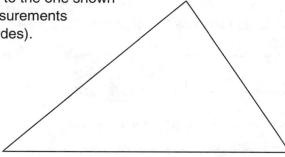

   b) What if you were allowed to make <u>three</u> measurements? Which measurements would
   you make?

2. Construct triangles with the measurements given below. Then try to construct a second
   non-congruent triangle with the same measurements. In which cases is this possible?

   a) base - 7 cm; base angle - 40°   b) base angle - 50°; base - 6 cm; base angle - 45°

   c) side - 8 cm; side - 5 cm   d) side - 6 cm; side - 9 cm; angle between the two sides - 30°

3. Answer the following "true / false" questions. Given a counter example if the statement is false:

   a) If two rectangles have the same area, they must be congruent.

   b) If two quadrilaterals are congruent, their perimeters must be equal.

   c) If two parallelograms have corresponding sides that are equal, they must be congruent.

   d) If two triangles are congruent, their corresponding sides must be equal.

   e) If two parallelograms have corresponding angles that are equal, they must be congruent.

4. Can you construct a copy of this triangle,
   using only a compass and a ruler?
   HINT: ∠ABC = 90°

   C

   A   B

5. Draw a triangle in your notebook. Describe the triangle to a partner and ask them to draw
   a congruent triangle without looking at yours. Try to describe your triangle using the fewest
   number of measurements.

A **line of symmetry** divides a figure into two congruent parts: if the figure is folded along the line of symmetry, the parts must fit onto each other exactly.

This dotted line *is* a line of symmetry:

The two parts are congruent and fit exactly.

This dotted line *is not* a line of symmetry:

The two parts are congruent but do not fit.

1. Complete the picture so that the dotted line is a line of symmetry:

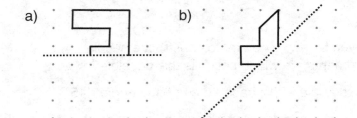

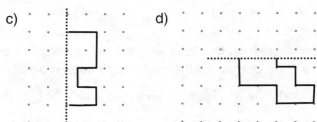

a)   b)   c)   d)

2. Draw <u>all</u> the lines of symmetry for each shape. Then complete the chart below:
    NOTE: "Regular" means having all angles and sides equal.

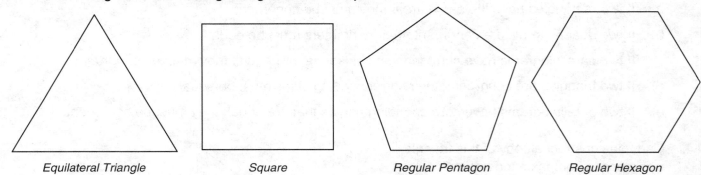

Equilateral Triangle   *Square*   *Regular Pentagon*   *Regular Hexagon*

a)

Figure	Triangle	Square	Pentagon	Hexagon
Number of edges				
Number of lines of symmetry				

b)   In your notebook, describe any relation you see between the number of lines of symmetry in a regular polygon and the number of edges it has.

3.   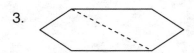   Brenda says the line shown here is a line of symmetry. Is she correct?
     Explain in your notebook.

4.   On grid paper, draw a figure with <u>exactly</u> two lines of symmetry. Explain how you know there are exactly two lines of symmetry.

1. Using your ruler, measure the sides of the shapes below. Circle those that are equilateral:

    NOTE: A shape with all sides the same length is called <u>equilateral</u>. ("Equi" comes from a Latin word meaning "equal" and "lateral" means "sides".)

    a)
    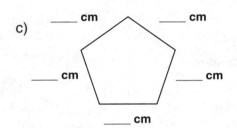
    ____ cm

    ____ cm   ____ cm

    ____ cm

    b)
    ____ cm
    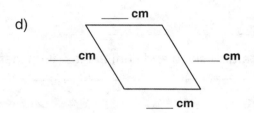
    ____ cm   ____ cm

    ____ cm

    c)
    ____ cm   ____ cm

    ____ cm   ____ cm

    ____ cm

    d)
    ____ cm

    ____ cm   ____ cm

    ____ cm

2. Complete the charts below, using shapes **A** to **J** in each. Start by marking the right angles and parallel lines in each figure. If you are not sure if a figure is equilateral, measure its sides with a ruler:

    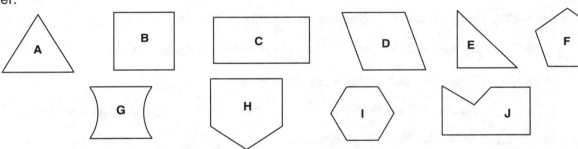

    a)

Property	Shapes with Property
Equilateral	
Not Equilateral	

    b)

Property	Shapes with Property
No right angles	
1 right angle	
2 right angles	
3 right angles	
4 right angles	

    c)

Property	Shapes with Property
No obtuse angles	
1 or more obtuse angles	

    e)

Polygon Name	Shapes with Property
Triangles	
Quadrilaterals	
Pentagons	
Hexagons	

    NOTE: Polygons must have <u>straight</u> sides.

    d)

Property	Shapes with Property
No parallel sides	
1 pair of parallel sides	
2 pairs of parallel sides	
3 pairs of parallel sides	

jump math
MULTIPLYING POTENTIAL.

E

G8-15: Special Quadrilaterals

A **quadrilateral** (that is, a shape with four sides) with two pairs of parallel sides is called a **parallelogram**:

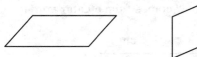

parallelogram
a quadrilateral with 2 pairs of parallel sides

Some other quadrilaterals have special names:

rhombus
a parallelogram with 4 equal sides

rectangle
a parallelogram with 4 right angles

square
a parallelogram with 4 right angles and 4 equal sides

trapezoid
a quadrilateral with only 1 pair of parallel sides

- -

1. Mark all parallel sides and right angles, then identify each quadrilateral:

    a)　　　　　　　b)　　　　　　　c)　　　　　　　d)

    _____　　_____　　_____　　_____

2. a)　I have 4 equal sides, but no right angles. What am I? _____

    b)　I have 4 right angles, but my sides are not all equal. What am I? _____

    c)　I have exactly 2 right angles. Which special quadrilateral <u>must</u> I be? _____

3. Use the words "all", "some", or "no" for each statement:

    a)　_____ squares are rectangles　　b)　_____ trapezoids are parallelograms

    c)　_____ parallelograms are trapezoids　　d)　_____ parallelograms are rectangles

Answer the remaining questions in your notebook.

4. Write 3 different names for a square.

5. A shape has 4 right angles. Which two special quadrilaterals might it be?

6. A quadrilateral has all equal sides. Which two special quadrilaterals might it be?

7. On grid paper draw a quadrilateral with:

    a) no right angles　　　b) one right angle　　　c) two right angles　　　d) no parallel sides

    e) one pair of parallel sides　　　　f) two pairs of parallel sides and no right angles

8. Describe any similarities or differences between a trapezoid and a parallelogram

9. a)　Why is a square a rectangle?　　　b)　Why is a rectangle not a square?

    c)　Why is a trapezoid not a parallelogram?

A diagonal of a quadrilateral is a straight line that is not a side and that joins two vertices.

A diagonal **bisects** a shape if it cuts it into two congruent parts.

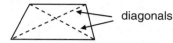
diagonals

----

1. For each of the quadrilaterals draw diagonals and fill in the chart below (write yes or no in the columns for each shape:

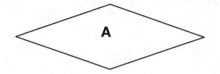
A

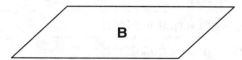
B

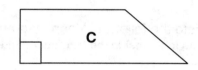
C

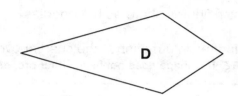
D

	Shape A	Shape B	Shape C	Shape D
Diagonals are perpendicular to each other				
Diagonals bisect each other				
Diagonals perpendicularly bisect each other				
Both diagonals bisect the shape				
One diagonal bisects the shape				
Both diagonals are angle bisectors				
One diagonal is an angle bisector				

Answer the following questions in your notebook.

2. Construct the shapes given below and make a chart like the one in Question 1 for the shapes:

a)
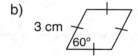

b)
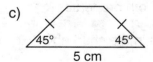

c)
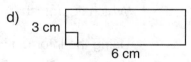

d)
3 cm

6 cm

3. For each statement below draw several squares and check if the statement holds true. Do you think the statement is true for all squares? If not, can you find a counter example?

   a) The diagonals of a square are equal in length.

   b) The diagonals of a square are perpendicular.

   c) The diagonals of a square bisect each other.

4. Repeat Question 3 for:

   a) a rhombus   b) a parallelogram   c) a trapezoid

1. Using pairs of properties that a figure might have (for instance, "I have 4 vertices" and "I have a vertical line of symmetry"), we are going to sort the following figures using Venn diagrams:

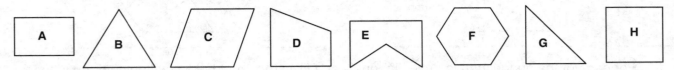

a)

Property	Figures with this property:
1. I am a quadrilateral	A, C, D, H
2. I am an equilateral	B, C, F, H

Which figures share both properties? _____

Using the information in the chart above, complete the following Venn diagram:
NOTE: If a shape does not have either property, write its letter inside the box, but outside both circles.

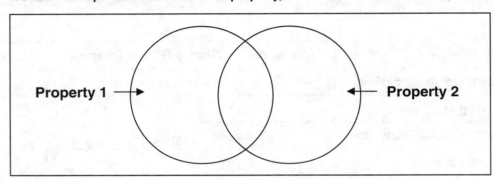

In parts b) and c), complete both the chart and the Venn diagram:

b)

Property	Figures with this property:
1. I am an equilateral	
2. I have <u>no</u> right angles	

Which figures share both properties? _____

Using the information in the chart above, complete the following Venn diagram:

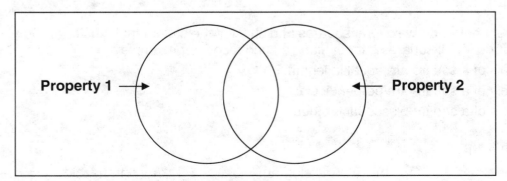

c)

Property	Figures with this property:
1. I have 4 or more vertices	
2. I have 2 or more obtuse angles	

Which figures share both properties? _____

Using the information in the chart above, complete the following Venn diagram:

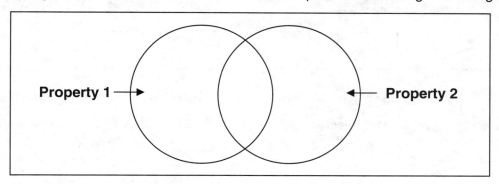

2. Record the properties of each shape. Write "yes" in the column if the shape has the given property. Otherwise, write "no":

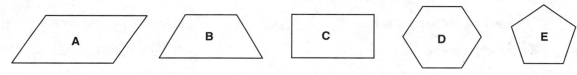

Shape	Quadrilateral	Equilateral	Two or more pairs of parallel sides	At least one <u>right</u> angle	At least one <u>acute</u> angle	At least one <u>obtuse</u> angle
A						
B						
C						
D						
E						

3. Using two properties of your own, make a chart and a Venn diagram for the figures in Question 1. Show your work in your notebook.

You might want to choose from the following:

✓ Number of vertices

✓ Number of pairs of parallel sides

✓ Number of edges

✓ Number of right, acute or obtuse angles

✓ Lines of symmetry

✓ Equilateral

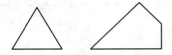

4.   Write **T** (for true) if *both* figures have the property in common.   Otherwise, write **F** (for false).

Both figures have...

a)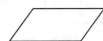

____ 4 vertices   ____ no parallel sides

____ 4 sides   ____ 1 right angle

b)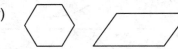

____ 3 vertices   ____ 5 sides

____ no right angles   ____ equilateral

c)

____ 3 sides   ____ 1 pair of parallel sides

____ 1 obtuse angle   ____ at least 1 acute angle

d)

____ 4 sides   ____ 1 pair of parallel sides

____ 2 right angles   ____ 4 vertices

e)

____ quadrilateral   ____ at least 1 right angle

____ at least 1 pair of parallel sides

____ 2 pairs of parallel sides

f)

____ 6 vertices

____ at least 2 pairs of parallel sides

____ no right angles   ____ equilateral

5.   a)   I have three sides. All of my sides are the same length. I'm an...

_____

b)   I have three sides. Two of my sides are the same length. I'm an...

_____

c)   I am a quadrilateral with two pairs of parallel sides. I'm a...

_____

d)   I am a quadrilateral with exactly one pair of parallel sides. I'm a...

_____

Answer the following questions in your notebook.

6.   Describe each figure completely. In your description you should mention the following properties:

✓ Number of sides   ✓ Is the figure equilateral?   ✓ Is the figure equilateral?

✓ Number of vertices   ✓ Number of right angles   ✓ Number of lines of symmetry

✓ Number of pairs of parallel sides   ✓ Number of acute angles

a)   b)   c)

7.   Name all the properties the figures have in common. Then describe any differences:

a)   b)